The Roman Emperors of Britain

The Roman Emperors of Britain

Tony Sullivan

First published in Great Britain in 2024 by
Pen & Sword History
An imprint of Pen & Sword Books Limited
Yorkshire – Philadelphia

Copyright © Tony Sullivan 2024

ISBN 978 1 39906 441 5

The right of Tony Sullivan to be identified as
Author of this Work has been asserted by him in accordance
with the Copyright, Designs and Patents Act 1988.

A CIP catalogue record for this book is
available from the British Library

All rights reserved. No part of this book may be reproduced or
transmitted in any form or by any means, electronic or mechanical
including photocopying, recording or by any information storage and
retrieval system, without permission from the Publisher in writing.

Typeset by Mac Style
Printed in the UK by CPI Group (UK) Ltd, Croydon, CR0 4YY.

Pen & Sword Books Limited incorporates the imprints of After
the Battle, Atlas, Archaeology, Aviation, Discovery, Family History,
Fiction, History, Maritime, Military, Military Classics, Politics,
Select, Transport, True Crime, Air World, Frontline Publishing, Leo
Cooper, Remember When, Seaforth Publishing, The Praetorian Press,
Wharncliffe Local History, Wharncliffe Transport, Wharncliffe True
Crime and White Owl.

For a complete list of Pen & Sword titles please contact

PEN & SWORD BOOKS LIMITED
47 Church Street, Barnsley, South Yorkshire, S70 2AS, England
E-mail: enquiries@pen-and-sword.co.uk
Website: www.pen-and-sword.co.uk
or
PEN AND SWORD BOOKS
1950 Lawrence Rd, Havertown, PA 19083, USA
E-mail: uspen-and-sword@casematepublishers.com
Website: www.penandswordbooks.com

Contents

Figures vi
Tables viii
Sources ix
Introduction xi

Chapter 1 Veni, vidi, vici: The First Invasion of Britain 1

Chapter 2 Claudius and the Invasion of Britain 15

Chapter 3 Vespasian and Titus 35

Chapter 4 Emperor Hadrian 60

Chapter 5 Pertinax and Clodius Albinus 82

Chapter 6 The Severans 107

Chapter 7 The Gallic Empire and the Pirate King of Britain 126

Chapter 8 The House of Constantine 141

Chapter 9 Usurpers and Tyrants 149

Chapter 10 The End of Empire 166

Sources for Images 180
Notes 183
References 191
Index 195

Figures

Figure 1	Roman Republic governmental structure	2
Figure 2	Imperial governmental structure	3
Figure 3	Career paths of senators and equestrians	4
Figure 4	Julius Caesar's second invasion 54 BC	9
Figure 5	Bust of Julius Caesar (Wikimedia Commons)	14
Figure 6	Map showing the possible invasion routes in AD 43	20
Figure 7	Camulodunum: Map of the Iron Age settlement and the first Roman fort	24
Figure 8	Map of typical Roman camp layout of legionary size	28
Figure 9	Bust of Claudius (Wikimedia Commons)	34
Figure 10	Legion command structure in the second century	40
Figure 11	Map of Vespasian's campaign in the west	45
Figure 12	Reproduction of Roman ballista (Wikimedia Commons)	47
Figure 13	Drawing of a Roman onager (Wikimedia Commons)	48
Figure 14	Aerial view of Maiden Castle (Wikimedia Commons)	49
Figure 15	Ramparts at Maiden Castle (Wikimedia Commons)	49
Figure 16	Roman *testudo* formation from Trajan's column (Wikimedia Commons)	51
Figure 17	A typical Roman legion formation in the first century AD	53
Figure 18	Bust of Vespasian (Wikimedia Commons)	54
Figure 19	Bust of Titus (Wikimedia Commons)	55
Figure 20	Map of major concentration of Roman villas in Britain	57
Figure 21	Map of Roman Britain c. 150 (Wikimedia Commons)	58
Figure 22	Bust of Emperor Hadrian (Wikimedia Commons)	61
Figure 23	A cross-section of Hadrian's Wall, ditch and vallum	68
Figure 24	Hadrian's Wall forts	69
Figure 25	Cross-section of The Antonine Wall	79
Figure 26	The Antonine Wall forts	80
Figure 27	Aerial view of Housesteads Roman Fort, Vercovicium (Wikimedia Commons)	87
Figure 28	Map of the incursion of 182	89
Figure 29	Aerial view of London (Wikimedia Commons)	95

Figure 30	London in second to third century (Wikimedia Commons)	95
Figure 31	Civil and military administrative structure of Britannia in the second century	96
Figure 32	Bust of Pertinax (Wikimedia Commons)	97
Figure 33	Bust of Clodius Albinus (Wikimedia Commons)	102
Figure 34	Battle of Lugdunum 197	104
Figure 35	The Severan family tree	108
Figure 36	Bust of Septimius Severus (Wikimedia Commons)	109
Figure 37	Map of northern campaign of Septimius Severus c. 208–11 (Wikimedia Commons)	114
Figure 38	Bust of Publius Septimius Geta c. 208 (Wikimedia Commons)	117
Figure 39	Map of Roman York	119
Figure 40	Layout of Roman fortress of Eboracum	120
Figure 41	Bust of Caracalla c. 212 (Wikimedia Commons)	122
Figure 42	Map of the first division of Britannia from c. 213	123
Figure 43	Gold aureus of Postumus in a pendant (Wikimedia Commons)	127
Figure 44	Gold aureus of Carausius, minted at London (Wikimedia Commons)	131
Figure 45	Roman copper coin of Allectus c. 293–6. Reverse with Galley (Wikimedia Commons)	134
Figure 46	Map of the invasion of Britain, 296	135
Figure 47	Gold coin of Constantius I (Wikimedia Commons)	136
Figure 48	Map of the second division of Britannia	138
Figure 49	Bust of Constantius Chorus (Wikimedia Commons)	141
Figure 50	Family tree of the Tetrarchy	142
Figure 51	Statue of Constantine the Great in York (Wikimedia Commons)	147
Figure 52	Bust of Constans I (Wikim…..//edia Commons)	148
Figure 53	Gold solidus of Magnentius from Trier (Wikimedia Commons)	149
Figure 54	The organisation of the late Roman Empire in the west	151
Figure 55	Valentia, the fifth province	155
Figure 56	Gold solidus of Theodosius I minted in Constantinople, 379–383 (Wikimedia Commons)	156
Figure 57	Roman Miliarensis of Magnus Maximus (Wikimedia Commons)	159
Figure 58	Gold solidus of Constantine III (Wikimedia Commons)	163

Tables

Table 1	Auxiliary unit types	41
Table 2	Auxiliary units and forts under Hadrian	70
Table 3	Auxiliary units from second to fourth century	71
Table 4	Auxiliary units on the Antonine Wall	79
Table 5	Emperors of the Gallic Empire	127
Table 6	The Tetrarchy c. 306–8	144
Table 7	Timeline of the last years of Roman Britain	164
Table 8	Units under the Comes Britanniarum	167
Table 9	Troops and Offices of the Count of the Saxon Shore	167
Table 10	Troops and Offices of the Dux Britanniarum	167
Table 11	Military commands of Roman Britain	169

Sources

CIL The *Corpus Inscriptionum Latinarum* collection of ancient Latin inscriptions
RIB Roman inscriptions of Britain
Bellum Gallicum, The Gallic Wars, by Julius Caesar, 100–44 BC
Geographica, Geography, Strabo c. 64 BC–AD 24
Naturalis Historia, Natural History, Pliny the Elder, AD 23–79
Bellum Judaicum, The Jewish War, Titus Flavius Josephus, AD first century
De Vita Caesarum, The Lives of the Twelve Caesars, Suetonius AD 69–122
De vita Julii Agricolae, The Life of Agricola, Tacitus AD 56–120
De origine et situ Germanorum, On the Origin and Situation of the Germans, Tacitus AD 56–120
Historiae, Histories, Tacitus AD 56–120
Ab excessu divi Augusti, The Annals, Tacitus AD 56–120
De Munitionibus Castrorum, Concerning the fortifications of a military camp, unknown, first to second century
Ektaxis kata Alanon, The order of battle against the Alans, Lucius Flavius Arrianus (AD second century)
Strategemata, Stratagems, Polyaenus AD second century
Historia Romana, Roman History, by Cassius Dio c. AD 155–235
History of the Roman Empire since the Death of Marcus Aurelius by Herodian c. AD 170–240
Liber De Caesaribus, Life of the Caesars, Aurelius Victor, c. 320–390
Historia Augusta anonymous author, fourth century
Epitoma rei militaris, Concerning Military Matters, by Vegetius, fourth century
Res Gestae, The History, by Ammianus Marcellinus c. AD 330–400
Breviarium Historiae Romanae, Summary of Roman History, Eutropius, late fourth century
De Bello Gothico, The Gothic Wars, in *De Bellis*, On the Wars, Procopius of Caesarea, AD sixth century
De mortibus persecutorum, On the Deaths of the Persecutors, Lactantius, fourth century
Vita Constantini, The Life of Constantine, Eusebius, fourth century
De Consulatu Stilichonis, Panegyric on Stilicho's Consulship, Claudian, early fifth century
Historiae Adversus Paganos, History Against the Pagans, Orosius, c. 380–420
Historia Ecclesiastica, History of the Church, Sozomen, c. 400–450
Historia Nova, New History, Zosimus, c. 500
De Bellis, On the Wars, Procopius, c. 500–565

Chronica Gallica CCCCLII, Gallic Chronicle 452 anonymous
Chronica Gallica DXI, Gallic Chronicle 511 anonymous
De Vita sancta Germani, The Life of Saint Germanus, Constantius of Lyon, c. 480
De Excidio et Conquestu Britanniae, On the Ruin and Conquest of Britain, Gildas, early sixth century

Introduction

Like many readers my first introduction to the Romans was at primary school. For me this was nearly half a century ago and I was immediately drawn to the might of the Roman army, the weapons and the armour. In terms of the actual history, I came away with a very superficial knowledge: the Romans came, they saw, they conquered. Then they stayed. For 350 years. Then they left. Into that 'void' stepped the Anglo-Saxons, and then history lessons took me quickly through the Vikings to the Normans and 1066 and all that. Later, in secondary school, we learned a little more about Roman achievements: roads, towns, law, baths and aqueducts.

However, aside from the revolt of Boudicca in AD 61, there was little about the many political upheavals, rebellions and usurpations that occurred in Britain throughout the period. St Jerome, writing in the early fifth century, claimed that Britain was a land 'fertile in tyrants'. As we shall see this was not an unreasonable point. In the century and a half before the end of Roman rule Britannia broke away several times, sometimes alone, sometimes along with other regions. In 306 Constantine was declared emperor at York and went on to eliminate all his rivals and unite the empire under one emperor once again. In AD 383 Magnus Maximus attempted the same feat when he was declared emperor by his troops in Britain, but met his end in AD 388 outside the city of Aquileia in Northern Italy. Less than a decade before Jerome made his observations, three usurpers were declared emperor in Britain in the same year.

A century before Roman rule began, Julius Caesar found a patchwork of tribes with different cultural identities. Many of these tribes, but not all, were hostile to Roman intervention and fought vigorously to push them back into the sea. For ninety years after Caesar left, the Britons looked warily across the channel for when the Romans might return. Return they did, this time under Claudius. Following Caesar's footsteps, Claudius also visited Britain. He wasn't to be the last emperor to do so.

If one were to ask people to name any of these emperors, usurpers or 'tyrants' who visited or began their 'career' in Britain, I suspect even the most well-versed readers might be surprised at the final list. Some might start with Julius Caesar before it's pointed out he wasn't actually an emperor. Later he was a *dictator* in the technical, Roman, sense of the word, but never an *augustus*. I suspect a quick show of hands might produce Hadrian, Septimius Severus, Constantine I and perhaps our final emperor, Constantine III, doomed to die with his son on the road to Ravenna. This a year after Rome was sacked by the Goths and the western emperor, Honorius, had instructed the Britons to 'look to their own defences'.

However, there have been many others who served in Britain in their early careers. Vespasian was a legionary commander for legio II Augusta in the invasion of AD 43. He led the second across southern Britain, storming hill-forts in his subjugation of the Britons. His son Titus was a legionary tribune in Britain just after Boudicca's revolt of AD 61. Pertinax served there three times: first as a legionary tribune of the Sixth legion at York, second as an auxiliary commander in the north, and finally returned as provincial governor two decades later.

More obscure figures might be less well-known. How many could have named Carausius, our enigmatic 'Pirate King', before the publication in 2020 of Simon Elliott's excellent book *Roman Britain's Pirate King: Carausius, Constantius Chlorus and the Fourth Roman Invasion of Britain?* Less still Allectus, his second in command, defeated during the invasion of another emperor to set foot in Britain, Constantius I, father of Constantine.

There have been many books about the Romans in general and Roman Britain in particular. Much of Britain experienced more than 350 years of direct Roman rule. This had a huge impact on the south and east of the island. These areas experienced the most urbanisation and 'Romanisation' during this period. It is interesting to note it was these same areas that received the greater share of Germanic material culture as well as settlement in the century directly after Roman rule ended. This is a point we will come back to at the end of this book. It will show there was a significant change in cultural identity.

There have also been many books about Roman emperors. Often this has focused on the 'official' emperors, with those classed as usurpers and tyrants a mere footnote, written by the victors. Roman history is full of such men. The year AD 69 saw four emperors vie for the throne, with Vespasian emerging victorious. As noted he is one of the emperors posted to Britain in his early career who we will be covering. The 'Year of the Five Emperors' in AD 193 gives us three such men: Pertinax, Clodius Albinus and Septimius Severus, all of whom came to Britain at one point. Much has been written about the first and last of these but very little about the reign of Albinus.

This book will attempt to address this discrepancy. For Britain was indeed not only 'fertile in tyrants' but also played host to a number of legitimate emperors, both during their early careers and when they were emperor. Some were declared emperor in Britain; some as a result of political events within the province. Emperors served, fought, died and were raised to the throne in Britain. Their stories offer a unique perspective of both Roman Britain and the wider empire.

Chapter One

Veni, vidi, vici: The First Invasion of Britain

The well-known phrase *veni, vidi, vici* (I came, I saw, I conquered) has been attributed to Julius Caesar by the greek historian Appian. Rather than referring to his campaigns in Britain, it is more accurately dated to 47 BC in a letter to the senate concerning a campaign against the kingdom of Pontus in the east. This was a year after he had defeated Pompey at Pharsalus, although the civil war rumbled on for another two years. This war began when Caesar crossed the Rubicon in 49 BC, an event that would lead him to be appointed *dictator*, first for just a period of eleven days and later for ten years.

The distinction between dictator and Emperor is important to understand as it highlights the change from the Republican Rome to Empire. To see how this evolved, we must look at the early history of Rome. The traditional date for the founding of Rome is 753 BC, on seven hills above the Tiber sixteen miles from the coast of the Tyrrhenum sea. Two separate foundation myths became fused together. The first is the familiar legend of Romulus and Remus abandoned as infants and suckled by a she-wolf before being rescued and raised by a shepherd. The second myth makes them descendants of Aeneas, a prince of Troy who escaped the city after its fall at the hands of the Greeks. Romulus is the first of seven kings, the last being Lucius Tarquinius Superbus dated to c.509 BC.

The overthrow of this last king and establishment of the Republic was seared into the Roman consciousness. So much so that an accusation of wanting to be a 'king' was a deep insult and potentially fatal to a political career. Indeed, one of the first acts of the man responsible for the overthrow of Tarquinius was to swear an oath that Rome would never again be ruled by a king. The message was very clear: one man should not have all the power and if such a man emerged it was one's civic duty to put an end to him. This man's name was Brutus and, legend or not, the coincidence would not have been lost on many Romans when another Brutus led the conspiracy against Julius Caesar.

Our first Brutus decreed that Rome was to be ruled by two consuls, appointed each year, with 300 senators. The consuls performed some of the same tasks as a king but crucially they were voted by the people, held office for a year and presided over the election of their successors. In an emergency the senate could vote powers to a dictator for a limited time. Such an emergency occurred twice in the fifth-century BC and Lucius Quinctius Cincinnatus stepped up each time for fifteen, and later twenty-one days, before handing power back. The concept of civic duty, stepping up when required but handing power back willingly when the task is completed, was very prominent in the Roman psyche.

This idea of handing power back to the senate did influence how later emperors ruled, with the more successful ones perhaps maintaining appearances even if the reality of where the power lay was very different. The concept features in Ridley Scott's 2000 film, *Gladiator*, with Richard Harris as Emperor Marcus Aurelius urging his general, Maximus Decimus Meridius, to restore the republic. In reality Marcus Aurelius did no such thing and in fact groomed his son Commodus for the succession. However, history has painted a very different picture of their reigns and in many ways this was due to their relationship with the senate. Marcus maintained the pretence he was merely 'first among equals' and was careful to have a good working relationship. With Commodus the relationship quickly broke down into a series of factional plots and murders, which ended with the emperor strangled in his bath by his wrestling partner on the orders of his inner circle.

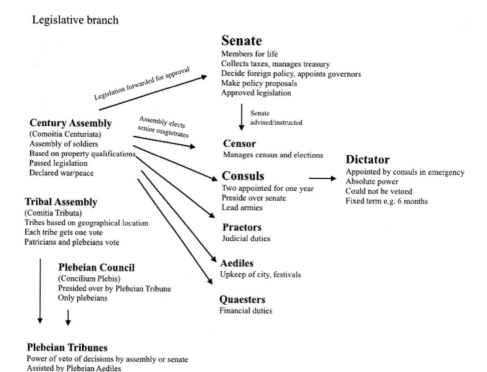

Figure 1. Roman Republic governmental structure.

The letters SPQR represent *Senatus Populusque Romanus*, 'the Senate and People of Rome', and this phrase embodies the ideal, if not the reality, of Roman government even in the Imperial period. The republic lasted several hundred years and during that time the small city state grew its territory and influence considerably. Its victory over Carthage consolidated its position as the major power across the Mediterranean. As Rome expanded, its system of government also evolved. It became difficult to administer this wide geographical area from what was a city state.

It would later move from a republican form of government to the imperial system. In brief, the emperors took on a similar role of the former official temporary post of *dictator*. Powers moved from the senate to the emperor, but emperors were careful never to declare themselves king, despite the political reality. It was Emperor Augustus, 27 BC to AD 14, who consolidated this system, introducing a number of reforms and incremental changes:[1] senatorial decrees were given the force of law along with Imperial pronouncements, which together formed the basis of Roman legislation. The difference between senators and equestrians was consolidated with the former being made hereditary for three generations, although with no obligation of taking office. These senators became an arm of the state and subordinate to the emperor. We can see how the system of government changed in the figures below.

Julius Caesar appears on the stage a generation before these changes took place. He rose up the *cursus honorum* ('course of honours'), serving as a military tribune, quaestor, aedile, praetor and consul. We can see the career paths of both senators and equestrians laid out in figure 3. In 58 BC he was given the prized post of provincial governor. The *lex Vatinia de provincia Caesaris* awarded Caesar Cisalpine Gaul and Illyricum, to which was later added Transalpine Gaul. This

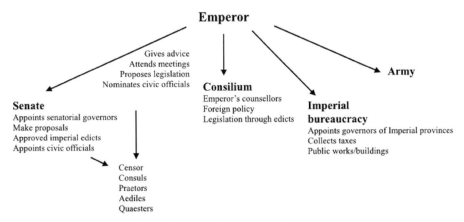

Figure 2. Imperial governmental structure.

4 The Roman Emperors of Britain

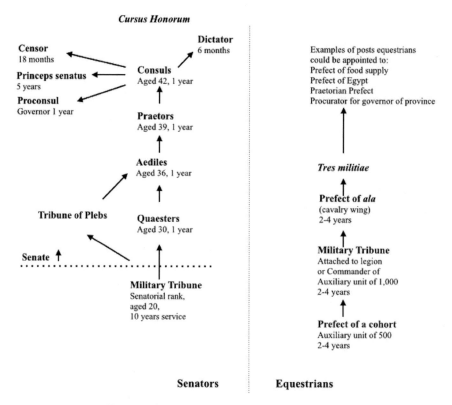

Figure 3. Career paths of senators and equestrians.

gave him the platform to extend the empire's borders, as well as his own power, to the north. It is this subsequent subjugation of Gaul that brought him into contact with the Britons.

The first invasion 55 BC

By 56 BC, after two years of fighting, the situation in Gaul had stabilised. During the winter months, Julius Caesar decided Britain was to be his next target. It was claimed the tribes from the island had provided military aid to the Gauls, although no mention of any significant help from the Britons was mentioned in Caesar's description of campaigns against the Veneti and other coastal tribes. There had been trading links across the channel and rumours of rich natural resources may have influenced the decision. More important perhaps was the glory and glamour of leading a Roman army to unexplored lands, especially one across the sea and on the edges of the known world.

Later that year Caesar moved south and wintered in Cisalpine Gaul. In the spring two Germanic tribes, the Usipetes and Tencteri, crossed the Rhine and Caesar marched north to head them off. After their defeat Caesar led an expedition across the Rhine, building a bridge he describes in great detail in the *Commentarii de Bello Gallico,* also known as *Bellum Gallicum,* the Gallic Wars. After eighteen days he was back in Gaul and dismantled the bridge.

It wasn't until late summer of 55 BC that he could consider sailing for Britain. Two legions, the Seventh and the Tenth, numbering approximately 8,000 men, accompanied him. In addition to his warships he had 100 transports. Eighty of these he filled with his infantry, perhaps 100 per vessel.[2] Eighteen transports were set aside for the cavalry. They likely set sail from modern Bolougne. A certain Caius Volusenus made a reconnaissance voyage to scout a good landing place and returned five days later.

Meanwhile, the Britons had learned of the Romans' intentions and envoys were sent to Gaul from some tribes to offer alliances and hostages. Caesar sent Commius, a Gallic chieftain who had been king of the Atrebates, back across the channel. No word returned as Commius had been imprisoned on arrival.

When the wind turned in Caesar's favour he decided he could wait no longer and ordered his ships out of the harbour. It was by now late August and he must have been aware of the potential for bad weather both at the time and for any potential return. In fact the cavalry transports never made it. Late to dispatch, the weather turned and they were unable to proceed. The infantry transports had left before dawn and sighted the coast by late morning. It was likely near Dover as the beach was overlooked by cliffs, lined with warriors. Caesar waited at anchor a few hours for all his available ships to arrive. In the late afternoon he advanced about seven miles up the coast looking for a suitable landing beach, possibly near Deal or Walmer. This part of the coast offered wide beaches not dominated by high cliffs.

However, the transport ships were not able to get close enough and many grounded some way out. The legionaries had to jump into the sea and wade ashore, carrying their equipment. The Romans were vulnerable to missiles while cavalry and chariots were able to pick off stragglers as they came ashore. Caesar ordered his warships in close to give covering support from artillery, slings and archers. Still the assault floundered until the actions of a single soldier helped turn the tide. Caesar himself wrote of the dramatic moment the soldier jumped down and exhorted the men to follow him.

The man was the eagle-bearer of the Tenth Legion and after offering a prayer to heaven he cried in a loud voice:[3] 'Leap down, soldiers, unless you wish to betray your eagle to the enemy; it shall be told that I at any rate did my duty to my country and my general.' He then cast himself into the surf and waded towards the shore holding the eagle aloft. The legionaries could not bear to allow the disgrace of losing the eagle and so followed their comrade and jumped in after him. Their comrades on the ships nearest seeing these did likewise and closed on the Britons on the beach.

Heavy fighting continued but a ragged line began to form and hold. The Britons, relying on cavalry and chariots, were more suited to hit-and-run tactics and were unable to hold a position or take a strong defensive formation. They wheeled away to fight another day. The Romans were able to take the beach and, after driving off the Britons, constructed a camp. Local tribes were cowed enough to offer hostages and grain, and Commius was released.

Four days after the landing the cavalry transports arrived but were driven off by a storm. Worse was to come as twelve of his own ships were destroyed and the rest damaged. The allied chieftains, sensing a change in fortunes, slipped out of the camp and cut the grain supply. The legionaries, forced now to search for wheat to harvest, were ambushed by chariots and cavalry. Caesar personally led two cohorts, just 1,000 men, to the rescue.

Caesar had displayed personal bravery several times before.[4] As a young man he had repeatedly refused Sulla's command to divorce Cornelia. Even after financial punishments and a clear threat of execution. He was awarded the highest awards for gallantry and bravery, the *corona civica*, when Mitylene on Lesbos was stormed. On this occasion his force managed to relieve their beleaguered comrades.

The Britons harassed and followed them back to camp and prepared an assault. Rather than wait to be besieged, Caesar formed his men up outside with a small troop of cavalry from Commius and his allies. Here the Romans were at an advantage and the Britons were beaten off. The Britons once more sued for peace and Caesar demanded double the hostages, adding the stipulation that they be taken across the Channel to Gaul.

Perhaps sensing he should quit while he was ahead, and fearing a turn in the weather would leave him stranded in Britain, Caesar took his entire force back across the channel around the September equinox. He now only had sixty-eight transports in addition to his warships but he managed to get the entire army back, leaving at midnight. Two of his ships floundered in Gaul and were attacked and plundered by the Morini. Caesar sent his cavalry, who rescued the men without a single casualty.

In some ways this first invasion was a disaster. A Briton might crow that Caesar had poked his nose across the channel and been thoroughly bloodied. Forced to scurry back a few short weeks later with his tale between his legs. Caesar of course presented it entirely differently. He'd crossed to an unknown land, won a battle, taken hostages and opened up new possibilities for the Roman world. The Romans lapped up the news and the Senate awarded him twenty days of public thanksgiving. Caesar spent the winter preparing for a return.

The second invasion 54 BC

The preparation for the second invasion was far better. Around 600 ships were built, with oars and sails, along with new twenty-eight new war galleys. To these were added 200 locally chartered transports and the eighty from the year before. The fleet gathered at Portus Itius, near modern Boulogne. The invasion force was also larger: five legions and half his available auxiliary and cavalry.[5] They left at sunset on 6 July. Met with low winds they drifted off course. The provision of oars was validated along with more suitable transports that allowed men and horses ashore straight onto the beach. By noon Caesar had secured his beach-head unopposed. It is likely the location of this initial landing was again near Deal. A marching camp has been found, 20 hectares in size, big enough to accommodate two legions.[6] Located at Ebbsfleet near Pegwell Bay in East Kent just over six miles north of Deal, it had a defensive ditch five metres wide and two metres deep. This would suggest Caesar anchored his ships in the Wantsum Channel between the Island of Thanet and Kent.

The Britons had again formed up on the high ground, but seeing the size of the force retreated. Caesar left 10 cohorts and 300 cavalry to guard the camp. He marched out at night with 40 cohorts, nearly 20,000 infantry, and 1,700 cavalry. The Romans covered twelve miles and found the Britons waiting behind a river, probably the Stour near Canterbury. The main force sheltered in a walled enclosure on a wooded hill, likely Bigbury Wood hill-fort.

The Britons launched cavalry, chariot and skirmishing attacks from the fort but were brushed aside by the cavalry. The Seventh Legion then assaulted the hill. A single ramp was built up to the wall and the legionaries used the *testudo*, or tortoise, formation to storm the fort. This involved a body of men overlapping shields above their heads, and to the sides of those on the outside, to form a tank or tortoise-like protection. The Britons fled and the Romans stopped for the night. The next morning Caesar sent out three columns to seek the enemy. But they were quickly recalled. A storm had destroyed forty ships and damaged many others. Caesar was forced to return and lost ten days due to repairs. The camp was enlarged to include the beach itself, where the damaged ships were dragged ashore. A message was sent to Gaul requesting craftsmen from the legions left with Labienus.

Several of the tribes had come together and appointed Cassivellaunus as their leader. The little information we have suggests he came from north of the Thames, most likely where the Catuvellauni ruled. Caesar advanced and was constantly harassed by chariots and horsemen. While they won concentrated or prolonged engagements, the Britons were able to lure them into ambushes from which the Romans suffered badly. The Britons then launched a major attack as the Romans constructed a camp at the end of a march. Caesar had to send an additional two cohorts to protect the outposts and a tribune was killed.

The next day Caesar sent three legions out to forage but they were attacked again by cavalry and chariots. They were able to regroup and drive off the enemy but the Romans must have feared a repeat of the year before where they risked being left with little grain.

Caesar decided to aim his attack at the homeland of the enemy chieftain. They forded the Thames and again brushed aside the Britons who defended the far bank. The exact location is disputed but recent evidence suggests it was further east than previously thought. One possibility is at Tilbury, the lowest fordable point in Roman times.[7] This would have brought them into the territory of the Trinovantes tribe centred around modern Essex and Suffolk. Cassivellaunus had placed sharpened stakes along the north bank and below the water line. Ballistae, slingers and archers from war galleys peppered the Britons as engineers dealt with the defences. The infantry and cavalry were able to ford the river and attack at the same time, driving the Britons off. The Romans were now north of the river.

Caesar claimed 4,000 chariots were sent against him and he suffered losses from skirmishing and foraging for much-needed food. The Britons conducted a scorched earth policy and destroyed or hid food and livestock. However, Caesar was able to divide the Britons. The Trinovantes, to the east of the Catuvellauni, surrendered. A prince of this tribe, Mandubracius, was able to tell Caesar where the *oppida*, a large fortified Iron Age settlement, of Cassivellaunus could be found. It lay in a heavily wooded area protected by marshes.

One possibility is Wheathampstead in Hertfordshire where 30-metre-wide and 12-metre-deep defences are still visible today. Five other tribes quickly followed the Trinovantes, leaving the Britons divided. The stronghold was stormed and captured, along with significant resources including cattle. The Romans again used the *testudo* formation, attacking on two sides under covering fire from ballistae and slingers. Meanwhile, an attack by the Kentish tribes on the main camp had been repulsed with major losses for the Britons.

By the end of September Cassivellaunus sued for peace, facilitated once again by Commius of the Atrebates. Annual tribute was agreed along with hostages and a promise not to attack the Trinovantes. Caesar, now satisfied, was eager to return to Gaul before bad weather set in. With some ships still damaged he decided to make two crossings as he had to wait for some of the ships to return. The initial crossing went smoothly but due to poor weather they were unable to return quickly and Caesar was forced to wait several days.

Fearing an attack, or being stranded on the wrong side of the Channel during winter, he once more took a risky decision. The remaining men were crammed

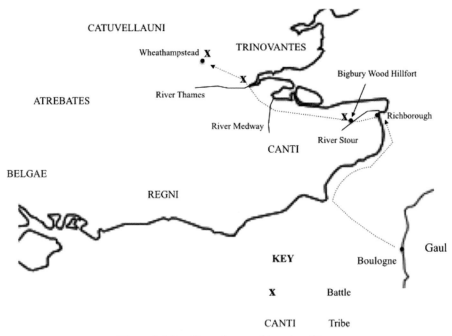

Figure 4: Julius Caesar's second invasion 54 BC.

into the few ships they had and they left at night to reach Gaul by dawn. Again his luck held. Trade with Britain now increased, shifting markedly eastwards to Kent and away from the south-west peninsula. But Caesar was never to return. It was more than eight years before they did.

According to Julius Caesar, a great victory had been won and the Britons, the southern tribes at least, were now friendly to Rome and paid a tribute. Whether any tribute was actually paid is unknown but the Romans secured their hold over Gaul. Julius Caesar was assassinated in 44 BC and Rome lurched into civil war. The result of these upheavals was the end of the republic and birth of the empire. The next time the Romans came in force to Britain would be under the emperor Claudius. Before we turn to him it would be useful to look at this land and people at the edge of the Roman world.

The Britons

Cunliffe, in *Britain Begins*, describes pre-Roman Britain as experiencing waves of immigration.[8] The first of these people appeared after the ice-sheets retreated c. 9600 BC. New practices in agriculture, especially barley and wheat, and animal husbandry of domestic cattle, ships and pigs occurred c. 4200–3000 BC. The following millennia and a half introduced new skills of metal working and an increase in trade and mobility. The period c. 1500 to 800 BC was one of population growth, land clearance and the development of a unique culture with close trade links to northern and western Europe. The late Bronze Age gave way to the Iron-Age c. 800–60 BC.

It is during this period that Britain experienced what Cunliffe describes as a 'descent into regionalism'.[9] Villages and 'open' settlements dominated in the east, with defended or enclosed homesteads in the west and north. A hill-fort-dominated zone predominated in the south and parts of the west. The land was dotted with a patchwork of rival tribes with distinctive cultures and practices. It is this world that confronted Caesar when he first landed in Britain.

It has been suggested by philologists that Indo-European languages, of which Celtic is one, spread from the east around north of the Black Sea or Anatolia. Early Greek and Roman sources point to the Celtic people inhabiting the west, such as Narbonne in southern France and the Iberian peninsula. The same sources suggest Britons shared a similar language and culture. It is not always simple to identify ethnicity or 'a people' through archaeology. Cultural practices change, evolve and are adopted from elsewhere.

However, language offers us some clues. Cunliffe suggests a photo-Celtic language moved westwards into southern Europe after around 6000 BC.[10] It moved north into the Iberian peninsula and the western British Isles in c. 3000 BC. The spread of 'Bell Beaker ideologies' accompanied a movement of peoples c. 2700–2400 BC, which spread the language into central Europe. He thus offers an 'Atlantic origin' for the development of Celtic languages as opposed to a 'myth of the eastern origins of the Celts'. Interestingly, he suggests this movement of people in the mid-third millennium as explaining the difference between Giodelic (Q-Celtic) and Brythonic (P-Celtic), with the former dominating the west and north. By this model the Britons confronted by Caesar would have spoken a Celtic language more closely linked to the language in Gaul.

One of the earliest references to Britain may have been by the Greek historian Herodotus in the fifth century BC. He can say little about these islands off the west coast of Europe except that it was known for its trade in tin, giving it the name *Cassiterides*, 'tin islands'. A poem from the fourth century AD, *Ora maritima*, 'The Sea Coast', claimed to contain an even earlier reference from a Greek navigational manual from the sixth century BC. This describes two islands inhabited by two peoples, the Hierni and Albiones, referring to Ireland and Britain respectively.

Our first eye-witness account is from c. 320 BC in *On the Ocean*, when the Greek explorer Pytheas travelled from Massalia to Armorica and from there circumnavigated Britain. The book did not survive but was referenced by later writers. One such was another Greek, Diodorus Siculus, in the first century BC.

He called the island *Pretanni*, making the Britons the *Pretani* or *Priteni*. This can be translated as the 'painted ones' or 'tattooed folk', which ties in with Caesar's observation of the use of woad, a blue paint used in body decoration.

Strabo in the first century AD uses the spelling *Pretannia*, but Britannia was by now being used as an alternative. Pliny the Elder refers to the cluster of islands as *Britannias* but the largest of them as *Albion*. The survival of the P-spelling may be heard in the later name for the tribes in the north, the *Picti*, and the Welsh name for Britain, *Prydain*. Ptolemy in the second century AD refers to *Brettania* and it was the B-spelling that became dominant.

Strabo, a young man when Caesar invaded Britain, gave a detailed description in *Geographica*.[11] Triangular in shape, Britain lies opposite *Celtica*, Gaul, and is 4,300 *stadia* in length. A stadia was roughly 157 metres, which equates to 675 kilometres or 420 miles. The distance from Kent to Lands End is about a hundred miles shorter but Strabo seems to be measuring the northern coast of Gaul from the Rhine. He names four main crossing points: from the mouths of the Rhine and Seine facing Britain and the Loire and Garonne on the western Atlantic coast of Gaul.

The island is described as flat but with some regions hilly and 'overgrown with forests'. It produces grain, cattle, gold, silver and iron, which are exported along with hides, slaves and hunting dogs. These latter they use in war, as do the Celti in Gaul. Compared to these the Britons are taller with a 'looser build' and 'not so yellow-haired'. Strabo claims he saw 'mere lads' in Rome, presumably slaves, 'half a foot above the tallest people in the city'. Yet they are 'bandy-legged and presented no fair lines anywhere else in their figure'. They had similar customs to the Celts but were 'simpler and more barbaric'. According to Strabo, they have no knowledge of gardening or 'agricultural pursuits' and place their cities in forests, fencing in a 'spacious circular enclosure with trees which they have felled and in that enclosure make huts for themselves and also pen up their cattle'. Strabo claims these are only temporary camps and goes on to comment about the weather: 'Their weather is more rainy than snowy; and on the days of clear sky fog prevails so long a time that throughout a whole day the sun is to be seen for only three or four hours round about midday.'

Strabo was writing during the reign of Augustus and makes an interesting comment about the treaty arrangements existing at the time, presumably a result of Caesar's second invasion. Chieftains from Britain sent embassies and 'dedicated offerings in the Capitol, but have also managed to make the whole of the island virtually Roman'. Heavy duties on imports and exports from Britain bring in much gold, the former from Gaul consisting of 'ivory chains and necklaces, and amber-gems and glass vessels and other petty wares' of that sort). The Britons are so subdued that Strabo states there is no need to garrison the island. In fact only 'one legion, at the least, and some cavalry would be required in order to carry off tribute from them, and the expense of the army would offset the tribute-money'. As we shall see, Claudius was to bring four legions and a similar number of auxiliary troops.

Some of this we must take with a pinch of salt, as we see from his description of Ireland. The inhabitants, even more savage than the Britons, are cannibals and 'openly have intercourse, not only with the other women, but also with their mothers and sisters'. However, he admits he has no trustworthy witnesses. He also mentions Thule, thought to be the Orkneys or Shetland islands, where the people live on 'millet and other herbs, and on fruits and roots; and where there are grain and honey', the latter of which is used to make a beverage.

Julius Caesar provides a fascinating first-hand account of events but also a glimpse into how the Romans viewed Britain.[12] He believed that 'in almost all the Gallic campaigns' the enemy had received support from Britain. He describes the coastal tribes as having migrated from northern Gaul and taken their names with them, suggesting the Belgae and Atrebates. The population is 'innumerable' and unlike Strabo, Caesar describes a rich agricultural tradition similar to Gaul with 'farm-buildings very close together', and a 'great store of cattle'. Gold and bronze coins or iron 'tallies' are used. The weather gets a better press than with Strabo: 'The climate is more temperate than in Gaul, the cold seasons more moderate.' He too describes a triangular island with a smaller one to the west (Ireland) and inbetween an island called Man. He states that the people of Kent are the most civilised while those in the interior 'do not sow corn, but live on milk and flesh and clothe themselves in skins'. We then get a famous descriptor of the physical appearance of the Britons: they 'dye themselves with woad, which produces a blue colour, and makes their appearance in battle more terrible. They wear long hair, and shave every part of the body save the head and the upper lip.' Households of ten or twelve men, often related, hold wives in common. Any children are said to belong to the house.

Yet the Britons were not a culturally homogenous society living peacefully side by side. Caesar tells of 'continuous wars' between Cassivellaunus and the other tribes. While the Britons came together and appointed him as leader, Caesar was eventually able to exploit these differences. A century later, Claudius was confronted with the same patchwork of competing tribes.

Tacitus, writing two generations after the invasion of AD 43, provides more information.[13] The soil is fertile and the weather rainy and cloudy, though the temperature is moderate. The red-haired, large-limbed Caledonians, Tacitus claims, are Germanic in origin. The Silures in south Wales have a swarthy complexion and curled hair. Those in the south-east resemble the Gauls and share some of their sacred rites and superstitions and the language is similar, though perhaps importantly not the same. The Britons are more ferocious in war than their Gallic cousins but even here some have been softened by peace.

Their strength lay in their infantry, while some tribes use chariots, the 'most honourable person guides the reins', while others fight from the platform. The Britons had kings and chieftains but were fractious and their disunity allowed the Romans to divide and conquer. The conquered Britons submitted to levies and tributes 'if they are not treated injuriously'. Tacitus was writing after Agricola's victory at Mons Graupius in c. AD 83, by which time much of southern Britain had been under Roman rule for several decades.

We see here how the Romans slowly won hearts and minds to their cause. A liberal education was provided for the sons of the chieftains and the Britons 'who lately disdained to make use of the Roman language, were now ambitious of becoming eloquent'. Roman habits began to be emulated and 'held in honour'. The toga became common and they became used to luxuries of baths and dining. This slow seduction by Roman civilisation is noted by Tacitus as causing the Britons' enslavement. All this was in the future. Tacitus appears more doubtful as to Julius Caesar's legacy. Caesar won some battles and gained the shore but he 'discovered rather than possessed the island'.

Then the island was neglected by successive emperors until an abortive attempt by Caligula. It was left to Claudius to finally accomplish the undertaking.

Julius Caesar: appearance and personality

Before we end this chapter on the 'first contact' between the Britons and the military might of Rome, we will take a brief look at the man who instigated it. Julius Caesar was born c. 100 BC into a Republic that was already prone to political instability and violence. In his childhood 'The Social War' was fought between the Roman Republic and some of its autonomous allies, resulting in much of Italy becoming 'Romanised' and a significant increase in Roman citizenship. As a young adult he survived Sulla's civil war and served with distinction in the army. In his mid-twenties, on his way to Rhodes to study, he was captured and later ransomed by pirates. It is likely he served as a military tribune during the rebellion of Spartacus in the 'Third Servile War', 73–71 BC.

His appearance and personality is described by Suetonius in *The Lives of the Twelve Caesars*:[14] He was 'tall of stature with a fair complexion, shapely limbs, a somewhat full face, and keen black eyes'. His health was good except towards his later years he was 'subject to sudden fainting fits and to nightmare as well'. Twice he was attacked by 'the falling sickness' on campaign, very likely epilepsy. He took care of his appearance and shaved both his face and excess body hair. Troubled by his baldness, he combed his 'scanty locks forward' to cover it.

He was fond of 'elegance and luxury' and often wore a senator's tunic with fringed sleeves with, unusually, a girdle around it. He is described as 'unbridled and extravagant in his intrigues' and also a ladies-man: 'he seduced many illustrious women… had love affairs with queens too', most famously Cleopatra. This appetite did not extend to food and drink, both of which he was indifferent to. Popular with the troops, he was 'highly skilled in arms and horsemanship, and of incredible powers of endurance'. Time and again he proved his personal bravery by leading his men into battle, placing himself in positions of great personal danger. His oratory skills were as high as his generalship. We can see a contemporary sculpture picturing his likeness in figure 5.

Figure 5. Bust of Julius Caesar (*Wikimedia Commons*)

Our next emperor to set foot in Britain was a very different man, both physically and temperamentally. Julius Caesar started his career gambling his life when he crossed the Rubicon and advanced on Rome. Many times before and after this momentous decision he'd placed himself in harm's way at critical moments in battles. Our next emperor began his reign very differently: hiding behind a curtain in the palace shaking with fear as praetorian guards went on a murderous rampage following the assassination of their beloved emperor, Caligula.

Chapter Two

Claudius and the Invasion of Britain

Tiberius Claudius Nero Germanicus was born at Lugdunum in Gaul in 10 BC He was the youngest son of Drusus the Elder, the brother of Emperor Tiberius. He was also the grandson of Mark Antony. His older brother, Germanicus, had an illustrious military career, married into the imperial family (a daughter of Tiberius's second wife) and was adopted by the emperor, becoming the natural heir to the throne. When Germanicus died in AD 19 some suspected poison. Tiberius was to rule for a further eighteen years, after which the son of Germanicus, Gaius Caesar Augustus Germanicus, became emperor. We know him today as Caligula. At the beginning of his reign the sources are as kind to him as they were to his father. Four years later, after his assassination, the sources widely condemn him for his cruelty.

Suetonius[1] states Caligula was 'sound neither of body nor mind' and had the ability to have both 'extreme assurance and, on the other hand, excessive timorousness'. His acts and words were equally cruel and he indulged in 'reckless extravagance' and 'unspeakable cruelty'. Even before he was emperor it was said 'he could not control his natural cruelty and viciousness, but he was a most eager witness of the tortures and executions of those who suffered punishment, revelling at night in gluttony and adultery'.

What then of Claudius, uncle to the now reviled Caligula? He grew up during the reign of the first emperor and was in his mid-twenties when Augustus died. He lived through the reign of Tiberius and saw the rise of his young nephew Caligula. Yet Claudius himself played little part in the political struggles of the day, held no notable civic posts and did not have a military career, let alone one to rival his brother. He was a most unlikely emperor when greatestnedd was thrust upon him by the praetorian guard at the age of 50. He was perhaps an even less likely conqueror of Britain.

He was a sickly child and Suetonius tells us this dulled 'both his mind and his body'.[2] So much so that even when he reached adulthood he was not thought capable of any public or private office and retained a guardian. His own mother, Antonia, called him 'a monster of a man, not finished but merely begun', and when insulting others would say they were 'a bigger fool than my son Claudius'. His grandmother Augusta also treated him with contempt. When learning of his ascension his sister Livilla 'openly and loudly prayed' that Rome would be spared her brother's rule.

Suetonius quotes a letter from Augustus to his wife Livia where he discusses the 'Claudius problem'. He suggests they decide once and for all if he is fit for public office. If he is 'wanting and defective in soundness of body and mind' then they should avoid the potential ridicule and embarrassment. However, he finishes noting 'where his mind does not wander, the nobility of his character is apparent enough'. Ultimately, Augustus decided Claudius just wasn't up to it and he served no offices except a priesthood. It wasn't until his nephew was emperor that he held high office as joint consul.

Caligula was stabbed to death by multiple assailants in a scene reminiscent of the murder of Julius Caesar. Caligula's guard went on a killing spree to avenge their fallen emperor. Innocent bystanders were caught up as well as some of the murderers and co-conspirators. In the bloodletting Caligula's wife, Caesonia, was stabbed by a centurion, while his daughter's brains were dashed out against a wall. The future conqueror of Britain was found cowering in hiding. While the praetorians sacked, looted and murdered anyone they came across, a single guardsman wandered through the palace and noticed toes poking out the bottom of some curtains. Drawing them back, he found Claudius shaking with fear and the fate of the empire hung on the guardsman's decision.

Writing a few decades later, Suetonius tells us Claudius 'fell at his feet in terror' but the soldier hailed him as emperor and dragged him to his comrades, who continued to run amok in 'purposeless rage'. It's easy to imagine Claudius being killed then and there and history may have taken a different turn. Perhaps no invasion of Britain at all and a completely different list of emperors. But the soldiers placed him in a litter and carried him to their camp. Claudius was apparently terrified and held overnight in despair. A standoff ensued, with the consuls and senate holding the Forum and Capitol. They ordered Claudius to attend but his message back claimed he was held 'by force and compulsion'. The senators descended into bickering and factionalism. Suetonius tells us it was the people themselves who called for Claudius, who, it is implied, reluctantly allowed the army to swear allegiance to him. The price was 15,000 sesterces each.

The invasion very nearly didn't happen. There was an abortive attempt on his life in 42 and at least six further attempts during the rest of his reign.[3] Scribonianus had revolted in Dalmatia but his legions refused to support the coup, earning them the title *Claudia Pia Fidelis* ('Cladius' own, loyal and true'). By the end of 42, with the ringleaders dead and confident that the legions were behind him, he had decided the invasion was on.

This was not the first time Rome had cast its eyes across the ocean since Julius Caesar had received the surrender of several tribes in 54 BC. The Catuvellauni had been required to agree not to invade their eastern neighbours, the Trinovantes of Essex. Within sixty years these two tribes had been unified under the Catuvellaunian king, Cunobelin, making the Trinovantian capital, Camulodunum, modern Colchester, his base. This might indicate Rome's influence had waned over the decades. Caesar had also demanded tribute, although there is debate about if it was ever collected, and if so, for how long. It has been suggested it was these events that put the Romans and Britons on a collision course. Three of Cunobelin's sons played a part: Adminius, who fled to Rome during the reign of Caligula; and Caratacus and Togodumnus. These latter two had a very different attitude towards Rome than their brother or father. It was their hostility and attack on Verica, a king of Atrebates who were friendly to Rome, that was ultimately to bring the legions to Britain.

There were several other times when Rome considered following up on Caesar's last expedition in 54 BC.[4] Augustus called off a planned invasion in 34 BC due to a Dalmatian revolt. Seven years later another proposed expedition was called off due to unrest in Gaul. Cassius Dio reports that Augustus had set out to 'make an expedition into Britain' but, after heading north, lingered in Gaul. The reasons given were twofold:[5] First, the Gauls were still unsettled with civil wars among the subjugated tribes; and second, the Britons seemed likely to make terms.

Just two years later Cassius Dio reports the Britons reneged, but this time Augustus was thwarted by a revolt of the Salassi in Liguria and Cantabri and Astures in Northern Spain. It has been suggested this marks the cessation of the tribute payments agreed by Caesar.

Augustus himself in *Res Gestae Divi Augusti*, 'The Deeds of the Divine Augustus', records two British kings who also requested aid: Tincommius of the Atrebates and Dubnovellaunus of the Trinovantes. Both tribes were under pressure from the Catevellauni, the very tribe Julius Caesar had forced a sort of non-aggression agreement on. Here then we have two further instances that might have persuaded the Romans to invade. It wasn't until the reign of Caligula that another potential invasion was planned.

Suetonius tells us Caligula had just the one experience of war. This quickly descended into farce. He was seized with the idea of a campaign into Germany and gathered together legions and auxiliary units. Clearly no fan, Suetonius described him as 'lazy and luxurious', insisting on being carried in a litter by eight bearers. The roads ahead were ordered to be swept and sprinkled with water to keep the dust down. However, he found himself with very little to do apart from antagonising the army. He dismissed generals and long-serving centurions just days from retirement, and reduced the pay of those reaching full service. Finding no one to fight, he resorted to faking skirmishes, once by sending his bodyguard ahead to pretend to be barbarians.

It was at this point events across the channel presented the Romans with an opportunity. The Catuvellaunian king, Cunobelin, had quarrelled with his son Aminius, who fled across the sea. The arrival of Aminius allowed the emperor to save face by giving him both a purpose and an excuse. But the army was reluctant to cross the ocean to mysterious island. Caligula, no doubt angered by his men's disobedience, drew up a line of battle on the shore of the ocean, placing his ballistas and artillery facing the sea. Many were no doubt concerned what new outrage the emperor might indulge in. Caligula suddenly ordered his men to gather shells, filling their helmets and the folds of their tunics and cloaks, calling them 'spoils from the Ocean, due to the Capitol and Palatine'.[6]

Cassius Dio adds to the account of Suetonius: Caligula 'set out as if to conduct a campaign against Britain, but turned back from the ocean's edge'.[7] The soldiers were drawn up on the beach while the emperor sailed past on a trireme. Returning to the shore, he sat on a 'lofty platform' and gave the order to collect sea-shells. Trumpeters urged them on as the proud legionaries scrambled about across the beach. Caligula we are told became 'greatly elated, as if he had enslaved the very ocean; and he gave his soldiers many presents'.

All these efforts only resulted in the official surrender of Aminius, effectively a prince without a kingdom. News of this great victory along with a letter and the shells were sent to the consuls and the senate. He erected a lighthouse, presumably at Gesoriacum. At his triumph he paraded his captives, many of whom were actually deserters. Choosing the tallest, he made to 'dye their hair red and to let it grow long' but 'also to learn the language of the Germans and assume barbarian names'. He even had the triremes he had intended to use carried overland to Rome.

This aborted invasion likely occurred in AD 40. Caligula was assassinated the following January. It was at this point we get the dramatic scene at the start of this chapter, with Claudius, a relatively old man shaking with fear behind a curtain. Little did the guardsman who found him know that the fate of Britain as well as the empire rested on his actions. The soldier stayed his arm and just over two years later Roman legions were marching across southern Britain.

The invasion

Caligula left behind a fleet of ships and a large port. These ships formed the core of the 900 the Romans were to use and later became the *Classis Britannica* regional fleet. The opportunity to use these resources came quickly. The Catuvellaunian king, Cunobelin, died in late 40 and was succeeded by his sons Caratacus and Togodumnus. Bad enough that they did not share their father's policy of good relations with Rome, but they attacked the friendly Atrebates in the Thames valley. Their king, Verica, fled to Rome where he found a sympathetic ear with the new emperor. Claudius had the means of a large fleet and now was presented with a motive.

Suetonius gives us a slightly different reason for the invasion. He tells us Claudius sought an imperial triumph and chose Britain as the best place for gaining it.[8] He describes the Britons as 'in a state of rebellion because of the refusal to return certain deserters'. Sailing from Ostia, hugging the coast as they went, violent storms nearly sank the ship twice before they had even reached Massilia, modern Marseille. Docking at the port on the southern coast of Gaul, he journeyed across land to Gesoriacum, Boulogne-sur-Mer. It was from this port, just thirty miles from the cliffs of Dover, that he made his crossing. Suetonius states there was no battle or bloodshed and he 'received the submission of a part of the island'.

The immediate objective was likely returning friendly client kings to power in tribes along the southern coast. Strabo, writing during the time of Tiberius, estimated just one legion and some cavalry could subdue the island. However, he also stated that more was gained from customs than tribute once the cost of a potential garrison was deducted.[9] A few decades later Claudius had more on his mind than economics. He had four legions at his disposal: Legio II Augusta, legio XIV Gemina, legio XX Valera Victrix and legio IX Hispana. The latter's commander, Aulus Plautius, was placed in charge of the army. The future Emperor Vespasian was the leading legionary legate and played a major role as we shall see in the next chapter. This was one legion less than Julius Caesar. However, they brought more auxiliary units, especially cavalry, to bring his total force up to about 40,000.

These legions were to provide the initial garrison. Much later legio XIV Gemina would be replaced by legio II Adiutrix, which itself returned to the continent in 87. This left the Second, Twentieth and Ninth legions. The Sixth legion arrived in the early second century and it is thought the Ninth left a few years later, returning the garrison to these three legions throughout the second, third and fourth centuries: II Augusta; XX Valera Victrix and VI Victrix. All this was in the future as Plautius prepared the Second, Fourteenth, Twentieth and Ninth legions, approximately 20,000 legionaries, for embarkation. A similar number of auxiliary troops were also prepared. The normal type of ship was a liburnian bireme galley, with two banks or oars on each side.[10]

The troops were nervous. They had heard stories of the mysterious island and were reluctant to board. They had no doubt heard tales from Caesar and Strabo of tall, ferocious Britons covered in blue dye. Tales of cannibals and sun-less days full of cold fog and rain would have added to the unease. Cassius Dio tells us Plautius had difficulty: 'inducing his army to advance beyond Gaul. For the soldiers were indignant at the thought of carrying on a campaign outside the limits of the known world.'[11] In the end they were shamed into action. Tiberius Claudius Narcissus was a member of the emperor's advisory council, the *Consilium Principis*. He was also a former slave. He boarded the nearest ship, shouting *Io Saturnalia!*. This was a reference to the role reversal performed at the end of the year festival. The soldiers were stirred into action and followed the former slave aboard.

A widely accepted view is that Plautius sailed from Gesoriacum to Richborough near Pegwell Bay in East Kent.[12] A landing spot further west near the Isle of Wight hasn't gained as much support, although as we shall see Vespasian later did capture the island. We can see the two possible invasion routes on the map in figure 6. The landing was unopposed. In 43 the Isle of Thanet was a true island with the navigable Watsum Channel separating the island from East Kent by two miles of water. Later a grand monumental arch was erected by Domitian at Richborough. Extended ditch and bank fortifications have been identified here. All this lends support that the area just north of Sandwich was the main landing point.

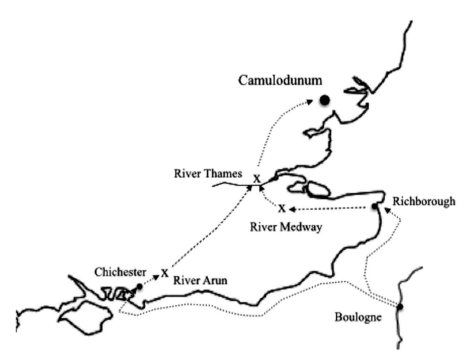

Figure 6. Map showing the possible invasion routes in AD 43.

An initial success near the River Stour allowed a fort to be constructed and they marched inland.

When they reached the Medway they found the Britons, led by Togodumnus and Caratacus, massed on the western bank. Plautius sent across Vespasian with his brother Sabinus. The Britons were taken by surprise and suffered many casualties but they did not break, attacking the Romans the next day. The defenders retreated to the Thames with Plautius hot on their heels.

Dio describes the place as follows: 'a point near where it empties into the ocean and at flood-tide forms a lake. This they easily crossed because they knew where the firm ground and the easy passages in this region were to be found.' This is thought by some to be near Westminster; however, Elliott makes a very good case for the Higham to Tilbury area as this is the lowest fordable point on the Thames in the first century.[13]

The modern Thames is about fifteen feet higher than the level at the time of the invasion.[14] At low tide Plautius would have looked out across mud flats interspersed with fresh water streams that shifted and changed course as the tides came and went. Evidence of a ferry crossing in the Middle Ages suggests this may have been the likeliest spot for a crossing centuries before. From Church Street, Higham in Kent to the northern bank at East Tilbury in Essex. Once again the Romans forced a crossing, attacking from several sides at once. The Britons managed to escape through the swamps in which the pursuing Romans, not knowing the terrain, lost a number of men.

With both these battles we have a fair amount of detail. Claudius was not present but Vespasian was. For that reason we will cover the battles in the next chapter. Once he secured the northern bank Plautius stopped. We are told Togodumnus died soon after the second battle, leaving Caratacus to fight another day. Dio tells us the Britons did not give up but united to avenge his death.

Then Plautius apparently 'became afraid, and instead of advancing any farther, proceeded to guard what he had already won sending for Claudius'. It is at this point we get the first mention of elephants: 'For he had been instructed to do this in case he met with any particularly stubborn resistance, and, in fact, extensive equipment, including elephants, had already been got together for the expedition.'[15]

Cassius Dio would have us believe the emperor himself took command and won a great victory, advancing on the Catuvellaunian capital at Camulodunum. He then won over many tribes 'in some cases by capitulation, in others by force'. He was 'saluted as imperator several times… deprived the conquered of their arms and handed them over to Plautius'. Leaving his general to subjugate the remaining districts, he hastened back to Rome. He sent his sons-in-law, Magnus and Silanus, ahead to give word to the senate, which honoured him with the title *Britannicus*.

Dio continues that 'portions of Britain, then, were captured at this time' and that Claudius returned to Rome after just six months. Importantly we are told he spent only sixteen days in Britain. It is thus likely he sailed from Gesoriacum and made land near Tilbury before advancing on the tribal capital at modern Colchester about forty miles to the north east of Tilbury. This would be just two days' march for a legion or a day's hard ride for a unit of cavalry. However, an invading army, unfamiliar with the terrain and trying to avoid swamps, inlets and rivers, could take considerably longer. Wagons drawn by oxen carrying artillery might only manage five miles a day.

It is therefore far more likely that after the victory at the Thames, Plautius simply took this opportunity to summon the emperor from Gesoriacum, a day's journey by boat. If he had summoned him from Rome as the sources imply it would have taken weeks for Claudius to receive the message and travel over a thousand miles on land and sea. It is likely he made the short journey across the channel, then down the Thames, arriving at the Roman camp by the end of July. There isn't a lot of time within a sixteen-day period to imagine Claudius personally leading a campaign and battling through to take Camulodunum.

It does sound more likely that Plautius secured the northern bank and the route to the tribal capital. Once the Romans stormed the *oppidum* and pacified the area they would have built a fort. The emperor needed to decide whether to march overland from Tilbury or travel by boat the short distance up the coast. Claudius received a triumph back in Rome and an arch was constructed on which the names of eleven kings of the Britons were inscribed.[16] It is possible a similar triumph, albeit on a much smaller scale, was arranged at Camoludunum. One can imagine the local chieftains being forced to endure their conqueror's triumphal entrance into the former tribal capital, whilst the victorious legions marched behind their emperor.

Camulodunum

What then did Iron Age Camulodunum look like? The Romans described the main urban settlements they encountered as *oppidum* (plural *oppida*), meaning 'enclosed space'. Julius Caesar named twenty-eight such sites in Gaul and while they are left undefined, they were centres of economic or political power. Strabo, referring specifically to Britain, states: 'The forests are their cities; for they fence in a spacious circular enclosure with trees which they have felled, and in that enclosure make huts for themselves and also pen up their cattle.'[17] We get a hint of this from Julius Caesar's own writing concerning his second invasion.[18]

Concealing themselves in the woods, the Britons fortified the approaches by 'a great number of felled trees'. The Seventh legion had to form a *testudo* using their shields to form a 'tortosie-like' formation. They then built a ramp against the fortifications and took the position.

Later in the campaign he learned of the location of the stronghold of Cassivellaunus 'fenced by woods and marshes'.[19] He tells us the 'Britons call it a stronghold when they have fortified a thick-set woodland with rampart and trench, and thither it is their custom to collect, to avoid a hostile inroad'. The Romans found it 'thoroughly fortified by nature and by handiwork'. The Britons tended to live in farmsteads, which were often enclosed by an outer ditch and wall.[20] The buildings were generally round with thatched roofs, wattle-and-daub walls and timber posts. Large farmsteads had a number of such buildings, likely for an extended multi-generational family group. These were often enclosed within a 'sub-rectangular' compound defended by a bank and ditch. One example found at Stansted in north-west Essex had eleven such round buildings within a square enclosure.[21]

The Iron Age settlement at Camulodunum was well chosen. It was protected by rivers on three sides: the Colne to the north and east; and the Roman River to the south. The earthworks defended the western gap between these two rivers. Eastern earthworks protected attack from the east across the River Colne. The name is thought to derive from a Brythonic Celtic name, *Camulodunon*, meaning 'the stronghold of Camulus', the British god of war. The area between the earthworks and rivers was a massive 1,000 hectares, nearly 4 square miles. In comparison, modern Heathrow airport covers 1,227 hectares. It is likely that farmsteads and other buildings were spread out within the *oppidum*. This was much larger than the site at Wheathampstead, which is thought to have been the stronghold of Cassivellaunus in Caesar's second invasion. That was only 35 hectares. The later Roman town at Camulodunum covered about just 43 hectares, demonstrating just how huge the pre-Roman site was.

The settlement can be dated to around at least 25 BC with coins dated to 10–15 BC.[22] There is no way of knowing if the site was in existence during Caesar's invasion but it seems fairly likely. Evidence of a farmstead has been found at Gosbecks to the south west of the site. This was a large high-status building believed to be home to a chieftain. Part of the complex was a large, square enclosure surrounded by a deep, wide ditch. The area around it was primarily agricultural.

The northern Sheepen site on the banks of the River Colne contained a large industrial zone with extensive iron- and leather-working activity. A port gave access to the river. Coins found there depict sailing vessels, the only known ones from Iron Age Britain. Imported pottery and amphorae demonstrate trade was an important part of the economy. To the west a series of earthworks protected the western approach. In the east a further bank and ditch added to the protection from the River Colne as it curled round to offer protection from the north.

If we include the earthworks it covered approximately 10 square miles between the valleys of the Colne and Roman River.[23] The dykes themselves measured 12 miles if placed end to end. They consisted of a V-shaped ditch with a bank behind. The largest ditches were 13 metres deep with a similar-sized bank rising behind it. This would have proved extremely difficult for cavalry and impenetrable for chariots.

It was a flat, rural landscape of pasture, cultivated fields and woodland. Crops such as wheat, barley, oats, peas and beans were grown, Livestock was predominantly cattle but pigs, sheeps and goats were also common. We know it was the Trinovantes who occupied the area because Tacitus tells us they specifically lost land to Roman settlers at Camulodunum. We can see the extent of the settlement together with the first Roman forts on the map in figure 7.

It has been claimed that Camulodunum was Britain's oldest recorded town or even Britain's first city. Pliny mentions the town in his *Natural history*[24] '… in Mona [Anglesey], which is about 200 miles from Camelodunum, a town of Britain'. A second-century inscription in Rome gives the name as '… *colonia Victricensis* which is at Camulodunum in Britannia …' ('… *coloniae Victricensis quae est in Brittannia Camaloduni* …').

It was described by Tacitus as being founded in 49: 'a colony was settled on conquered lands at Camulodunum by a strong detachment of veterans, who were

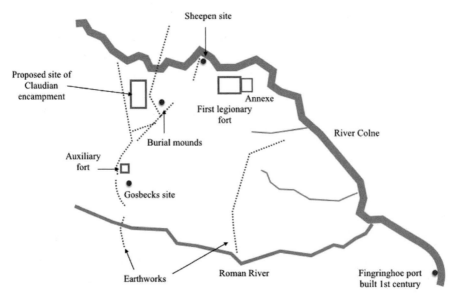

Figure 7. Camulodunum: Map of the Iron Age settlement and the first Roman fort.

to serve as a bulwark against revolt and to habituate the friendly natives to their legal obligations.'[25] Tacitus tells us again that by 61, the year of the Boudican revolt, Colchester (a *colonia*) and St Albans (a *municipium*) were chartered Roman towns. London at this point was a mere trading-post. He blames the veterans for creating the 'bitterest animosity' among the natives. They acted as though they owned the entire island and drove people from their homes and lands, treating them as 'captives and slaves'.

Adding insult to injury the newly built temple of the deified Claudius stood like 'a citadel of an eternal tyranny'. Importantly Tacitus tells us at this point, just eighteen years after the invasion, the colony was 'unprotected by fortifications'.[26] Of course none of this was there when Claudius arrived in 43. Instead there was an iron-age settlement fortified by ditches and covering a wide area.

Wacher, in *The Roman Towns of Britain*, lays out the initial phases of occupation.[27] The site at Sheepen near the River Colne appears to have been converted into a works depot. Nearby an auxiliary fort was constructed covering about four acres. A legionary fortress was constructed very early, c. 43–4, and overlooked the Colne to the north. This was garrisoned by the Twentieth legion. To the east of this a large annexe was built. In late 48 the new governor of Britain, Ostorius Scapula move the Twentieth west to assist in his camping against the elusive Caratacus and the Silures. It was at this point a new *colonia* of retired veterans was established. The fortress was abandoned and the defences levelled with the ditches filled in. This was to prove a disastrous decision a decade later.

Many buildings remained and were adapted for civilian use. The famous temple of Claudius was built in the annexe area to the east of the area where the fortress had stood. Tacitus refers to a *curia*, council or senate house, at the time of the revolt. Later, walls encompassed the entire area where these former buildings stood, including the initial fortress. There is some debate whether this was soon after the revolt or much later in the third century. All this was in the future and the sight Claudius would have been presented with would have looked very different. Before we look at the emperor's grand entrance to receive the surrender of the British kings there is one long standing story we need to address.

Emperors and elephants

Sky Atlantic's popular TV show Britannia, as entertaining as it is, is hardly an accurate historical account. In the opening episode of season 2 we see Emperor Claudius arriving on the back of an elephant. Seated in a box with red curtains matching the soldiers' cloaks and centurion's helmet plumes. Gold braid edging catching the sun. To the front and rear legionaries march in columns five wide.

Crowds of on-lookers cheer him through a stone arch whilst inside the fort several buildings are under construction with some already finished. Some tourist websites go along with this tale.[28] Wikipedia also eludes to the event: 'The first historically recorded elephant in northern Europe was the animal brought by emperor Claudius, during the Roman invasion of Britain in AD 43, to the British capital of Colchester'.[29] Barbara Levick in *Claudius* describes the parading troops and elephants giving the Britons and awe-inspiring display.[30]

It's a story I vaguely remember hearing, seeing or reading about as a child. The question is did this actually happen? The only reference to elephants in Cassius Dio is when Plautius stops north of the Thames and awaits the arrival of the emperor: 'For he had been instructed to do this in case he met with any particularly stubborn resistance, and, in fact, extensive equipment, including elephants, had already been got together for the expedition'.[31] Does this mean Plautius had already utilised them? Or were the elephants in reserve and came over with Claudius? It sounds like the latter, if they came at all.

Polyaenus, writing in the third quarter of the second century tells us it was in fact Julius Caesar who first brought elephants to Britain.[32] We are told the Britons defended the far bank of a large river with large numbers of cavalry and chariots. This seems to be during the second invasion but which river crossing does it refer to? Two possibilities present themselves: the Stour near Canterbury or the Thames. As the British king Cassivellaunus was leading the defenders at this point it would seem to be the latter. The elephant is described as mailed in scales of iron, with a tower on its back. Archers and slingers were able to rain down fire from this elevated position. The Britons must have been filled with fear and wonder at such a sight but the horses were terrified. Polyaenus tells us that horses will flee even unarmored pachyderms. With armour shining in the sun and a huge tower from which arrows and slings fired deadly missiles was 'a sight too formidable to be borne'. The Britons fled allowing the Romans to take the far bank, the battle decided by the mere sight of a single elephant.

Nearly a century later in 43 few Britons had likely ever seen an elephant even if they had heard tales of the former invasion or from traders who may have glimpsed one on their travels. If the sources are correct then elephants were certainly part of the force prepared for the invasion. It seems reasonable to suggest that Plautius intended to make rapid progress and then call on further resources once he had a sufficient bridgehead. Having secured the south-east as far as the Thames this was accomplished. If this was the moment the emperor came with reinforcements then perhaps the elephants came with him. A study of similar use of elephants in warfare of the period would suggest they numbered a few dozen rather than one or two or hundreds.[33]

Claudius, let us remember was by now 53 years old and was not a physically fit man. Even if we accept Suetonius' account that he was relatively healthy he also had bad knees and had difficulty at times walking. It seems unlikely he would have been willing or able to ride on the back of an elephant. It is far more likely his entrance would have been similar to his triumph which is described below where he entered riding on a chariot. Even so the sight of several elephants, towers on their backs with archers and slingers, plodding into the settlement would have filled the Britons with awe.

Forts

One of the strengths of the Roman army was it's ability to quickly construct defensive fortifications. Vegetius, writing in the fourth century, described three types of camp:[34]

1. Where there's no immediate danger or for one night: A three-feet-deep fosse or ditch is cut five-feet wide with the turves stacked up on the inside edge.
2. A 'stationary camp': A temporary fosse nine-feet wide and seven-feet deep.
3. When more serious forces threaten a twelve- to seventeen-feet wide and nine-feet-deep fosse is built. Then inside an embankment four-feet high overlooks the fosse making it thirteen-feett deep.

They should be located near a good supply of water, firewood and fodder, avoiding swampy areas and those overlooked by higher ground. These 'marching camps' could be built in just a few hours at the end of a days march. This usually began just after dawn. Twenty miles might take about five hours using the 'military step'. But they could cover twenty four miles at 'full step'.[35] The distance would be completed by the afternoon leaving sufficient time to build the camp.

In hostile territory half the infantry and most of the cavalry would stand ready allowing the others to complete the camp before evening. Legionaries carried stakes which they could place in a fixed line to protect the construction or to line the top of the bank in a quickly constructed earthwork. An outer ditch, the *fossae*, six-feet deep and five-feet wide was dug and the soil used to build this rampart, approximately six-feet high by eight-feet wide. This placed a legionary at least twelve feet above the bottom of the ditch. These ramparts were reinforced with logs and a palisade built on top with possibly battlements and turrets added to provide a fighting platform. Attackers were faced with a six-foot ditch, and a six-foot rampart topped with a six-foot wooden palisade. Wide gates, protected by towers, were added, sometimes forty-feet wide, to allow rapid deployment against an attacking force.

28   The Roman Emperors of Britain

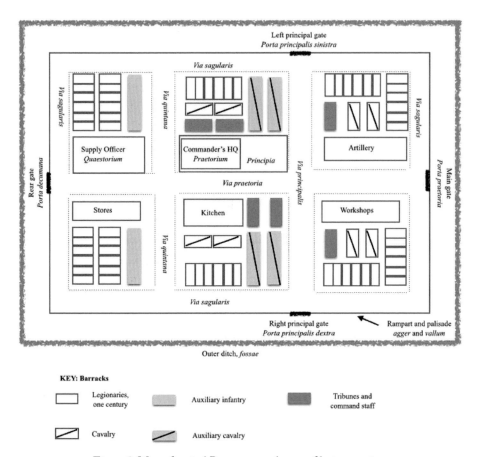

Figure 8. Map of typical Roman camp layout of legionary size.

Inside the wall a road, the *via sagularis*, ran around the perimeter of the camp allowing access to the ramparts from any part of the camp. Camp size obviously depended on the size of the force.

Most of the camps along the Antonine Wall, for example, were about two hectares, or just over three football fields. The camp at Carnuntum on the Danube was home to four legions and covered about ten hectares. We can see an example of a basic camp layout for a single legion in figure 8. Whatever the size a visiting dignitary, or emperor, would be received, and perhaps stay in, the *praetorium* at the centre of tree camp.

A more contemporary but anonymous Roman writer details slightly smaller dimensions compared to the later Vegetius:[36] A ditch, five-feet wide and three-feet deep surrounded a rampart nine-feet wide and six-feet in height. A second century source, *De Munitionibus Castrorum*, 'Concerning the fortifications of a military camp', gives a detailed description of the typical camp layout, generally a square or rectangular 'playing card' shape. This became common from the time of Claudius.

Each side had a gate with two main roads connecting the gate opposite. These converged on the *principia*, at the centre of the camp. Here lay the commander's headquarters and an open courtyard or forum with a raised platform to address the troops. Within the headquarters was the *aedes*, or shrine, where the legion or unit's standards were kept. Under this a strongroom was dug to hold the troops coins. Also here were armouries, *armamentaria*, and even rooms for officer recreation, *scholae*. Established camps would have had baths, granaries and even shops with local settlements growing up around them. However, a marching camp in enemy territory would have no such luxuries.

Attached to the legions were a variety of specialists, *immunes*. Legionnaires with specific skills could also perform these vital functions; however, non-military personnel often accompanied the legions, adding considerably to the numbers. Larger and more established camps would have had a considerable number of these personnel. A list of some examples is instructive as to what a camp might have included:[37] surveyors, *mensores*; medical orderlies, *medici*; wound dressers, *capsarii*; veterinaries, *veterinarii*; master-builder, *architectus*; artillery makers/operators, *ballistrarii*; craftsmen, *fabri*; arrow makers, *sagittarii*; bow-makers, *acuarii*; blacksmiths, *ferrarii*; bronze-smiths, *aerarii*; lead-makers, *plumbarii*; carpenters, *carpentarii*; sword-makers, *gladiatores*; hydraulic engineers, *aquilices*; stonemasons, *lapidarii*; hunters, *venatores*; armourers, *custodes armorum*; and millers, *polliones*. Specialist builders, shipwrights, ships' pilots, bridge-builders and artillery specialists were also present, as were priests to officiate at ceremonies and staff to look after sacrificial animals. Repair shops and manufacturers needed officers, managers and a sizeable workforce of skilled labourers. Clerks of various kinds were also needed for the granaries, general book-keeping; and for the deceased.

Large elaborate camps took time to construct although a well trained legion could build a basic fort in a few hours even under enemy pressure. In 52 BC at Alesia Julius Caesar took just three weeks to construct ten miles of fortifications. The question is what sort of sight greeted the emperor on his arrival? Claudius very likely sailed first to Richborough in East Kent where the Emperor Domitian later built an arch to celebrate the conquest forty two years later. This also supports Pegwell Bay area as the main landing site in 43. The journey from Richborough to Tilbury, if that was the site of Plautius's base, is a two day march or a day by boat. A carriage would have taken considerably longer and giving the time constraints (we recall Claudius was in Britain for just 16 days) a boat is more likely.

The next stage of the journey from Tilbury to Camulodunum is forty miles overland. This is two days march for hardened legionaries but considerably longer for the ailing emperor who would be forced to be carried in a litter or by carriage. Sailing straight to the settlement from Gesoriacum would take less than two days and from Tilbury a few hours. Whatever the case it is likely some sort of fort had already been constructed to protect and allow the emperor to recuperate from his journey.

Claudius may well have rested at the camp at Tilbury and again for a few nights at Camulodunum. If that is the case then he would have stayed in the *principia* of the main camp before travelling to Camulodunum. There he would have entered an enormous *oppidum*, passing through the impressive earthworks. Cassius Dio would have us believe it was Claudius himself who defeated the defenders and captured Camulodunum. But as we have noted previously it is far more likely Plautius secured the victory, and the capital, before informing Claudius who was waiting just across the channel.

Claudius was cautious and wary of danger so I would suggest the site was already secure with a fort constructed guarding the area and as a place of refuge should the Romans come under attack. Philip Crummy in *City of Victory: The Story of Colchester – Britain's First Roman Town*, suggests a temporary fort was first placed at Triple Dyke which can be seen in map in figure 7.[38] The earthworks here are 45 metres across and 1.5 km long. Evidence of an auxiliary fort with a likely capacity for 500 infantry was also found near Gosbeck's site.

Perhaps it was at the larger fort the visiting chiefs and kings were forced to watch the arrival of the Twentieth to their new home. Protected by dykes on three sides and the river to the north. Julius Caesar had a tent measuring 200 foot square when campaigning in Gaul which gives an indication the size of tent which a visiting emperor might expect at the very least. Alternatively the large flat area inside the *oppidum* would have allowed a significant display of Roman martial power. One can imagine the scene, a wide expanse, flanked by soldiers, with kings and chieftains waiting to receive the emperor. Slowly a procession would wind itself through the entrance and into the centre of the *oppidum*.

What must the Britons have felt when they saw the might of Rome march into their former centre of power? Perhaps followed by these huge lumbering beasts some had only heard rumours of. Topped by towers with archers and slingers. And finally this 'emperor-god', purple-cloaked and adorned with laurel leaves and a gold crown on a chariot. Some no doubt saw opportunity whilst others looked to their own interests. Others gritted their teeth and bided their time. Some of their children would return to Camulodunum a generation later. At their head would be a very different leader also riding a chariot. Her intention and the result would be very different.

Triumph

Claudius returned to Rome in six months later. The senate granted permission for him to celebrate a triumph and awarded the title *Britannicus* to both him and his son. They voted for an annual festival to mark the occasion and built two triumphal arches, one in Rome, dedicated c. 51–2, the other in Gaul. The latter was likely at *Gesoriacum* as Cassius Dio tells us it was from the place he set sail when he crossed to Britain. Part of the inscription of the arch at Rome still survives and it seems to corroborate he gained submission of a number of tribes by both force and diplomacy.

It was once thought it said eleven kings but this is now uncertain. Dedicated from the Senate and Roman people, it uses his full name, Tiberius Claudius Caesar Augustus Germanicus, and lists his titles: Pontifex Maximus, Tribunicia Potestas (for the eleventh time), Consul five times, Imperator (twenty two times), Censor and Pater Patria (father of the country). The inscription reads: '…he received into surrender eleven kings of the Britons conquered without loss and he first brought the barbarian peoples across the ocean under the authority of the Roman people'.[39]

Suetonius declares the emperor fought no battles and suffered no casualties. A century and a half later Cassius Dio states Claudius joined the legions at the Thames then crossed the river and defeated the Britons who assembled there. This seems at odds with the statement that Plautius crossed the river then called for imperial help. There is no archaeological evidence the Romans actually assaulted Camulodunum.[40] However literary sources record a show at the Campus Martius in Rome depicting a siege and capture of a British town along with the surrender of British kings. Claudius took the applause.

Who were these British kings that surrendered? Webster notes the eleven kings referenced on the arch in Rome and attempts to name some.[41] Three allies are named first: Cogidubnus of the Regni, Prasutagus of the Iceni and Cartimandua of the Brigantes. Kings from the Atrebates, Dobunni and Coritani of the East Midlands are also suggested. There may well have been kings from Kent and sub-kings of the Catuvellauni.

Prasutagus is well-known for being the husband of Boudicca. It was his death, and the Roman response to it, that sparked the uprising seventeen years later. Cartimandua of the Brigantes was the queen who famously handed Caractacus over to he Romans. Cogidubnus of the Regni is the same Cogidumnus, or Togidumnus, mentioned by Tacitus. He was said by Tacitus to have ruled several *civitates* and been loyal 'down to our own times'. An inscription at *Noviomagus*, Chichester, names Tiberius Claudius Togidubnus as 'great king of Britain'[42]

Governors of the provinces came to Rome to attend a 'triumph of great splendour'. A naval crown was placed on the gable of the Palace to show he had crossed and subdued the Ocean. There were no set rules for a Triumph but in general the booty and prisoners would be followed by the victorious general with the army at the rear. This would often end at the Temple of Jupiter Optimus Maximus where offerings could be made.

The general rode a chariot and wore a *toga picta*, purple tunic, covered with patterns. On his head was a laurel wreath and golden crown. In earlier times the face of the conqueror may have been painted red, a practice they may have died out by the time of Claudius. Behind the emperor rode Messalina, his third wife, in a carriage. Those who had won honours followed on foot in purple-bordered togas. The army brought up the rear, in full military garb and regalia. They would sing bawdy songs and cry *io triumpe* as they marched. Claudius ascended the Capitol on his knees supported by his sons-in-law.

What then can this tell us about the emperor's entrance into Camulodunum? It would obviously have been on a smaller scale than the grand parade in Rome. As noted previously Claudius would more likely have been riding a chariot than an elephant. Perhaps he was preceded by booty and captured Britons to make a point. Those friendly to Rome, awaiting his entrance, may have benefitted both with a share of the spoils and from any vacant positions of power. Cogidubnus seems one such figure. Given the grandness of the palace uncovered at Fishbourne, near Chichester, he seems to have taken to Roman life rather quickly.

Yet such a spectacle would have impressed upon them the extent of Roman power. Those who had capitulated earlier may have congratulated themselves on their wise decision as columns of soldiers marched past, followed by the cavalry and lumbering elephants with towers and men on their backs. The legionaries would have felt a certain amount of pride in a job well done although many of their comrades would have fallen along the way. But the fighting was not yet over.

Claudius left Britain a little more than a fortnight after his landing. The Romans consolidated the south-east but were quickly on the march again. Pushing north and west, the main thrust was lead by our next emperor, Vespasian. In 43 he was still legionary legate of the Second legion and it was to him Plautius turned for the next attack.

Post-invasion

Within four years of the fall of Camulodunum Plautius had secured much of southern and central Britain. This new province of Britannia extended to a border marked by the Fosse Way, linking Exeter in the south west to Lincoln in the east.

In 43 Vespasian lead was ordered to lead his single legion and auxiliaries to the west, capturing hillforts and the Isle of Wight. The Durotriges and Dumnonii tribes were subdued after much hard fighting. By the year 47 Vespasian had reached and occupied the area around modern Exeter.

Between 47–53 the expansion continued under Ostorius Scapula. The fourteenth advanced into the Midlands and was based first at Manduessedum, Mancetter and then Viroconium, Wroxeter. The Ninth marched north to Lindum, Lincoln whilst the Twentieth remained at Camulodunum. Later it was to move west to Gloucester to support the advance into Wales. The Second Augusta we will cover in the next chapter which covers Vespasian and Titus. His son was also to serve in Britain as a legionary tribune shortly after Boudicca's revolt. Before we turn to their reign we must briefly take one last look at Claudius.

Claudius: appearance and personality

He was described by Suetonius as tall and well built with an 'impressive face' and 'handsome' white hair. He possessed 'majesty and dignity of appearance' although this was confined to when he was standing still or sitting. When he walked his knees often gave way. His laughter was 'unseemly' and his anger 'disgusting' and he would foam at the mouth and his nose would run. He stammered and his head shook, especially when he exerted himself. His health had been poor throughout his life but improved when he was emperor, except for attacks of heartburn which caused him extreme discomfort.

He loved good food and drink and slept little. He was 'devoted to gaming' and took great pleasure from watching beast hunts and gladiatorial contests. He had a darker side in that he enjoyed watching the fallen die. There 'was nothing for which he was so notorious as timidity and suspicion' and insisted he was heavily guarded at all times and visitors searched, even woman and children.

Suetonius. commenting on his private life, said men 'marvelled at his absent-mindedness and blindness' although Claudius had awareness enough to declare it had been 'his destiny to have wives who were all unchaste, but not unpunished'. He was often 'heedless in word and act' and had a 'tendency to wrath and resentment'. Yet he also could be conscientious and reasonable. Whilst he had his faults he was not a homicidal maniac as Caligula is portrayed.

One interesting anecdote comes from a display of a naval battle was put on by the Emperor Claudius in AD 52 at a natural lake, Faucine, outside Rome. The lake was surrounded by a raft and breastworks lined with ballistas and catapults. The lake was large enough to allow ships to manoeuvre and use their battering rams. The mock battle between Sicilains and Rhodians involved 19,000 men. It is here we find the oft-quoted line *ave Caesar, morituri the salutant*, 'Hail Caesar. Those who about to die salute you'. Yet this is the only record of its use. There is no record of it being used in any other context, not at individual gladiatorial contests, the Colosseum or anywhere else.[43]

He was the first emperor to give the praetorian guard a large gift of money. This set a precedent that was to prove disastrous a century and a half later when the throne was auctioned off to the highest bidder in AD 193 after the murder of Emperor Pertinax. Married four times, his last wife was his niece, Julia Agrippina, mother of a twelve year old son, the infamous Nero, who Claudius later adopted. This was to prove fatal for Britannicus, the presumptive heir, and son of his third wife, Messalina.

Figure 9. Bust of Claudius. (*Wikimedia Commons*)

Suetonius reports a 'general belief' that he was poisoned: either by his taster, the eunuch Halotus, at a banquet; or at a family dinner where his wife Agrippina served him mushrooms. One report has him vomiting the first poison and being given a second dose in his gruel. A second has him immediately losing the power of speech and suffering excruciating pain all night, dying before the sun came up the next day.

Cassius Dio offers a different story. Agrippina was eager for her own son, Nero, to inherit the throne. She learnt that her husband was about to name his son Britannicus from his third wife Messalina. She sent for a 'famous dealer in poisons' a woman named Lucusta who administered it to a plate of mushrooms. He was taken from the banquet apparently drunk and never awoke. Britannicus died soon after, and if the sources are to be believed also poisoned by Agrippina and Nero. He was only 13 years old.

Nero's reign ended in disaster, civil war and suicide. The subsequent 'Year of the Four Emperors' marked the end of the Julio-Claudian dynasty and the beginning of the Flavian period. We see a perhaps flattering image of Caludius in figure 9.

Chapter Three

Vespasian and Titus

Titus Flavius Vespasianus was born in the year AD 9 at Reate, to the north of Rome. His parents were both of equestrian rank but his uncle became a senator elevating the family's fortunes. Both Vespasian and his brother Sabinus also entered the senate. He had a distinguished military career, serving in Britain during the invasion and earning the insignia, *ornamenta*, of Triumph. He received the consulship in 51 but fell out of favour with Claudius' wife, Agrippina, mother of the future emperor, Nero. It was sometime before he was called on again and he came out of semi-retirement in 63 to be proconsul of Africa. Four years later he was the governor of Judea and suppressed the First Jewish Revolt, known to the Jews as the First Roman War.

The Year of the Four Emperors

Nero's reign ended in 68. Vindex, governor of Gallia Lugunensis revolted and encouraged his friend Galba, in Hispania, to take the throne. Galba's troops proclaimed their legate emperor, supported by Otho, governor of nearby Lusitania. Vindex was defeated but when more legions defected the senate proclaimed Galba emperor and Nero was forced to commit suicide with the help of his private secretary, Epaphroditus. Galba quickly made enemies and he lost the support of the legions on the Rhine who declared for a new contender, Vitellius, on January 1st 69. Fatally he also lost the support of Otho who he had overlooked in declaring an heir. Within two weeks of Vitellius being declared emperor, Galba was dead, murdered by Otho. Otho supported by the senate and praetorian guard marched out to meet the usurper. On the 14th April in northern Italy Otho was defeated at the First Battle of Bedriacum. Otho killed himself the next day and Vitellius was quickly appointed emperor by the senate.

However the new emperor lacked support outside his own legions. Vespasian, legate in Syria, attracted support from legions on the Danube as well as supporters of the two fallen emperors. On July 1st in Alexandria he was proclaimed emperor and marched on Rome. Vitellius was dead before he got there. The legions of the Danube were closer and they defeated Vitellius at the Second Battle of Bedriacum in October. Vitellius fled back to Rome and attempted to abdicate but was killed by a mob and his headless corpse flung in the Tiber. By 70 Vespasian's position was secure. He was to reign for a decade and give his name to the period known as the Flavian dynasty, being succeeded in turn by his sons, Titus (79–81) and Domitian (81–96).

This book is concerned with his time in Britain and so we must wind the clock back a generation. His son Titus was only 3 years old and would grow up to also serve in Britain. Vespasian was 31 when Caligula was assassinated. He was appointed legate of *Legio II Augusta* in Germania by Claudius at the start of the new emperor's reign. Two years later he was urging his men onto the transport ships in northern Gaul under the command of Aulus Plautius.

Vespasian and the battles for Britannia

Plautius landed at Richborough and marched inland looking for a fight. The Britons wisely avoided open battle and resorted to guerrilla tactics. Using the swamps and forests they performed hit and run attacks and retreated before, what must have seemed to them, like a massive force. The first major river was the Stour and initial defences were brushed aside. A fort was constructed protecting their line of supply and retreat. The next major obstacle was the Medway and it is likely here we first learn of Vespasian's involvement.

For this we must turn to Cassius Dio.[1] In his account we learn that the Romans landed in three divisions. They caught the Britons ill-prepared and landed unopposed. Yet Plautius was able to defeat first Caratacus and then Togodumnus. The next line is rather interesting as Dio claims the Romans then 'gained by capitulation a part of the Bodunni, who were ruled by a tribe of the Catuellani'.

The Catuvellauni we recall were the tribe of our two British kings, noted above, and was situated north of the Thames. However if the Bodunni can be identified as the Dobunni this raises an interesting question. The Dobunni were located east of the Severn valley and quite a distance to the west of where it is assumed the main invasion took place. This could be a case of mistaken identity. However if this is the same tribe then either the Romans were much further west than is thought or a far-away tribe took the opportunity to gain their independence. If that is the case this was to prove illusory.

The Romans, leaving a garrison in the territory of their new ally, advanced farther inland and came to a river. The Britons assumed they were safe, protected by the wide expanse of water, and camped on the western bank, spread out in a 'rather careless fashion'. But Plautius had a secret weapon: A unit of Germanic auxiliaries who were 'accustomed to swim easily in full armour across the most turbulent streams'. Dio describes an operation that sounds like a commando assault. Instead of attacking the Britons they targeted the horses, specifically the ones that pulled the chariots. These they wounded rather than killed caused mass confusion among the enemy.

It was at this point Paulius sent the Second Augusta lead by Vespasian across. He was accompanied by his brother Sabinus who was acting as his lieutenant. We are not told how or where they crossed the river only that they took the Britons by surprise and killed many. Vespasian, and Second Augusta, may have felt they had secured a bridgehead. The Britons returned the next day and very nearly pushed the Romans back across the river.

The battle was close and at first indecisive, with another legate, Gnaeus Hosidius Geta only just escaping capture. This suggests the presence of another legion and it seems it was this, rather than the Second, which eventually won the day. For it was Geta and not Vespasian who was praised for the victory and received the *ornamenta triumphalia*.

The Britons retreated to the Thames and we have noted the most likely site was at Tilbury, the lowest fordable point on the Thames in the first century.[2] The Britons knew the safe paths across at low tide and the Romans were forced to stop. Once again Paulius called upon his Germanic commandos who swam across. This time we are told they were supported by others who crossed by a bridge a little way up-stream. The Britons were then attacked from several sides at once. We aren't told if the Romans built the bridge. They were certainly capable of it as we shall see in the next section. It is intriguing to imagine the Britons had constructed it and the Romans simply utilised it.

Whatever the case the Britons were defeated again and driven off. The Romans lost a number of men in the pursuit through the swamps. It was soon after this battle that Togodumnus was killed and the Britons united under Caratacus. The Romans camped north of the river and awaited the arrival of Claudius. If the route to Camulodunum was secured prior to his arrival we are not told what part Vespasian and the Second played. It is possible all four legionary legates were present at some point to greet their emperor. If so the most likely occasion would have been his triumphant entrance into the *oppidum* at Camulodunum. Vespasian's western campaign was yet to come. First we will turn to bridges and Roman engineering.

Bridge building

In the last section w mentioned the bridge utilised by the Romans in their assault across the Thames. This could have been a simple matter of a pontoon bridge or the use of ships lashed together. However they were capable of much grander engineering projects and at remarkable speed too. In 55 BC Caesar, just months before his first invasion of Britain, he was campaigning in Gaul and Germania.[3] He decided to cross the Rhine at Coblenz where today the river is about 400 yards wide and averages 5 to 25 feet in depth.

Here Caesar was able to construct a timber bridge 36 feet wide. He caused 'pairs of balks eighteen inches thick' to be rammed into the river bed at a slight angle in the direction of the flow. Another pair were similarly placed 40 feet to the side. All this was done from rafts. Two foot thick joists connected these trestles. Timber and wattle-work laid at right angles made the platform across which the legions and cavalry could cross. Further piles were placed in front of the bridge to protect from 'trunks of trees, or vessels, were launched by the natives to break down the structure'.

This immense undertaking took just ten days which included cutting down and preparing the timber. Caesar took his army across, burnt villages, destroyed crops, and just eighteen days later, having satisfied 'both honour and expediency' he withdrew into Gaul. He then destroyed the bridge, leaving nothing behind the Germanic tribes could use.

The Thames near Tilbury today is about 500 yards at it's narrowest and In the first century it was about fifteen feet lower.[4] However, whilst the river may have been narrower, at high-tide especially, there would have been far more swamps, tidal pools and shifting sands making paths across difficult and ever-changing. The determining factor would have been time. A pursuit, followed by a quick assault, which seems the most likely scenario, required a rapid crossing.

This makes it more likely a bridge was already in place or the Romans built quick pontoon bridge. What this battle demonstrates is the efficiency an organisation of the roman military machine. They were able to bring several elements together: legion, auxiliaries and naval units. This required organisation, training and logistics. The backbone of this machine was the legions. It is to that we will now turn, remembering that at this point in our narrative Vespasian is the commander of this vital part of the Roman army.

The legion

In the first century a legion numbered approximately 5,500. These were professional volunteers drawn from Roman citizens. Under Augustus there were about twenty five legions and these steadily rose over the next two centuries, reaching thirty five under Caracalla (211–7), another emperor who fought in Britain.

There was a clearly defined hierarchy: This legion commander was titled *legatus legionis*, a man of senatorial rank, who served for an average of three to four years. This man answered to the provincial governor, the *legatus Augusti pro praetore*. Where there was only one legion present in a province the *legatus legionis* was also the governor. There were exceptions to this which I will detail later. As we have seen Vespasian was *legatus legionis* of *legio II Augusta* and Gnaeus Hosidius Geta was a legate of one of the other legions. Both reported to Aulus Plautius who became the first governor of the new province, *Britannia*.

The second in command was the senatorial tribune, *tribunus laticlavius*, 'military tribune of the broad stripe', which referred to the toga worn by senators. This was usually an inexperienced young man, often the son of a senator following in his father's footsteps. As we shall see Titus, son of Vespasian, did just that then he served as Tribune in his early twenties in Britain in the early 60s. Advising both the commander and his young subordinate were five military tribunes, *tribuni angusticlavii*, 'military tribune of the narrow stripe'. These men were of equestrian rank and were normally experienced, battle-hardened men. This formed the last rung on the ladder of promotion for equestrians at the time, the *tres militiae*. Under Claudius the path consisted of *praefectus cohortis – praefectus alae – tribunus militum*. We will cover equestrians and auxiliary units a little later. Third in command was the *praefectus castrorum*, camp prefect. Thus the senior officers of a legion consisted of the following:

First in command: Senatorial legionary commander, *legatus legionis*.
Second in command: Senatorial tribune, *tribunus laticlavius*.
Advisors: Five equestrian military tribunes, *tribuni angusticlavii*.
Third in command: Camp prefect, *praefectus castrorum*.

One further person was allowed to sit in the command tent and that was the *primus pilus*, or 'first spear'. This was the lead centurion of the legion. The legion itself was made up of ten cohorts with cohorts two to ten divided into six centuries of eighty men, thus 480 per cohort. The lead centurion of each was called the *pilus prior*. The first cohort, however, consisted of five double centuries of 160 men totalling 800 men. The lead centurion of this elite cohort was the *primus pilus*, who led the first century, *centuria*, of the first cohort. He obtained equestrian class on retirement.

There were therefore fifty-nine centurions in a legion, each with an *optio* as second in command. Each century was made up of ten (or twenty in the first cohort) eight-man 'tent groups', *contubernium*, who shared a mess tent and a mule.[5] Each century had a *signifier* who carried the standard for the century. He was also responsible for the troop's pay and savings. Accompanying him was a *cornicen* or horn blower, and a *imaginifer*, carrying an image of the emperor to remind the men of their loyalty. One last point concerns battle standards. The *aquilifer* carried the legion's standard or eagle. The legions used three main types of military signals: the voiced; the 'semi-voiced', with bugle, horn or trumpet;

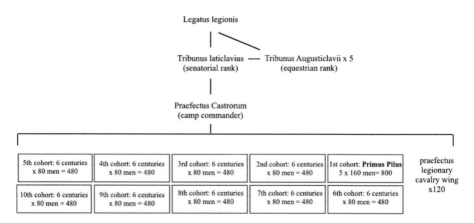

Figure 10. Legion command structure in the second century.

and the 'mute signals', with eagles, dragons, ensigns and plumes.[6] While the eagle was the standard of the Roman legions, later cohorts had their own 'dragon-bearer'.[7] In addition to the 5,120 infantry, the legion had a 120-man *alae*, cavalry, attached called the *eques legionis*, used as scouts and messengers.

Auxiliaries

Under Claudius both the organisation of auxiliary units and career path of equestrians became more organised.[8] Prior to Claudius auxiliary commands were given to senators, equestrians or *primipilares* in an ad hoc fashion. Now they were part of a set career path for equestrian officers. Units had often been temporary and named after the commander or tribe. Now they became permanent and given ethnic names such as Cohors I Tungrorum. These ethnic names remained with the unit and were not always an indication of the ethnic make up of the unit.

In battle the legions provided the heavy infantry but it was the auxiliaries who provided the bulk of the light troops and cavalry. They were often deployed first and, if the enemy broke, the cavalry and light troops would pursue. If this failed however the enemy could be lured onto rows of heavy legionaries and an impenetrable wall of wood and iron. In some battles, such as Agricola's great victory at Mons Graupius, it was the Germanic auxiliaries who won the day. The legions held back and weren't needed at all. At the Medway and Thames under Plautius Germanic units attacked first and then legions closed in.

Auxiliary troops became more important as time went, numbering as many as 440 units by the mid-second century, half of which were stationed along the Danube provinces.[9] There were three main types of these units: Infantry; cavalry;

and mixed. Each of these could be a standard unit of around 500, *quingeneria*, or a larger unit termed a *milliaria*. This latter one was not always literally one thousand but varied in size as we can see in the table below.

Table 1. Auxiliary unit types.

Unit	Description	Number	Composition
Cohors quingeneria peditata	Infantry	480	6 centuries of 80
Ala quingenaria	Cavalry	480	16 turmae of 30
Cohors equitata quingeneria	Mixed	600	480 infantry, 120 Cavalry
Cohors milliaria peditata	Infanrty	800	10 centuries of 80
Ala milliaria	Cavalry	720	24 turmae of 32
Cohors equitata milliaria	Mixed	1040	800 infantry, 240 cavalry

In the early principate a *primus pilus* could move on to command an auxiliary unit. However, by the second century nearly all auxiliary commanders came from the established equestrian class, often beginning their careers as magistrates in Italian, and later provincial, municipal cities.[10] Most unit commanders were termed *praefectus* although some were of tribune rank. Claudius standardised a career path for equestrians so that one could command an infantry unit, *praefectus cohortis*, then a cavalry unit, *praefectus alae*, followed by finally a military tribune, *tribunus militum*, advising the legate and his subordinate, the *tribunus laticlavius*. The period of service for the commander was not fixed, but was usually two to four years. Later emperors were to make the praefectus alae the senior role. Thus we will see Pertinax in the late second century serving first as Tribune of the Sixth legion at York before leading an auxiliary unit.

Claudius began granting bronze diplomas giving auxiliaries Roman citizenship after 25 years service. This grant was extended to their wives and children. Two other kinds of units are worth mentioning.[11] First, *numeri* was a term used for a body of irregular troops. One example was of a unit of Britons posted to the German frontier manning a series of watchtowers. Another example is a *numerus* of bargemen from the Tigris at South Shields on the Tyne in northern Britain. Second, *cunei* appears to be specifically a Germanic irregular unit. Literally meaning 'wedge', Tacitus refers to this Germanic tactic of attack, and applies it to the Batavii in the civil war of 69.

After the surrender of Camulodunum Vespasian led his legion westwards and a number of auxiliary units would have been attached to the Second Augusta. In peace time these same units would have occupied their own forts and reported to the provincial governor rather than come under the command structure of the nearest legionary base. In war they were the advance troops of Vespasian's thrust westwards.

Senators, equestrians and plebs

To understand the difference between officers of senatorial rank and those of the equestrian order it is necessary to look at the social hierarchy of the Roman empire. The plebeians formed the bulk of the population and beneath them came freedmen and, lastly, slaves. Freedmen were not automatically made Roman citizens and even if they were granted citizenship they were generally barred from holding office. From early Republican times there had been a distinction between patricians, the wealthiest leading families, and plebeians in Roman society. The definition of patrician evolved and divided into a stratified upper-class of wealthy aristocrats, senators and equestrians. The difference became more important as time went one.

Augustus reduced the number of senators to around 600. From these men were chosen provincial governors and legionary commanders. Equestrians numbered as many as 30,000 and from these were chosen military and civilian officials to help run the empire.

The career ladder of the senatorial class, the *cursus honorum*, gave aspiring nobles a route to high office. The first step on this ladder was often as a military tribune, *tribunus laticlavius*. From there they progressed through the following: quaestor – aedile – praetor – consul. These all had different roles and minimum ages which can be seen back in figure 3. Governors and legionary commanders were chosen from praetors and consuls hence terms such as propraetorian or proconsul governor. Senatorial status required one to have one million sesterces and was hereditary for three generations with no obligation of taking office.

The qualification for equestrian class was 400,000 sesterces. The career path of the equestrian class, the *tres militiae*, began with command of an infantry unit. In the reign of Claudius the next step was command of a cavalry regiment before military tribune of a legion, *tribuni angusticlavii*. Later emperors were to reverse these last two making a cavalry commander the senior post. From there an equestrian could obtain a position as procurator. This was a type of financial officer who reported directly to the emperor. Finally came one of the four great praefectures:

- Prefect of the grain supply, *praefectus annonae*, again based in Rome.
- Prefect of the Vigiles, *praefectus vigilum*, commanding seven cohorts, also in Rome.
- Prefect of Egypt, *praefectus Aegypti*, controlling the strategically important province of Egypt with its number of legions and importance of its grain supply.
- Praetorian prefect, *praefectus praetorius*, based in Rome and consisting of usually nine cohorts.

These last two posts became increasingly important in the empire. Praetorian prefects in particular became the kingmakers in transition of power.

Most plebeians could only dream of such riches. A legionary soldier received 1,200 sesterces a year. However the army was often the main route for social mobility. A man could rise through the ranks to centurion. If he became *primus pilus* he qualified for equestrian status on retirement. Equestrians too could find themselves promoted to the senate. One remarkable example involves one of our emperors who served in Britain. Pertinax, the son of a freeman (a former slave) was able to obtain a patron and a commission in the army. He served as an equestrian tribune in Britain and had a distinguished military career fighting on the Danube. After gaining senatorial rank he returned to Britain as governor and just a few years later obtained the throne after the death of Commodus.

Governors and procurators.

It's useful at this point to understand how the provincial system functioned in the first century of the empire. There were two main types of provinces: Senatorial and Imperial. Senatorial provinces were administered by governors of senatorial rank who reported direct to the senate. Imperial provinces were also generally run by those of senatorial rank but they reported to the emperor. These men were ex-consuls or praetors hence the title proconsul or propraetorian. Legionary commanders were also appointed by the emperor and provinces with one legion were administered by the same man, the pro praetorian legate of the emperor, often seen on inscriptions as *legatus Augusti pro praetore*.

Each province also had a financial procurator. This man was of equestrian rank and reported direct to the emperor regardless of what sort of province it was. There were some exceptions regarding provincial governors. Some minor provinces were run by an equestrian procurator. The important province of Egypt was administered by an equestrian reporting direct to the emperor, the *praefectus Aegypti*. This was one of the four great prefectures of Rome and often the pinnacle of an equestrian's career aside from perhaps the Praetorian Prefect.

Britain, being an important province with multiple legions, was always an imperial province in the first two centuries of it's existence. It thus had a senatorial governor reporting direct to the emperor. The legionary legates also owed their appointment to the emperor. A senatorial Iuridicus handled legal matters whilst the equestrian procurator reported separately to Rome.

All this was in the future for Britain as Plautius secured the initial areas of conquest in the south and east. It is interesting where he directed the next stage of the campaign. We recall there had been suggestions one of the three prongs of the initial invasion was to the west. In addition the Bodunni, possibly the Dobunni, had quickly capitulated. Vespasian was dispatched to the west taking the Second and some auxiliary units with him.

Vespasian's campaign

We recall from Suetonius that Vespasian was given command of a legion in Germany by Claudius on the advice of his counsellor Narcissus. He then went to Britain with Plautius and it is Tacitus who informs us this legion was the Second Augusta. Suetonius informs us he fought thirty battles, reducing to subjection 'two powerful nations, more than twenty towns (*oppida*), and the island of Vectis' (the latter being the Isle of Wight).[12] The question arises who were these warlike tribes and where were these twenty *oppida*?

Taking all the sources together it would appear this western campaign came after Claudius had left Britain on his return journey to Rome. This would suggest Plautius remained in the south-east of Britain securing what was to become a new province. He then sent Vespasian west to secure the southern coast and his western flank before he pushed into the interior of the island.

The Isle of Wight is slightly to the west of the territory of the Regni and to the south of the Atrebates. Both these tribes were friendly to Rome with the Catuvellaunian incursions of the latter's territory being the excuse for the invasion. We recall Verica, a king of Atrebates, and Cogidubnus of the Regni. This leaves the Durotriges, in modern Dorset, as one of the most likely candidates for one of the 'two powerful nations' conquered by Vespasian. The Durotriges territory likely extended to the River Exe. Further west the territory of the Dumnonii of Devon and Cornwall was not compromised until the 50s with a legionary fortress established at Exeter in c. 55.[13]

For the second tribe we have a number of choices. Whilst part of the Dobunni under the control of the Catuvellauni surrendered before the fall of Camulodunum it is possible a part of Dobunni territory remained hostile. Alternatively the Belgae, a tribe centred on Winchester, *Venta Belgarum*, is the only other likely possibility.

The Durotriges must have been the greater threat. There are over fifty hill-forts spread across what is thought to have been their territory on the southern coast of England. South Cadbury, Spettisbury Rings, Hod Hill, Maiden Castle have all shown evidence of assaults alongside massacres of the defenders.[14] Some evidence is uncertain. At South Cadbury the remains of thirty men, women and children appear to have been left to rot although their injuries could have been caused by animals.[15] Radio-carbon dating of charred wood gave a date

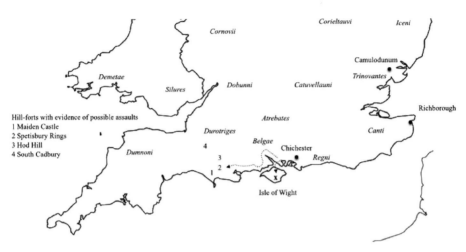

Figure 11. Map of Vespasian's campaign in the west.

range of 45–61 but the evidence points to the upheavals of 61 with Boudica rather than Vespasian's campaign.

At Hod Hill it appears the defenders attempted to strengthen the defences before abandoning it half way through.[16] A new outer ditch ends suddenly for no apparent reason. Inside the fort we find signs of the possible cause. Fifteen *ballista* bolts were found, seemingly directed at the chieftain's hut. The Roman's must have occupied the area as a Roman fort was built into the north-west corner. The best evidence lies at Maiden Castle.

We can see one suggested route of Vespasian's campaign in the map in figure 11. Just four of the many scores of hill-forts in this part of the country are noted: Maiden Castle, Spetisbury Rings, Hod Hill and South Cadbury. Assaulting a hill-fort was no easy task. The defences were formidable. We will focus on just one of those *oppidum* shortly. But first it is worth looking at the sort of weapons the Romans had available.

Artillery

We recall in Caesar's first landing the Britons opposed them from the beaches, even entering the surf to hurl their spears. Caesar ordered his warships to move to the exposed flank of the enemy. From there they drove them off with slings, arrows, and artillery. The defenders, unfamiliar with the ships or weapons, were forced to withdraw. One type of artillery the Romans had were ballista.

The early Roman *ballistae* used torsion-power to ratchet a a bow-string back. This twisted rope springs made from animal sinews. When released a bolt or stone could be thrown several hundred metres. The engines could be also placed in carts drawn by horses, towers on forts, siege towers or on ships. A form of light artillery, *carroballistae* were mounted on carts drawn by mules.

Another type of Roman artillery was the scorpion. There were two main types of Roman *scorpio*. The first was a horizontal version using torsion-power to shoot a bolt or stone. The second type, an onager, consisted of a vertical arm which sprung forward to fire a rock or other missile. This could deliver a stone weighing 25 kilos 440 metres. Archaeological finds of artillery stones in the north of Britain weigh up to 50 kilos. The effects of these weapons were gruesome and armour provided little to no protection.

Vegetius describes how each legion had ten *onagri*, one for each cohort, transported on oxen-drawn wagons. This would slow down progress considerably. A legion could march twenty miles in a day but oxen drawing a heady carriage would be lucky to travel half that in the same time. Nor was it suited for battering down thick stone walls. It could break down wooden structures and thin stone walls. As an anti-personnel weapon in a fixed position it could create havoc and panic in an attacking force. It was very well suited as a defensive weapon and we see this at the fort at Bremenium where the stone platforms measuring 7.5 m by 10 m were attached behind its walls.

Ammianus describes one example as follows:[17] Between two posts a long iron bar is fixed which projects out 'like a great ruler'. To this is attached a squared staff 'hollowed out along its length with a narrow groove'. In this groove the gunner places a long wooden arrow tipped with 'a great iron point'. The arrow, 'driven by the power within, flies from the ballista … before the weapon is seen, the pain of a mortal wound makes itself felt.' He goes on to describe the scorpion or 'wild-ass'. A wooden arm, capable of holding a large stone, rises vertically (looking like a scorpion's sting) but can be pulled horizontally using iron hooks with tension supplied via the twisting of ropes. When released, the arm returns to the vertical with a violent kick (like an ass) and the wooden beam strikes a 'soft hair-cloth' cushion. Another name he gives is an 'onager'.

The Romans also used light artillery and these could more easily be utilised on the battlefield. The ballista could fire stones or bolts of up to a foot in length, with one example from Spain estimated to have had a range of 300 metres.[18] We can see examples of *carro-ballistae* on Trajan's column where the artillery is mounted on carts. Similar artillery pieces would have been utilised by the Sixth and been present at many of the forts and camps across the northern frontier.

Josephus was a first-century Romano-Jewish historian and military leader who initially fought against the Romans before surrendering to Vespasian's army in 67 towards the end of Nero's reign. Josephus served as translator to Titus in the siege of Jerusalem in 70 (eventually taking the name Titus Flavius Josephus). He gives a vivid account of the effects of Roman artillery under

Vespasian at the siege of Jotapata.[19] The general set up one hundred and sixty engines throwing stones, lances, arrows, darts and fire at the walls.

The Romans constructed a bank to reach the wall which caused the defenders to raise the height. The defenders attempted to protect themselves from missile attack by animal hides attached to poles. Still the 'darts and stones' kept up their deadly rain of fire killing the defenders 'one upon another'. The force of the stones was so great that they 'hurt several at a time' and 'carried away the pinnacles of the wall, and broke off the corners of the towers'. Josephus himself was standing by a man near a the wall when he was struck by a stone and 'his head was carried away… and his skull was flung as far as three furlongs'. This is nearly 2,000 feet or 670 yards, over a third of a mile. The noise of the stones and darts was tremendous. A pregnant woman was hit so violently the unborn child was ripped from her stomach and landed 300 feet away.

Procopius, in writing in the sixth century, tells of *ballistae* that reach over 'two bow-shots'. Given Roman archers trained with targets set at about 180 metres we can estimate perhaps 400 metres. When it hits a tree or even a rock it pierces it easily.[20] Slings or 'wild-asses' were placed on the parapet walls of Rome to throw stones similar distances. The power of these weapons was described in vivid terms. At the siege of Rome in the sixth century a large Gothic archer stood apart from his comrades shooting arrows up at the Roman defenders. A bolt was fired from a tower to his left and punched through his chest and embedded itself in a tree leaving his corpse hanging.[21]

Figure 12. Reproduction of Roman Ballista. (*Wikimedia Commons*)

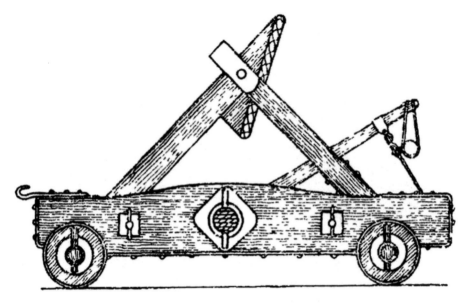

Figure 13. Drawing of a Roman onager. (*Wikimedia Commons*)

This demonstrates the destructive power of Roman artillery. Also that Vespasian was personally well acquainted with the use of artillery. We can see how the Second Augusta might have gone about methodically preparing to assault a hill-fort in Britain. To look at this more closely we will turn to one of the most formidable, Maiden Castle.

Maiden Castle

Maiden castle lies two miles south of Dorchester in Dorset in the area controlled by the Durotriges tribe. It is the largest iron-age hill fort in Europe, covering 47 acres. The fort confronting the Romans had been built around 450–300 BC. It stands 130 metres above sea level and 40 metres above the surrounding land. The initial defences consisted of a V-shaped ditch and a rampart. Later, to the south, four ramparts and three ditches were added. The fourth did not extend all the way round because of the steepness of the northern side. Further earthworks were added to the eastern entrance. Entrances were not aligned making assaults more difficult. Wooden palisades would have been built along the rampart with gates protecting the entrance.

The initial bank was 2.7 metres high overlooking a shallow ditch. However the later development left a warrior standing in the bottom of a ditch facing up to 8.4 metres, or nearly 30 feet, of earth. A formidable barrier especially if topped with a wooden palisade defended by determined warriors able to rain

Figure 14. Aerial view of Maiden Castle. (*Wikimedia Commons*)

Figure 15. Ramparts at Maiden Castle. (*Wikimedia Commons*)

down stones, spears and other missiles. Once you reached the top, tired after the climb, you would struggle to hold a shield above your head whilst wielding a sword or spear. It would be difficult even to stand up-right and keep your footing. Even today the ramparts tower twenty feet above visitors.

Excavations uncovered a number of bodies of Iron Age warriors. They were buried with food and drink, possibly for their journey into the after life. Sir Mortimer Wheeler excavated the site in the 1930s and suggested evidence showed men, women and children had been savagely killed with the few survivors left to bury the dead. A skull had a square piercing which looked like the result of a Roman ballista-bolt. Another skeleton had an iron arrow-head still stuck in a vertebra. He also had a large cut to the head suggesting an injured carrier had been put out of his misery. Or perhaps a legionary was simply making sure of the fallen as he walked the battlefield after the hill fort's capture. However others have suggested the fire damage found in some buildings was from ironworking. Additionally the skeletons cannot be dated accurately and they seemed to have been laid to rest carefully suggesting this was no hurried post-battle burial. Yet three quarters of all the remains show signs of violence from sharp weapons or projectiles.

Webster in *The Invasion of Roman Britain*, provides further details.[22] Twenty eight graves contained the bodies of twenty three men and eleven women. Many had severe head injuries and some showed signs of being hacked after their death. The tops of the ramparts were deliberately pushed into the ditches and the gateways destroyed. The site then appeared to be abandoned. The nearby Roman town of Durnovaria became the modern town of Dorchester.

As formidable as these defences were they proved no match against the Roman war machine. Vespasian would have surrounded the hill-fort with a ring of death-delivering artillery, firing bolts and stones into the interior of the fort. One can only imagine the terror as the defenders huddled beneath whatever protection they could find as they watched an earthen ramp slowly crawl up the steep slopes and bridged each ditch and bank, one after another. Then the assault as hundreds of heavily armoured legionaries of the Second steadily advanced up the newly constructed ramp using *testudo* formation. Shields interlocked front, top and sides. We can see an example of this in figure 16 from Trajan's column.

We get a vivid description of this formation from both Plutarch and Cassius Dio. Plutarch tells us the first rank drops to one knee with the shield in front. Then each rank behind protects the head of the man in front forming a roof which protects them from missiles. Dio provides more detail:[23] During the Parthian campaign of Mark Antony in 36 BC the Romans walked into an ambush and received 'dense showers of arrows' from horse archers. The Romans joined their shields with presumably the front rank resting their left knee on

Vespasian and Titus 51

Figure 16. Roman *testudo* formation from Trajan's Column. (*Wikimedia Commons*)

the ground. The Parthians, thinking they had the upper hand, dismounted and went in for the kill. This was a fatal mistake as the Romans simply reformed their line and attacked the lightly armed and dismounted archers. We also learn that the oblong, curved, and cylindrical shields were drawn up on the outside whilst those with flat shields raise them above their heads so that nothing but shields can be seen. He claimed this is so strong that not only men can walk upon it but even horses and carriages.

Two scenarios are noted. The first is as a defence from archers where a whole army can be protected with even the horses being trained to lie down. The second is when assaulting a fort, enabling troops to scale the walls. Either from a ramp built across the defensive ditches or attacking the main gate of an *oppidum*. We will now take a brief look at the legion that tore through southern Britain and captured Maiden Castle and other *oppida*.

Legio II Augusta

The emblems of the Second legion Augusta were the Capricorn, the winged horse Pegasus and the war god Mars. In the late third century, only the Capricorn remained. There is some debate as to when it was formed: One suggestion is it was raised by Julius Caesar in 48 BC. An alternateve suggestion is it was formed around 43 BC by Octavian and the consul Gaius Vibius Pansa. It may have originally been called *Sabina* meaning 'from the Sabine country'. One of it's first campaigns is likely to have been at the battle of Philippi in 42 BC under the Second Triumvirate when Octavian, Mark Antony and Lepidus defeated an army led by Brutus and the other conspirators of the murder of Julius Caesar. The following year evidence of sling shot bearing the mark *Caesar Leg II* suggests it was present at the siege of Perugia.

After about 30 BC it was in Hispania Tarraconensis and fought in the Cantabrian War, 26–19 BC. After the disaster in the Teutoburg Forest in AD 9 it was moved to the Rhine where it fought under Germnaicus in 14–16. Sometime later it moved to a new base at Agentoratum (Strasbourg) protecting a major crossing point of the Rhine. It was noted for a victory against Gallic rebels in the year 21. In 43 it accompanied three legions and a significant numbers of auxiliary units in the conquest of Britain. We have noted the battles at the rivers Medway and Thames and the campaign against the southern tribes capturing several hill-forts and *oppida*.

It's first base was at Silchester but after the successful campaign in the south-west it was moved to Dorchester, Dorset. By 55 it had moved further west to Exeter where it remained for nearly two decades before the legion was posted to Gloucester. In the 'Year of the Four Emperors' in 69 a vexillation of Vespasian's old unit supported Vitellius when he marched on Rome, prompting Otho's suicide (Galba, the first of the four contenders having already been killed by the praetorian guard months before). Vespasian's subsequent victory sent these units back to Britain where the bulk of the second remained.

Around the year 75 it was moved to Caerleon where it remained for much of the rest its time in Roman Britain. Little evidence exists suggesting vexillations fought elsewhere, aside from Domitian's war against the Chatti in 83. That same year the bulk of the second was present at Mons Graupius when Agricola won a great victory. The legion played a significant role in the building of both Hadrian's and the Antonine Walls suggesting for a time only a skeleton force remained at Caerleon.

In 196 Clodius Albinus took much of the garrison with him to Gaul only to be defeated at Lugdunum the following year. The victor of that battle, Septimius Severus, sent the survivors back to Britain but still used the legion in his Caledonian campaign of 208–11. It shared a large fortress at Carpow on the River Tay with the Sixth legion from York. Later it received the name *Antonina*, implying its loyalty to either Caracalla or Elagabalus.

Its main base is believed to have still been Caerleon in the mid-third century. The reforms under Diocletian and Constantine I may have split it up into smaller units. The last known reference is from the early fifth century Notitia

Vespasian and Titus 53

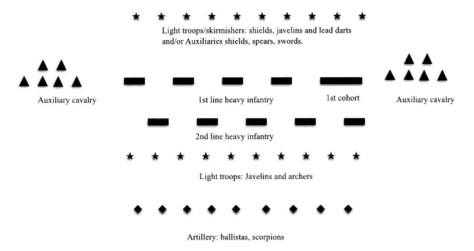

Figure 17. A typical Roman legion formation in the first century AD.

Dignatatum which lists a unit under the command of the *Comes Litoris Soxonicum per Britannias*, 'Count of the Saxon Shore': *Praefectus legionis secundae Augustae, Rutupis* (Richborough, Kent).

In the first century under Vespasian the Second Augusta would have had a paper strength of nearly 5,500. Heavy infantry numbering 5,120, command staff, 120 legionary cavalry and as well as a variety of people essential to maintaining a camp: engineers, craftsmen, vets, surgeons and many others. In reality units would have had a number of men sick or transferred to other duties. The legion would also operate in conjunction with auxiliary troops. Figure 17 shows just such a deployment. An auxiliary unit of 500 fronting the formation with another unit of 500 archers behind. Flanking are two units of cavalry with the Second Augusta standing like a wall of iron and wood against the enemy. Ready to receive an attack or move in to support the auxiliaries. All waiting on the word of their commander Vespasian looking on with his command staff.

Vespasian: Appearance and personality

Suetonius paints a picture of an unassuming and affable man who was forgiving and generally good-natured, especially after a bath and meal.[24] His health was excellent and in looks he was 'well-built with strong sturdy limbs' but with a stern and strained expression. He was known to be witty famously saying, as death drew near: 'Woe is me. I think I am turning into a god'. His last words are worth recording: At the age of 69 he had a severe case of diarrhoea that caused him to almost faint. He tried to struggle to his feet saying: 'An emperor ought to die standing'. But he could not stand and died in the arms of his helpers. The only thing for which he can fairly be censured was his love of money increasing taxes, tribute and selling offices. But even here Suetonius states this was partly due to the treasury's poor condition and he used the money well.

Vespasian had two sons, Titus and Domitian. Both would go on to reign though only Titus is recorded as serving in Britain.

Titus

Suetonius had much praise for Titus describing him as the 'delight and darling of the human race'.[25] Born in 39 he was three years old when his father lead the Second Augusta against the hill-fort at Maiden Castle. He served as military tribune both in Germany and in Britain, 'winning a high reputation for energy and no less integrity'. This must have been in the early 60s as he became quaestor in c. 65 and served under his father in Judea in 67, commanding a legion.[26]

Figure 18. Bust of Vespasian. (*Wikimedia Commons*)

He was brought up with his close friend Britannicus, the son of Claudius, who was allegedly poisoned by Agrippina. Britannicus died the day before his fourteenth birthday and the fifteen year old Titus was said to have been sitting next to his friend as he drunk the poison. Suetonius states that Titus also tasted from the same cup and was ill for some time. He never forgot his friend and years later set up a golden statue and dedicated another equestrian statue of ivory in his honour.

He had a 'handsome person' although he was 'not tall' and had a 'protruding belly'. Physically and mentally accomplished his memory was extraordinary. Skilled in arms and horsemanship and 'the arts, both of war and of peace' He also wrote verses and speeches in Latin and Greek. One quirky talent was the ability to write shorthand with great speed and imitate another's handwriting calling himself 'the prince of forgers'.

He fought in Judea capturing the cities of Tarichaeae and Gamala and at one point having his horse killed in. He gets a good press from Suetonius: He respected property, took 'nothing from any citizen' and wouldn't even accept gifts. Yet he was extremely generous. He had some bad luck, having to deal with three serious emergencies in his reign: the eruption of Mount Vesuvius; a fire in Rome which lasted three days and nights; and a plague 'the like of which had hardly ever been known before'.

When he died at the age of 41 Suetonius declared it 'the loss of mankind'. Just before he died he is reported to have said he had only one regret. Unfortunately he did not state what it was and so we are left to speculate. One suggestion at the time was he had slept with Domitia, his brother's wife. Both Suetonius and Cassius Dio rejects this with the latter suggesting that it was the fact 'he had not killed Domitian when he found him openly plotting against him'.[27] Dio goes on to say 'the whole populace mourned as they would for a loss in their own families'.

Figure 19. Bust of Titus. (*Wikimedia Commons*)

The position of *tribunus laticlavius* was the first step on the cursus honorum for a young man of senatorial rank. Titus would have been about twenty years off age. Taking Suetonius at face value he served in Germany first which would place him there from late 59 through 60. The Boudican rebellion is traditionally dated to 60 or 61. It is possible Titus was in Britain by 61. However it is likely the sources would have mentioned his presence during the rebellion and so it is more likely he was in Germany throughout this turbulent time in Britain. He would therefore have arrived after the events, perhaps in c. 62–3, and taken part in the re-pacification of the province. However it is worth looking at the battle that ended the revolt as it illustrates what a young tribune would have experienced.

The Battle of Watling Street

The revolt of Boudicca resulted in the destruction of Colchester, London and St Albans as well as an initial force sent against the Britons. The Roman governor of Britain, Gaius Suetonius Paulinus, had been campaigning on the island of Mona (Anglesey), a stronghold of the druids. General Suetonius arrived from North Wales with the Fourteenth Legion, detachments of the Twentieth and auxiliaries, numbering 10,000 troops. The Britons are said to have numbered as much as 230,000. This may be an exaggeration, but certainly it was many times that of the Roman force. Tacitus provides further details.[28] Paulinus chose a position 'approached by a narrow defile and secured in the rear by a wood'. The legionaries formed up in 'serried ranks', with light-armed troops on the side flanked by cavalry. The Britons' forces deployed in 'bands of foot and horse ... moving jubilantly in every direction'. Clearly confident from their recent victories, Tacitus tells us they had brought 'even their wives to witness the victory', placing them in wagons on the edge of the plain which lay before the Roman front line.

Boudicca, 'mounted in a chariot with her daughters before her, rode up to clan after clan and delivered her protest': to avenge 'as a woman of the people, her liberty lost, her body tortured by the lash, the tarnished honour of her daughters'. She reminded them that Heaven was on 'the side of their just revenge' and that they had already destroyed a legion. Tacitus puts equally stirring words into the mouth of Paulinus. They should 'treat with contempt the noise and empty menaces of the barbarians' with 'more women than soldiers ... unwarlike and unarmed, they would break immediately'. Shakespeare put similar words into Henry V's mouth at Agincourt: 'The fewer men, the greater share of honour ... We few, we happy few, we band of brothers'. Tacitus claims the general advises his men: 'it was but a few men who decided the fate of battles; and it would be an additional glory that they, a handful of troops, were gathering the laurels of an entire army.'

We then read something of the formation and tactics: 'Only, keeping their order close, and, when their javelins were discharged, employing shield-boss and sword, let them steadily pile up the dead and forget the thought of plunder: once the victory was gained, all would be their own.' The Romans stood their ground, using the defile as protection. When the Britons came within range they exhausted their missiles and charged. We can imagine 10,000 pila from the fourteenth legion alone. If the auxiliaries were similarly armed we can double that. A pilum weighed on average between 0.9–2.3 kilograms. If we estimate just 10,000 pila at 1.5 kilo each that means the advancing Britons were met with about 15 tonnes of wood and iron raining down.

The Roman advance was a wedge-like formation, legions and auxiliaries alike. The cavalry, 'with lances extended, broke a way through.' This seems to have caused an immediate flight. However, escape was difficult and blocked by the cordon of wagons at the far end of the plain. The panic appears to have been total and the Romans gave no quarter. Women and even baggage train animals were 'added to the pile of bodies'. Tacitus tells us a little less than 80,000 Britons were killed and only 400 Romans died with a similar number wounded. Boudicca ended her days by taking poison.

Aftermath

Roman rule was extended west and northwards achieving a high-water mark with Agricola's campaign in c. 84. He then retreated a considerable distance consolidating the border along the Stanegate Road. Just north of this road would be constructed one of the most famous walls in history, ordered by the subject of our next chapter. Agricola was governor under Domitian, younger bother of

Figure 20. Map of major concentration of Roman villas in Britain.

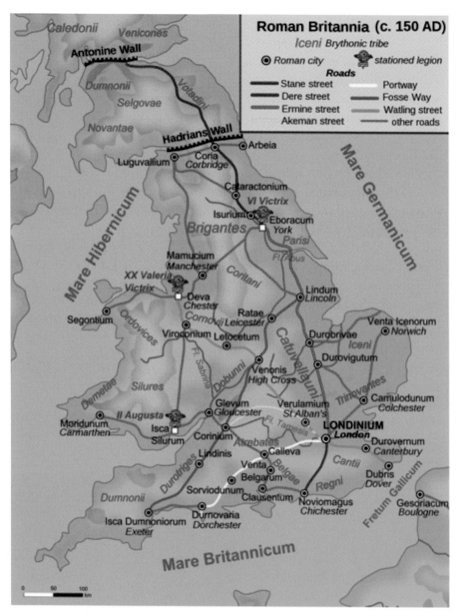

Figure 21. Map of Roman Britain c. 150. (*Wikimedia Commons*)

Titus, who received a much worse press from contemporary historians compared to his father and sibling. He was assassinated by a court plot and succeeded by Nerva, regarded as the first of the 'Five Good Emperors'. The second of these was Trajan who expanded the borders into Dacia and Pathia. It is the third of these 'good' emperors we will turn to next.

Before we do it is worth noting how the Roman province had evolved over the decades. By the beginning of the second century the province was criss-crossed by miles of roads connecting new urban centres. Roman authority was established through *civitates*, often based on tribal areas. For many Britons life continued as before. The majority of the population remained rural and farmers continued to farm. Yet significant pockets of urbanisation appeared, changing the economic and social life of people. Villas appeared and elite Britons aped their Roman masters.

Figure 20 gives us the spread of known Roman villas found so far. We can see they are concentrated in the south and east. Figure 21 is a map of Roman Britain in c. 150 and shows the major roads and towns that covered the province. Here we are getting ahead of ourselves as it includes both Hadrian's and the Antonine Walls. Additionally the former map includes villas built after the first century and throughout the Roman period. Nevertheless these two maps give a good indication of the extent of Romanisation across the province when Hadrian inherited the empire in 117.

Chapter Four

Emperor Hadrian

Publius Aelius Hadrianus was born c. 76. The family originated from Picenum in northern Italy. His grandfather married Ulpia who was aunt to the emperor. This gave him important connections to the imperial family. Hadrian's father died before his tenth birthday and he was entrusted to two guardians, Publius Aelius Attianus and Marcus Ulpius Trajanus, the future Emperor Trajan. As a young man he served as military tribune in various legions on the Danube and Rhine. When Trajan became emperor in 98, Hadrian was 22 years of age. Two years later he married into the imperial family by taking the hand of Matilda Augusta, the emperor's niece.

Hadrian is recorded as being tall and well built, bearded and austere looking. Physically active and energetic, he was skilled in weapons and hunting, once killing a lion with a javelin.[1] He put on lavish gladiatorial shows and hunting displays. Especially keen on lions he once killed a hundred in one display. He was also an able administrator, taking a keen interest in Roman law. He made important changes to governmental positions elevating the role of equestrians at the expense of freedmen. This expanded and opened up the career paths for equestrians. His policies prioritised peaceful, stable and controlled borders protected by a well-trained and disciplined army.[2]

However, the general view of his personality was negative. He was described as unpredictable, envious, fickle and cruel, once stabbing a slave in the eye with a stylus for a minor offence.[3] Soldiers and freedmen were executed for petty insults and he could be vengeful and vindictive. But perhaps the main reason for the negative view of him in the sources is he killed off many senators especially likely successors.

The militarily aggressive Trajan expanding the borders of the empire significantly. Hadrian rose up the *cursus honorum*, serving as a legionary commander during the Dacian Wars and as governor of Syria in the Parthian War of 114. He had received a suffect (part of a yearly term) consulship in 108 and was due a second term in 117 when Trajan died.

The day after Trajan's death it was announced the emperor had formally adopted Hadrian, a claim which was met with some suspicion at the time. However with the endorsement of the emperor's widow, Pompeia Plotina, and also the army, the senate had little choice. Like so many emperors he began by assuring the assembled senators of his good intentions. One of his first promises was to never to put any of them to death, a vow he broke within the year. A plot was uncovered and the perpetrators executed, although he claimed he was unaware of the orders.[4]

The new emperor abandoned Trajan's expansionist policies pulling back from Parthia and leaving a client king in Armenia. He remained in Dacia and turned his attention to the northern borders. This new policy of avoiding external military action meant a strengthening of the border defences. Legionary soldiers started to perform a number of other 'non-operational' tasks, one of which was large building and engineering projects.

Figure 22. Bust of Emperor Hadrian. (*Wikimedia Commons*)

Hadrian began a process of visiting provinces, strengthening the borders as he went becoming known as the 'greatest of all imperial travellers'.[5] He was the first emperor to see the empire from anything other than a Roman standpoint.

As he travelled he took a keen interest in army discipline which is reflected in his coinage, one example of which includes the words *Disciplina Augusti*.[6] He created a distinction between mobile and static troops which was copied by later emperors. This is evident later in Britain when we see auxiliary troops manning Hadrian's Wall with the Sixth Legion based at York, over seventy miles to the south.

The only serious war in his reign was the Jewish War of 132–6. Reprisals were severe: nearly 1,000 villages were razed to the ground and Cassius Dio numbered those killed to over half-a-million Jews killed in battle alone. Aside from the severe reprisals to that insurrection, Hadrian is not considered overly heavy-handed by historians even if senators at the time and later took a dim view of him.[7] His visit to Britain occurred in the first years of his reign and it is to that we will now turn.

Hadrian in Britain

There is some evidence of military problems in northern Britain at the start of his reign:[8] Sources tell us 'the Britons could not be kept under Roman control';

coins showing BRITANNIA issued in 119 appear in the record suggesting a successful campaign; and Fronto, writing in 162, refers to a large number of soldiers being killed in this period. Supporting this is an inscription in Italy, dated to the reign of Hadrian, which shows 3,000 men from three different legions were sent to Britain.[9] This in turn suggests a large number needed replacing and some have speculated the Ninth Legion was destroyed. However later evidence from the Rhine points to it's presence on the continent several decades later.

More coins issued c. 122–3 refer to *expeditio Augusti*. This must refer to Hadrian's presence in Britain which suggests, if taken at face value, a campaign whilst the emperor was present.[10] What these coins and literary sources tells us is that after Trajan's death significant unrest occurred in Britain. Whatever action took place in response must have been successful for coins to display BRITANNIA by 119. Was Hadrian's visit in c. 122 in response to further unrest? The sources are silent but the numismatic evidence points to another successful campaign with Hadrian present in Britain. It was this visit that prompted the transfer and arrival of one of Roman Britain's most famous legions, *Legio VI Victrix*, the 'Victorious Sixth Legion'. It also prompted the construction of arguably one of the most famous walls in history, *Vallum Aelium*, Hadrian's Wall.

Before we turn to that let us first look at the border before Hadrian arrived in Britain. As the legions pushed north and west in the first decades of Roman rule Legionary bases were built with those at York, Chester and Caerleon becoming the permanent base for most of Roman Britain. These bases were rebuilt in stone most likely under Trajan.[11] In addition to these colonies for veterans at Gloucester and Lincoln were added to the one at Colchester. Agricola's campaign in the north had culminated in the Roman victory at Mons Graupius c. 83–4.

However this was not to last and the withdrawal from north of the Forth-Clyde isthmus came shortly after c. 86. Coin deposits suggest it was complete by c. 88.[12] A generation later and the Romans had retreated again, this time to the Tyne-Solway isthmus. Tacitus presents a golden opportunity wasted: 'Britain was totally conquered, and then immediately let go'.[13] How different might British history have been if the Romans had conquered the entire island and even gone one step further and crossed the sea to Ireland?

In the late 80s the Romans consolidated their new border. A major road was built, the Stanegate Road, connecting two strategically important forts. Corbridge in the east and Carlisle in the west. The Roman zone of influence likely extended much further and further forts were constructed along this line and further south in support. It is to this border that Hadrian visited in 122. Whilst we have seen signs of unrest just prior to his visit other evidence suggests there were not serious military problems on the frontier in the years directly after Agricola's withdrawal.[14] Part of this evidence comes from one of the forts positioned half-way along the Stanegate Road.

Vindolanda fort

Vindolanda sat on an escarpment on the Stanegate Road thirteen miles west of Corbridge and twenty three miles east of Carlisle. Placing it roughly half way between the Solway Firth and the North Sea. Just a smile south of where Hadrian's Wall ran it is located near the picturesque village of Bardon Mill in Northumberland. The fort's name is Brythonic: *vindo* means 'white' or 'shining' and evolved into the Welsh *gwyn* or Irish *finn*. Although no evidence has been found of any prior settlement.

The first fort was built c. 85 by the First Cohort of Tungrians, an infantry unit of 500. A larger fort was constructed c. 95 when a mixed unit of 1,000 Batavians moved in. This was the Ninth Cohort of Batavians who, together with the Tungrians, are referenced in the famous Vindolanda tablets. Both of these auxiliary units fought at Mons Graupius in c. 83. It was Batavian auxiliaries that swam across the River Medway in 43 when Vespasian led the second legion to victory. The Tungrians returned to Vindolanda in the early second century and again a larger wooden fort was built. This unit moved north a generation later when the Antonine Wall was built. A stone fort later replaced the wooden one.

It is thought that the Tungrians were replaced in the mid-second century, c. 150–200, by a cohort of Nervians, *Cohors II Nerviorum Civium Romanorum*.[15] The final residents were the Fourth Cohort of Gauls, *Cohors IV Gallorum Equitata*, a mixed unit of 500, who remained until towards the end of Roman Britain.

Back in the first century a revolt by Batavian auxiliary units in 69–70 on the Rhine caused Rome major problems. Taking part in the final victory over the Batavians was legio VI Victrix who later accompanied Hadrian to Britain in 122. Some of the Batavian elite had remained loyal to Rome, including two cavalry commanders, Claudius Labeo and a Briganticus. The revolt was suppressed by Vespasian's son-in-law, Petillius Cerialis. The Batavian commander at Vindolanda was named Flavius Cerialis and he may well be the son of one of the loyal Batavians, named after their benefactor.[16]

The Vindolanda Tablets

One of the most incredible archaeological finds in Britain were excavated in the 1970s and 1980s at Vindolanda Roman Fort, a short distance south of Hadrian's Wall. Found up to four metres below the modern surface. Several 'tablets', thin pieces of wood (0.5 to 3mm), most about the size of a postcard (10 by 15cm) were discovered. Dated to c. 85–130 and known today as the 'Vindolanda tablets' they gave a range of fascinating insights into life in the Roman army of the first century. In total 117 items were found: letters, documents, *descripta* tablets, and what are described as 'texts of uncertain nature', some illegible or indecipherable.[17]

Two of the tablets refer to the indigenous *Brittones*. One tells of the economic relationship involving wagons and the supply of corn. The other is disparaging, using the word *Brittunculi*, 'wretched little Britons'. Tablet number 164 tells us the following: 'the Britons are unprotected by armour. There are very many cavalry. The cavalry do not use swords nor do the wretched Britons mount in order to throw javelins'. We get the impression of northern tribes still causing problems for the local garrisons.

On the other hand Tacitus writes that the Britons 'submit readily to conscription' and also implies Britons were fighting in Agricola's army at Mons Graupius.[18] It is likely this means auxiliary units as only citizens could join the legions. Indeed units of Britons, *numeri Brittonum*, are attested to on the German frontier by 140 and are thought to have arrived as early as 100.[19]

At he time many of these tablets were produced Hadrian's Wall had not been constructed. Agricola had withdrawn his forces to a line roughly between modern Newcastle and Castle. A road, the Stanegate Road, connected two important bases, Carlisle in the west and Corbridge in the east.

Many of the tablets refer to these and other forts in the north: Binchester, Catterick, Aldborough, Ribchester, High Rochester and York. London is also mentioned and possibly Lincoln.

We get a fascinating insight into the strength of a regular auxiliary unit, the First Cohort of Tungrians, based at Vindolanda. The commander, Iulius Verecundus, served *c.* 92–7. It is the only known example of a strength report of an auxiliary *cohors milliaria peditata* (tablet 154). Dated 18th May it states the unit strength is 752 of which only 296 are present at Vindolanda. The others are spread out at other postings: guards of the governor (at London?) 46; at Corbridge 337. Of those at Vindolanda, 15 are sick, 6 wounded and 10 'suffering from inflammation of the eyes'. This leaves just one centurion and 264 men fit for active service at the fort. Thus only a third of the unit is available at it's base fort.

The maintenance reports and leave requests would be recognisable to soldiers in the British Army today. A report of the ninth Batavians records 'all at their places who ought to be and their equipment intact'.[20] A leave request to Cerialis, Commander of the Ninth Batavians (tablet 169), reads. Tablet 175 reads 'I, Messicus ..., ask, my lord, that you consider me a worthy person to whom to grant leave at Coria (Corbridge)'.

We read of travelling expenses and provisions bought: wine, barley, wheat, wagon-axles, a carriage, vests, salt and fodder. The locations they travelled through: Isurium, Isurium, Cataractonium and Vinovia, all on the road from

York to Corbridge. Domestic items are listed: shallow dishes, 2; side-plates, 5; vinegar-bowls, 3; egg-cups; a platter a shallow dish; a strong-box; a bronze lamp bread-baskets; 4 cups; 2 bowls . Of the 200 persons named, around half, are Batavian or Tungrian, the two units known to have been present at the fort, and most have Celtic or Latin names.[21]

The soldiers weren't officially allowed to marry so presumably the next tablet is from an officer's wife. Claudia Severa, writes to Sulpicia Lepidina, wife of Cerialis, the same Cerialis commanding the ninth Batavians we met earlier (tablet 291). Claudia invites her friend to her birthday celebrations ion 11th September. She sends greetings from 'my Aelius and my little son' . She signs off: 'Farewell, sister, my dearest soul, as I hope to prosper, and hail'.

Out last tablet hints at a tale of corruption and violence.[22] The importance of it for this chapter is that there is a suggestion it can be dated to Hadrian's visit to the north of Britain. The presence of writing on the back suggests this was a draft and, given where it was found, perhaps not even sent.

> he beat (?) me all the more ... goods ... or pour them down the drain (?). As befits an honest man (?) I implore your majesty not to allow me, an innocent man, to have been beaten with rods and, my lord, inasmuch as (?) I was unable to complain to the prefect because he was detained by ill-health I have complained in vain (?) to the *beneficiarius* and the rest (?) of the centurions of his (?) unit. Accordingly (?) I implore your mercifulness not to allow me, a man from overseas and an innocent one, about whose good faith you may inquire, to have been bloodied by rods as if I had committed some crime.

The writer, apparently a civilian trader, addresses the letter *maiestatem*, which translates as 'majesty'. It would appear soldiers poured his goods away and gave him a beating. The intriguing possibility is that the use of the word majesty suggests it could have been addressed to Hadrian himself when he was present in Britain which would date the letter to 122. Whatever the case, it shows the attitude of the complainant. He feels his treatment was unjust as he was an innocent man and 'from overseas'. Does this imply a Briton could be beaten with impunity? There is clearly an expectation that his complaint would be considered although he states he received no 'satisfaction from the *beneficiarius* or the centurions'. Was it eventually received and discarded by the commander at Vindolanda? We are left to wonder what became of our complainant. Perhaps he received redress and the soldiers were punished. Or perhaps the discarded letter found nearly 2,000 years later is evidence of a complaint dismissed and the trader lucky he received just the one beating.

Actions in Britain

In 121 Hadrian was in Germania Inferior overseeing the construction of defences on the Lower Rhine limes. The local governor, Platorius Nepos, was a personal friend. After the Batavian Revolt in 69–70 a new legionary base was built at Neuss, on the Rhine in modern Germany, the former base of *legio XVI Gallica*. One of the victorious legions, VI Victrix, was to occupy the fort through to the first quarter of the second century. It was the Sixth legion that Platorius used to build the Limes in Germania Inferior. Hadrian was present in the province when he oversaw the construction of the new defences.

Once completed Hadrian turned his eyes to across the Channel: 'Then having reformed the soldiers in royal fashion [in Germany], he set out for Britain, where he corrected many things and, as the first to do so, built a wall for eighty miles, which was to separate the barbarians from the Romans'.[23] It is likely both Platorius, appointed the new governor of Britain, and VI Victrix accompanied Hadrian when he crossed to Britain in the early summer of 122.[24] Platorius remained governor for at least two years but was gone before 127.

We get little snippets of information concerning his stay in Britain. His journey across the sea no doubt started from Gesoriacum, Boulogne. As with previous emperors his likely arrival port was Rutupiae, Richborough in East Kent. When he arrived we are told he dismissed the guard prefect, Septimius Clarus, and the chief secretary, Suetonius Tranquillus, and 'many others', allegedly for disrespecting the emperor's wife.[25] The sources suggest a sense of paranoia with the emperor spying on many people, even his friends. If he dismissed officials these were likely in Londinium which by now had grown into a major Roman city.

The legionary commander of the Sixth in Lower Germany in 122 was Marcus Valerius Propinquus Grattius. He may have travelled with the legion to Britain as he is attested as governor of Aquitania the year after in 123.[26] In Britain he handed command to Tullius Varro Varro who led XII Fulminata in Cappadocia. It was rare to command two legions so there may have been a specific reason. By 127 Varro had served as proconsul of Baetica, Treasury Prefect and consul. So we can date him quite tightly to the first years of the Sixth's presence in Britain.

Did he have an expertise in large projects or was it his battlefield experience that made the emperor pick him? Around this time we see coins refer to Hadrian's *adventus* and *exercitus Britannicus*, so it appears that some sort of campaign took place when he was present.[27] This campaign can be dated to shortly after the arrival of the new governor, Platorius, and the Sixth legion, now led by Varro.

A senatorial military tribune, *tribunus laticalvius*, can be dated exactly to the crossing from Germany to Britain. his name was Marcus Pontius Laelianus

Larcius Sabinus, and he would have been about 20 years of age.[28] The same age and rank as Titus, sixty years before. Forty years later, Fronto praised the 'old-fashioned discipline' of possibly this same Laelianus. This he may well have learnt from his experience under Hadrian as we find an altar at Chesters Roman Fort dedicated to 'the Discipline of the Emperor Hadrian'.[29] Laelianus went on to have an illustrious career. First leading two armies under Antoninus Pius Upper Pannonia and then Syria between 138 and 161.[30] Under Marcus Aurelius he was senior advisor to Lucius Verus in the Parthian War of 161–6. With a reputation as a strict disciplinarian he was highly decorated and ended his career, aged approximately 70, fighting on the Danube in the 170s.

A dedication to another Sabinus, an equestrian praefectus, suggests he led a number of units on a British expedition and this appears to be dated to c. 122.[31] If so, this supports the proposal that Hadrian's visit may have been in response to some unrest in the north. Did he travel by road the nearly 300 miles to York? Or perhaps by sea, landing at Petuaria, modern Brough, on the Humber, a short distance to the south east of the Sixth's new home. The famous wall that bears the emperor's name was to be built a further seventy miles to the north.

Hadrian's Wall

The *Historia Augusta* tells us: 'Hadrian was the first to build a wall, eighty miles long, to separate the Romans from the barbarians'.[32] The building work on the *Vallum Aelium* began soon after the emperor's arrival in 122. Three elements made up the defences: a ditch to the front of the wall, the wall itself and another ditch, the *Vallum*, to the rear:

1. The ditch: Approximately 9–10 feet deep, ranging from about 26 to 40 feet in width. The distance between the wall and the ditch was about 20 feet.
2. The wall: Approximately 14 feet high. The width varied between 8 and 10 feet.
3. The *Vallum*: A flat-bottomed ditch, 20 feet wide and 10 feet deep.

Two-thirds of the Wall were constructed in stone. The western third was built in turf. Approximately every mile a 'mile-castle' was built with with double gates to front and rear. These were of varying sizes and held eight to thirty-two men. A number of forts were also added along the wall. They ranged in size from approximately 3.35–9.32 acres in size. The smallest could hold an auxiliary unit numbering 500 men (with the exception of Drumburgh at 2 acres).[33] The largest could hold a the larger *milliaria* units, potentially up to just over 1,000 men if a mixed unit, *Cohors milliaria equitata*.

These stone forts were built astride the wall with their front double-gates opening to the north. The earlier forts also had their eastern and western gates opening north side of the wall. Later forts just had their northern gate to the north. This enabled rapid deployment allowing the Romans to engage in the open field quickly which their tactics and training favoured. These larger forts were placed six to nine miles apart: Wallsend; Benwell; Rudchester; Halton Chesters; Chesters; Housesteads; Great Chesters; Birdoswald; Castlesteads; Stanwix; Bough-by-Sands; and Bowness-on-Solway.

To the rear the *vallum* was built after the forts. About 30 feet from the lip of both sides were two mounds, both 20 feet wide, thus creating a barrier 120 feet in total width. Access to the wall from the south was thus restricted to crossing points over the *vallum*. Later in the second century it was partially filled. It is possible its initial function was redundant and speed of access for the military heading north became important than defence from the south. At places the rear ditch was as much as 700 metres from the wall whilst in others in snaked much closer. The old Stanegate Road had run south of the *vallum*. A new road was constructed to the north of the ditch and south of the wall.

Forts at Corbridge and Vindolanda sat a short distance south of the Wall on the Stanegate Road. The former became a major supply depot and possibly the target of a major incursion under the reign of Commodus. North of the wall three outpost forts were built: Bewcastle, Netherby and Birrens. In the west forts, smaller 'fortlets' protected the Solway and Cumbrian coast, notably Beckfoot, Maryport and Meresby. A chain of towers and mileforts were placed twenty-six miles down the Cumbrian coast and there exists evidence of ditches and fences which likely controlled travel in a similar way to the wall. To the east, South Shields and smaller fortlets protected the south bank of the Tyne. Similar evidence of protection down the east coast has yet to be found.

It was a huge expense of time, manpower and money that took about six years to complete. It's purpose may not be as obvious as some people think. On

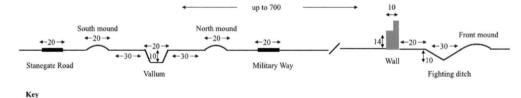

Key

20   All distances approximations in Roman feet.

Figure 23. A cross section of Hadrian's Wall, ditch and Vallum.

the Rhine frontier, part of which the Sixth legion had helped to build prior to 122, certain regulations restricted movement: One could only cross the barrier unarmed, under guard and on payment of a fee.[34] Thus the purpose of the wall in Britain was not primarily defensive or even to prevent the movement of people across a border but rather to control and tax that movement.

Support for this comes from the debate as to whether the wall itself could be used as a fighting platform. The parapet was two-feet wide, leaving only four to eight feet of space on the walkway. This allowed two men at most, no room for artillery and no provision for protecting towers. The preference of the Roman army was fighting in formation in the open. This suggests their main objective would have been to deploy quickly from the south to the north rather than fight from the wall itself.[35]

Epigraphical evidence exists detailing building activity at various forts and part of the Wall. One example at High House mile-castle on the wall state the 'The Sixth Legion, Dutiful and Loyal, built [this]'.[36] Another stone at Halton Chesters also tells us the Sixth were responsible for its construction and more importantly can be dated to 122–4 as it notes Aulus Platorius Nepos was pro-praetorian legate at the time.[37] A stone at Castlehill declares that the Sixth were responsible to a very precise 3,666½ paces of the wall.[38] At quarries by the River Gelt near Brampton two masons, both soldiers of the Sixth, left their names, Eustus and Amnio, carved into the rock.[39] Two altars found in the Tyne

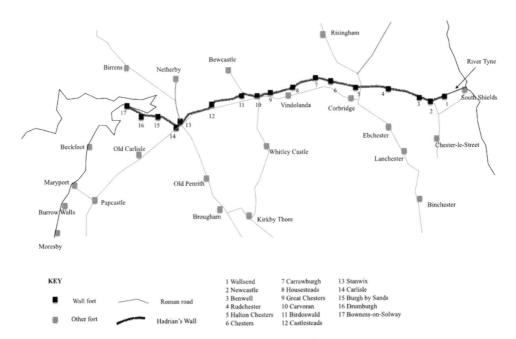

Figure 24. Hadrian's Wall forts.

riverbed at Newcastle are thought to mark the site of a bridge. Dedicated to Neptune and the Ocean, both record the 'Legion VI Victrix Dutiful and Loyal' as having 'set them up'.[40]

Figure 24 shows the forts along the Wall as well as the forts to the north and south. It also shows the major roads connecting these forts.

Auxiliary units and the Wall

It is important to note that the nearest legionary base at York was 70 miles to the south. The forts along to wall and those to it's north and south were auxiliary forts, each with a unit of 500 to 1,000, and commanded by it's own praefectus or tribune. These equestrian officers reported to the provincial governor rather than the nearest legionary legate. Whilst units could be attached to legions for specific campaigns in general the auxiliary units posted to forts should not be considered to be 'attached' to a specific legion.

Three cavalry units are thought to have been posted to the Wall: Chesters, Stanwix and Benwell. Three infantry units resided at Housesteads, Great Chesters and Birdoswald. The other units were mixed, *cohortes equitatae*.[41] The fort at Stanwix held the largest cavalry unit in Britain, *ala milliaria*, and protected the main route north of the western part of the wall. The commanding officer there was the most senior on the wall but we cannot assume he held any authority over the other commanders. The table below shows the size of the forts and I have rounded the units up to 500 or 1,000.

Table 2. Auxiliary units and forts under Hadrian.[42]

Fort	Size in acres	Estimated unit type and size under Hadrian
Wallsend	4	Mixed 500
Benwell	5	Cavalry 500
Rudchester	4.5	Mixed 500
Halton Chesters	4.3	Mixed 500
Chesters	5.75	Cavalry 500
Carrawburgh	3.9	Mixed 500
Housesteads	5	Infantry 1,000
Great Chesters	3.36	Infantry 500
Carvoran	3.6	Infantry 500
Birdoswald	5.33	Infantry 1,000
Castlesteads	3.75	Infantry 500
Stanwix	9.32	Cavalry 1,000
Burgh-by-Sands	4.9	Mixed 500

Fort	Size in acres	Estimated unit type and size under Hadrian
Drumburgh	2	Infantry 500
Bowness-on-Solway	7	Mixed 500
Beckfoot	2.55	Infantry 500
Maryport	5.8	Mixed 500
Moresby	3.6	Mixed 500

This gives us a total of between 8,000 to 9,000 troops. The next table shows known long term postings from the time of Hadrian to the end of the fourth century. It doesn't take into account any temporary posts or detachments but it does give an idea of the main units and their primary postings. There are significant gaps in our knowledge as can be seen below. However interestingly there is a degree of consistency with some units remaining in certain bases across two centuries.

Table 3. Auxiliary units from second to fourth century.

Fort	Hadrian	later 2nd century	3rd century	Notitia Dignitatum
Hadrian's Wall forts				
Wallsend	Cohors Quingenaria Equitata	Cohors II Nerviorum Civium Romanorum	Cohors IV Lingonum Equitata	Cohors IV Lingonum
Newcastle	-	-	Cohors I Ulpia Traiana Cugernorum Civium Romanorum	Cohors Prima Cornoviorum
Benwell	Ala Quingenaria	Cohors I Vangionum Milliaria Equitata	Ala I Asturum	Ala I Asturum
Rudchester	Cohors Quingenaria Equitata	-	Unknown (run down c. 270–370)	Cohors Prima Frisiavonum
Halton Chesters	Cohors Quingenaria Equitata	-	Ala Sabiniana	Ala Sabiniana
Chesters	Ala Augusta Ob Virtutem Appellata	Ala II Asturum	Ala II Asturum	Ala II Asturum

Fort	Hadrian	later 2nd century	3rd century	Notitia Dignitatum
Carrawburgh	Cohors Quingenaria Equitata	-	Cohors I Batavorum Equitata	Cohors I Batavorum Equitata
Housesteads	Cohors Milliaria Peditata	-	Cohors I Tungrorum (Numerus Hnaudifridi & Cuneus Frisiorum)	Cohors I Tungrorum
Vindolanda	Cohors I Tungrorum	Cohors II Nerviorum Civium Romanorum	Cohors IV Gallorum Equitata	Cohors IV Gallorum Equitata
Great Chesters	Cohors VI Nerviorum	Cohors Raetorum	Cohors II Asturum	Cohors II Asturum
Carvoran	Cohors I Hamiorum	Cohors I Hamiorum	Cohors II Delmatarum Equitata	Cohors II Delmatarum Equitata
Birdoswald	-	-	Cohors I Aelia Dacorum Milliaria	Cohors I Aelia Dacorum Milliaria
Castlesteads	Cohors IV Gallorum Equitata	-	Cohors II Tungrorum Equitata	-
Stanwix	Ala Petriana Milliaria	-	Ala Petriana Milliaria	Ala Petriana Milliaria
Burgh-by-Sands	Cohors Quingenaria Equitata	-	Cohors I Nervana Germanorum Milliaria Equitata, Numerus Maurorum Aurelianorum, Cuneus Frisionum Aballavensium	Numerus Maurorum Aurelianorum
Drumburgh	-	-	-	-
Bowness-on-Solway	Cohors Milliaria Equitata	-	Cohors Milliaria Equitata	-

Emperor Hadrian 73

Fort	Hadrian	later 2nd century	3rd century	Notitia Dignitatum
Other forts				
Beckfoot	Cohors Quingenaria Peditata	Cohors II Pannoniorum	-	-
Maryport	Cohors I Hispanorum Milliaria Equitata	Cohors I Delmatarum Equitata, Cohors I Baetasiorum Civium Romanorum	Cohors Milliaria	-
Moresby	Cohors II Lingonum Equitata	-	-	cohors II Thracum equitata
Ravenglass	-	Cohors I Aelia Classica	-	-
South Shields	-	-	Cohors V Gallorum	Numerus Barcariorum Tigrisiensium
Bewcastle	Cohors Dacorum Milliaria peditata	-	Cohors Milliaria	-
Netherby	-	-	Cohors I Aelia Hispanorum Equitata	
Birrens	-	Cohors II Tungrorum Milliaria Equitata	-	-
Risingham	-	Cohors IV Gallorum Equitata	Cohors I Vangionum Milliaria Equitata, Exilatio Raetorum Gaesatorum, Exploratores Habitancenses	-

Fort	Hadrian	later 2nd century	3rd century	Notitia Dignitatum
High Rochester	-	Cohors I Lingonum Equitata	Cohors I Fida Vardullorum Civium Romanorum Milliaria Equitata, Explatores Bremensienses	-

We also have the names of various commanders of the Sixth legion for this period. Lucius Minicius Natalis Quadronis Verus, can be dated to c. 130. A native of Barcino (Barcelona) in Tarraconensis, he served as tribune in three successive legions before becoming a legate to the pro-consul of Africa. He won the four-horse chariot race at the Olympic Games in 129.[43] Two late Hadrianic legates are Quintus Antonius Isauricus (c. 143) and Publius Mummius Sisenna Rutilianus (c. 146).[44] By this time the Sixth had been in Britain for a generation and no doubt some had already retired and settled in the growing new *vicus* appearing around the fort at Eboracum.

We recall the legions present in the initial invasion of 43: Legio II Augusta, legio XX Valera Victrix, legio XIV Gemina, and legio IX Hispana. The first two legions, the Second and Twentieth, remained in Britain throughout the Roman period. The fourteenth was replaced by the Second Adiutrix which returned to the continent in 87. This leaves the Ninth. We know the Sixth arrived in c. 122 with Emperor Hadrian. One question that has intrigued historians is what became of the Ninth legion?

The Ninth Legion

Simon Elliott in *Roman Britain's Missing Legion, What Really Happened to IX Hispana?*, summarises the evidence as follows:[45]

- The last reference to the legion is by Tacitus in 82 campaigning with Agricola in the north of Britain. (Agricola 25–7)
- The legion was present at the battle of Mons Graupius in c. 83–4
- The last inscription in Britain is dated to 108 at York. (RIB 665)
- A vexillation of the Ninth was posted to the legionary fortress at Nijmergen in Germania Inferior dated 104–120.
- The Sixth Legion arrived in Britain in 122.
- Inscriptions reference units of the other legions based in Britain building Hadrian's Wall c. 122–8.

- No such inscriptions exist for the Ninth suggesting they did not take part.
- The legion is missing from the *Collonetta Maffei* list in 168 (CIL VI.3492)

This places their disappearance sometime between 108–168. Elliott goes on to list various options which include:[46]

- They were destroyed during a serious military crisis in the north of Britain between Hadrian's accession and his arrival in Britain, 117–122.
- A 'Hadrianic War' in London based on archaeological evidence of hundreds of skulls dated to c. 120–160s but proposed to be during early years of Hadrian's reign.
- The legion was lost fighting on the Rhine near where vexillation was stationed.
- Alternatively it was destroyed in the east: Trajan's Parthian War of 115; the Third Bar Kokhba Jewish Revolt, 132–5; or the Parthian War of 161–6.

We can summarise the options as destroyed by military defeat, disbandment or *damnatio memoriae*. Elliott concludes the end possibly came in the north of Britain in the early years of Hadrian's reign. A combination of defeat and disbandment may have been the catalyst which prompted Hadrian's visit and the transfer of the Sixth. However an alternative explanation is possible.

Birley lists the careers of a number of its officers after it's apparent disappearance from the record in 108.[47] He notes references to *vexillatio Britannica* in Germania Inferior but also evidence from tile stamps at Carlisle. It is thus possible it was sent further north after the arrival of the Sixth at York. He suggests it may have remained in Britain for a further ten years or more and, possibly, was sent to the Jewish War of c. 134–6, or Cappodocia c. 137. Following from this latter date an unnamed legion was destroyed at Elegia in the beginning of the Parthian War of 161–6, led by the governor of Cappodocia. This suggests one option might be the Ninth remained in Britain for a few years before being removed to Germany and from there to the east where it was later lost.

Thus the mystery remains. Elliott lists the legions that are known to have been destroyed or disbanded and declares the Ninth is the only one whose fate is unknown.[48] We appear to be left with two leading contenders: It was lost in the north of Britain in the early years of Hadrian's reign, 117–122; or it left Britain and was lost most likely in the east before 168. This left Britain with three legions: the Sixth based at York; the Second Augusta at Caerleon; and the Twentieth at Chester.

The two walls

Hadrian was to reign for a little over 20 years, dying in the summer of 138. His death appears to have been welcomed by some. The *Historia Augusta* states that many spoke against him after his death and the senate wished to annul his acts. Only the intervention of the new emperor, Antoninus Pius forced them to give Hadrian the title 'the Deified'.[49] Cassius Dio gives a more balanced account:[50] 'Hadrian was hated by the people, in spite of his generally excellent reign, on account of the murders committed by him at the beginning and end of his reign, since they had been unjustly and impiously brought about'. Yet he goes onto state Hadrian did not have 'a bloodthirsty disposition' and could be magnanimous and refrain from punishing people at times, lightening the penalty if they had children.

Hadrian had wished to name Marcus Aurelius and Lucius Verus as co-emperors but their age prompted him to turn to an unlikely successor. Antoninus Pius was 51 years old and was a rather obscure choice. However it was these very reasons Hadrian chose him. He was seen as a temporary safe pair of hands to rule. With no heirs himself he was forced to adopt Marcus and Lucius as his sons. In fact he was to rule even longer than Hadrian. Unlike his predecessor he hated to travel and remained in Rome. Concerning Britain his reign is notable for two things: The building of the Antonine Wall and the retreat back to Hadrian's Wall twenty years later. Before we move on to our next emperor of Britain it is worth looking at these events more closely.

The Antonine Wall

Almost immediately on the ascension of Antoninus there are indications of unrest in northern Britain: 'For Lollius Urbicus, his legate, overcame the Britons and built a second wall, one of turf, after driving back the barbarians.'[51] Under Hadrian Urbicus had fought in the Bar Kokhba revolt, 132–5 and after was the governor of Germania Inferior. In 139 Antoninus appointed him governor of Britain. By the year 142 the new emperor had taken the title imperator, coins appeared with the word *Britannia* and Antonius praised Urbicus for 'completing the British war'.[52] All this strongly suggests a successful campaign in northern Britain at the beginning of his reign. A number of inscriptions place detachments of the Sixth Legion in the area from c. 139. A further inscription at Balmuidy, bearing the name of the governor, Lullius Urbicus, suggests construction of the first fort and part of the wall began around 142.[53]

This new frontier was approximately seventy-five miles further north. We signs of preparation with significant rebuilding work at Cordbridge dated to

c. 139. It is estimated governor Lollius Urbicus had a force of approximately 22,000, split equally between the legions and auxiliary units.[54] The Second legion was certainly present, likely with vexillations from the Sixth and Twentieth.[55] Cavalry and auxiliary units screened the main force and baggage train as it wound it's way for six miles through the northern countryside.

A number of sources detail the order of march.[56] Polybius, writing in the second century BC, lists it as follows: Elite troops at the head followed by the allied cavalry and infantry from right wing; behind these are pack animals and baggage; next comes the first legion and their pack animals and baggage; then the second legion and more pack animals and baggage; at the rear came the baggage of remaining allied troops followed by the allied infantry and cavalry from left wing.

Josephus recorded Vespasian's march into Galilee in the first Jewish War (66–73): In the vanguard was lightly armed auxiliary troops and archers followed by heavy Roman infantry and cavalry. Next came the camp builders, ten men from each century, with their tools. Behind these came the baggage train of the senior officers followed by the general himself and his personal bodyguard. Then came the legionary cavalry and mules with the siege equipment. The officers, legionary legates and tribunes and the auxiliary prefects, accompanied the eagles, standards and trumpeters. Behind all these marched the bulk of the legionaries, six abreast, followed by the servants and baggage with auxiliary and allied troops. A rearguard of light and heavy infantry and cavalry completed the spectacle.

A few years before Urbicus marched north Flavius Arrianus, the governor of Cappadocia, led a Roman army against an incursion by the Alani. This is perhaps our closest source to the time period in question. The main threat for Arrianus was horse archers but this is not too dissimilar to the hit and run tactics of the Britons recorded during the invasion of 43 or the Caledonian campaign of Severus in 208–11. One of the Vindolanda tablets (164) dated c. 97–105 makes no mention of archers but hints at a significant cavalry element: 'the Britons are unprotected by armour. There are very many cavalry. The cavalry do not use swords nor do the wretched Britons mount in order to throw javelins'.

Arrianus described the formation utilised when under attack as follows:[57] The army deployed, eight ranks deep, with spearmen in the first four ranks. The remaining ranks were armed with javelins.

The front ranks 'locked shields' and 'pressed their shoulders to receive the charge'. This formed an impenetrable wall which cavalry were unable to break. Attackers were pinned by the front ranks as javelins, arrows and other missiles rained down from the rear. Artillery pieces were placed on the rear with a screen of heavy infantry and archers. The cavalry was placed in eight 'wings' to the rear of the formation along with horse archers.

If they could have forced a pitched battle then a likely tactic would have been that used by Agrippa at Mons Graupius a few decades earlier: auxiliary units in front, flanked by cavalry and the legions forming a 'wall of iron and wood' behind. The auxiliary units pushed the Britons back up the hill as the calvary outflanked them. In the end the legions were not needed by Agrippa. There is no mention of a major battle under Urbicus so it is likely the campaign consisted of brushing aside ineffective ambushes. By 142 the new frontier had been stabilised enough to allow construction of the new wall to commence.

The central sector, climbing over Cray Hill and Bar Hill, appears to have been constructed first followed by the thirteen miles of the eastern sector and lastly the western portion.[58] Distance slabs give very precise lengths such as the 3,660⅘ paces built by the Twentieth at Castlehill. Similar slabs are found on both the north and south faces of the wall and are unusually ornate compared to Hadrian's Wall or the German frontier. One example, at Bridgeness on the Wall, shows someone making a sacrifice on behalf of the Second Legion. Interestingly evidence suggests the letters, LEG II AUG, had been painted red.[59] The wall generally adapted itself more to the country than its southern counterpart which had several straight stretches.

A fifteen-feet wide stone-base was laid to aid drainage topped by turf, earth or clay. The turfs measured a very precise 18 x 12 x 6 Roman inches, narrower and thicker than a modern paving slab. This earthen bank resembled the German limes with a fence but no rampart. More evidence this was a demarcation line rather than a defensive rampart.[60] In front was a ditch, 20 to 40 feet in width and 8 to 12 feet deep. At Watling Lodge in Falkirk the ditch is an impressive twelve-feet deep and forty-feet wide. One can imagine looking up from the bottom of the ditch. One would need five men standing on each others' shoulders to reach the top of the fence on the bank above. North of the ditch was a a low bank formed by the deposits from the ditch. To the rear of the entire construction, 120 to 150 feet behind, ran the Military Way. This road consisted of stones topped with gravel and side ditches to aid draining.[61] It was 16 feet wide allowing soldiers to march up to four abreast.

A number of inscriptions detail which units were responsible for specific sections. At Dunchoter a detachment of the Sixth was responsible for 3,240 feet.[62] A distance slab gives the emperor's full name, Emperor Caesar Titus Aelius Hadrianus Antoninus Augustus, and states, 'a detachment of the Sixth Legion Victrix Pia Fidelis did the construction of the rampart for 3,240 feet' (RIB 2,200). Some inscriptions allow us a glimpse at the ethnicity of the soldiers. At Castlecary soldiers of the Sixth and 'citizens of Italy and Noricum' erected a shrine'.[63] This is dated to the reign of Commodus, which would place troops back on the Antonine Wall twenty years after it was abandoned. An altar at

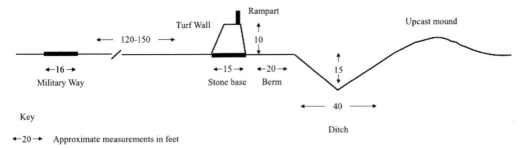

Figure 25. Cross section of The Antonine Wall.

Westerwood attests to the fact centurions and above could bring their wives with them: Quadriviae Vibia Pacata, wife of Flavius Verecundus, centurion of the Sixth Legion, has a name of North African origin.[64]

Once complete auxiliary units were posted to the various forts doted along the wall. We can see these in figure 26. Only eight units are attested to date and they can be seen in table 4 below. We can see that many were moved from Hadrian's Wall to the northern frontier and then returned after the Antonine Wall was abandoned. It is worth noting that evidence indicates it was not occupied concurrently with Hadrian's Wall.[65] It is therefore quiet likely, given auxiliaries served for 25 years, that some individuals marched north at the start of their career c. 140 only to march south again near the end. Some units returned to their old bases on Hadrian's Wall. Some are recorded as still being present in the late fourth century by the *Notitia Dignitatum*.

Table 4. Auxiliary units on the Antonine Wall.

Unit	Details
First Cohort of Hamian archers	Unit of 500 from Syria. Served at Carvoran on Hadrian's Wall and then Bar Hill on the Antonine Wall after 142. Returned to Carvoran and also Fort Housesteads.
First Cohort of Tungrians	Infantry unit of 800 raised in modern Belgium served at Vindolanda and Carrawburgh. Posted to Cramond and Castlecary on the Antonine Wall. At Fort Housesteads in the 3rd century.
First Cohort of Baetasians	Infantry unit of 480 raised in Germania Inferior in modern Netherlands, this unit of 480 infantry is thought to have been posted to the Manchester or Ribchester area prior to the building of the Antonine Wall.
Second Cohort of Thracians	Mixed unit of 600 based at Old Kilpatrick and later Bar Hill on the Antonine Wall. On the withdrawal south this unit was sent to the Cumbrian coast and relocated to Maryport. It is recorded in the fifth century *Notitia Dignitatum* at Reculver in Kent

Unit	Details
Fourth Cohort of Gauls	Mixed unit off 600 raised in Thrace posted to Mumrill's Fort on the Antonine Wall. In the 3rd century at Moresby Fort, Cumbria.
First Cohort of Vardullians	Mixed unity of 1,000 originating from Hispania Terraconensis posted to Castlecary on the Antonine Wall. Later evidence places it at Corbridge c. 161–3, Lanchester c. 175–6 and High Rochester and Cappuck c. 213.
Sixth Cohort of Nervian	Infantry unit of 480 from modern Belgium. Sent from Great Chesters to Rough Castle on the Antonine Wall. In the 3rd century at Bainbridge in North Yorkshire.
First Cohort of Batavians	Mixed unit of 600 from modern Belgium and Netherlands. Posted to Castlecary on the Antonine Wall. In the 3rd century at Carrawburgh.

Another point to note is that construction took about twelve years but almost immediately we get evidence of unrest. Coins dated to c. 155 refer to 'Britannia subdued' with suggestions of a revolt by the Brigantes in an unknown Genunian district.[66] A new governor, Gnaeus Julius Verus, arrived c. 154–8 with soldiers from 'each of the three British legions' who had 'contributed to the two German armies'. The evidence points to the Antonine Wall being abandoned soon after c. 158, just 20 years after Urbicus led an army of over 20,000 men north.[67] We then see evidence of re-occupation of Hadrian's Wall and also building work at the now major supply fort of Corbridge. Detachments of the Sixth dated to

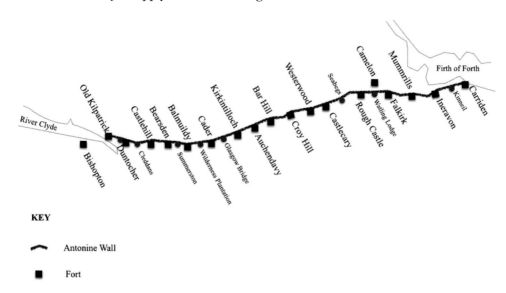

Figure 26. The Antonine Wall forts.

155–9 (RIB 1132) and also also under the governorship of Sextus Calpurnius Agricola (c. 163–6): 'To the Unconquered Sun-god, a detachment of the Sixth Legion Victrix Pia Fidelis made [this] under the charge of Sextus Calpurnius Agrippa, pro-praetorian legate of the Emperor.'[68] The abandonment began before Antoninus died in 161 and we see buildings and forts demolished and burned. Distance slabs were deliberately concealed, buried in shallow pits. We can only speculate as to the reason but unrest among the northern tribes is a likely culprit.

Antoninus was succeeded by Marcus Aurelius, the last of our 'good emperors'. His reign was plagued by wars on the Danube and with Parthia. We will cover that in more detail in the next chapter as the period gives us the backdrop on the rise of a remarkable man. From the son of a former slave to the highest position of all. The chapter will also introduce a lesser known Emperor of Britain. A man who fought and lost against one of the most formidable emperors of the time. An event that heralded the ascent of the Severans who we will cover in Chapter six. But first we meet Pertinax, the son of a freedman.

Chapter Five

Pertinax and Clodius Albinus

Emperor Antoninus Pius died in 161 and was succeeded by Marcus Aurelius who appointed his adoptive younger brother, Lucius Verus, as his co-emperor. Cassius Dio praises Marcus Aurelius for preserving the empire despite the 'unusual and extraordinary difficulties' he faced. This most philosophical and academic emperor was embroiled in wars throughout his reign. First the Parthian War which began in his first year. Second the Marcommanic Wars on the Rhine and Danube where more than one future emperor served and fought with distinction: Pertinax, Didius Julianus, Albinus, Clodius and Pescennius Niger. Cassius Dio tells us the one thing that disappointed Marcus Aurelius was his son, Commodus, famously observing when commenting on the succession: 'our history now descends from a kingdom of gold to one of iron and rust'.[1]

In late AD 161, Vologases IV of Parthia invaded the Roman client state of Armenia and installed his puppet-king, Pacorus. Severianus, governor of Cappadocia in eastern Turkey, led a legion to expel him, but his force was utterly destroyed after being trapped at Elegeia and he committed suicide. Marcus responded by first ordering Statius Priscus, governor of Britain, to the now vacant governor position in Cappadocia. He was replaced as governor in Britain by Sextus Calpurnius Agricola. The emperor's second act was to send Lucius Verus east to take command of the Roman response. The situation became even more urgent when the governor of Syria, Lucius Attidius Cornelianus, led another Roman army to defeat.

Verus organised a three pronged attack, the first led by Priscus directed against the Armenian capital at Artaxata. The central campaign was directed through Mesopotamia and the third towards the Parthian capital. All three campaigns were ultimately successful allowing the emperors to award themselves the titles of *Armeniacus* and *Pathicus*. It is likely Priscus brought some units from Britain and we have two inscriptions that hint this. The first comes from dedication slab. built by a detachment of the twentieth at Corbridge, erasing the Lucius Verus as 'conqueror of Armenia'.[2] Evidence suggests the Priscus captured the Armenian capital Artaxata by 163 and the slab is dated to shortly after. Coins appeared soon after bearing the words ANTONINVS AVG ARMENIACVS and L VERVS AVG ARMENIACVS with Verus first taking the title Armeniacus in 163.[3]

The second inscription comes from Great Chesters Roman Fort on Hadrian's Wall. A dedication slab erected by the Sixth Cohort of Raetians names both emperors as 'conquerors of Parthia, Media, and Armenia'.[4] This is dated after the end of the war in 166. It is possible vexillations of the legions in Britain and auxiliary units accompanied Priscus east and took part in the Armenian campaign, returning to Britain after. If so they returned with another significant figure. Pertinax was a young equestrian officer and he served with distinction in the Parthian War.

Further potential evidence comes from the memorial stone of Lucius Artorius Castus found at Epetium, near Salona (Dalmatia), in modern Croatia. The stone lists his military career through various centurion posts and then crucially:[5] 'prefect of the Sixth Legion Victrix, commander of three British legions against the Armenians'. In my 2022 book, *The Roman King Arthur? Lucius Artorius Castus*, I show there is no link between this historically attested Roman equestrian officer and the later Arthurian legends which appeared in the middle ages and I detail his career. The academic consensus places his floruit ending after one of the historically attested Armenian campaigns in 163, 215 or 233.

If it is the former timeframe as many experts believe, such as Loriot, Higham and Birley, then we have an intriguing possibility. Namely Priscus brought with him units of legions from Britain supported by the *praefectus castrorum* of the Sixth legion. Only natural for Priscus to take control of the army and a trusted officer to lead the troops from Britain. After the Armenians were defeated and Artaxata captured Priscus remained in the east whilst the wider Parthian war rumbled on. Castus retired and earned a promotion to procurator of Liburnia soon after the war ended in 166. Who then led any units back to Britain? Pertinax having earned his reputation in the central theatre against the Parthians would be a natural choice if he was posted to Britain.

Publius Helvius Pertinax was born on 1st August 126. He was a Ligurian from Alba Pompeia and that his father was said to be 'not of noble birth', the sources glossing over his even more lowly status as the son of a freedman.[6] To gain advancement in Roman society one often needed a mentor. Pertinax found one in Tiberius Claudius Pompeianus. Pompeianus is perhaps most famous for being one of the possible figures behind the fictional character Maximus Decimus Merdius in the 2000 film *Gladiator*. The history behind the film is covered in my book *The Real Gladiator: The True Story of Maximus Decimus Meridius* which demonstrates history is every bit as entertaining as anything the film industry can invent.

Pompeianus had also came from relatively humble origins, his father being an equestrian. He caught the eye of the new emperor, Marcus Aurelius and became one of his more trusted generals. Promoted to the senate he eventually married the emperor's daughter, Lucilla. It was under his patronage that Pertinax rose through the ranks, winning promotion promotion in the Parthian War of 161–6.

Simon Elliott in *Pertinax, The Son of a Slave who became a Roman Emperor*, dates his time in Britannia to before 166.[7] Pertinax is one of three known equestrian legionary tribunes of the Sixth: Antoninus Gargilianus and Publius Aelius Macrianus are referred to on tombstone in York. His next posting in Britain was as a praefectus of an auxiliary cohort, *cohors I Tungrorum milliaria*. This double-sized unit of 800 infantry was based at Castlecary on the Antonine Wall under the Emperor Pius. The next evidence places it at Housesteads on Hadrian's Wall in the third and fourth century. It is possible it returned there after the more northerly wall was abandoned prior to Pertinax arriving.

This suggests that Pertinax was sent to Britain before the end of the Parthian War in 166 and he left in time to distinguish himself in the late 160s when Pompeianus utilised him in the First Marcomannic War. This wasn't to be the last time he visited Britain awe shall see.

The Sixth Legion

A detailed history of the Sixth Legion is covered in my recent book, *The History of Roman Legion VI Victrix*. At this point we only need to cover the period up to the arrival of Pertinax in the 160s. The legion was founded by Octavian shortly after the assassination of Julius Caesar. The subsequent vicious civil war effectively ended at Philippi, where Brutus and Cassius, two of the chief architects of the assassination, committed suicide. This Second Triumvirate was an uneasy truce between Octavian and Mark Antony with the latter taking control of Egypt and the eastern provinces. Octavian took Rome and the west while the increasingly sidelined Lepidus was confined to North Africa.

The peace was broken by Mark Antony's brother, Lucius Antonius, who raised an army in Italy but was forced to surrender at Perugia in c. 40 BC. It is here we see the first evidence of the Sixth's existence: sling shots with the inscription 'VI'. The Sixth was next involved against Sextus Pompeius, son of Pompey the Great, who had occupied Sicily and threatened the grain supply to Rome. The shifting alliances brought Antony and Octavian together temporary but by 31 BC defeat at Actium had pushed Antony back to Egypt. The Sixth played little part. The next year they were sent to Hispania Tarraconensis in north-eastern Spain.

Here they remained for some time, fighting in the the *Bellum Cantabricum et Asturicum*, Cantabrian and Asturian, Wars, 29–19 BC. By the end of this war the republic had withered and died. Antony had died the year of Actium and in 27 BC Octavian had been named Augustus.

The Sixth was initially called *Hispaniensis*, meaning simply 'stationed in Spain', and there it stayed throughout the first decades of the principate. The name *Victrix*, or 'Victorious' is first attested during the reign of Nero, AD 54–68. When Galba declared himself emperor the Sixth supported their legate and provincial governor. The subsequent 'Year of the Four Emperors' resulted in Vespasian's reign. The following year he sent the Sixth to the Rhine to quell a revolt by the Batavians.

The Romans proved victorious at Xanten, near the legionary base Vetera, on the Lower Rhine. A monument, found near Vynen north of Xanten, was erected, dedicated to Vespasian and his son Titus:[8] 'Legio VI Victrix dedicated this, when Aulus Marius Celsus was pro-praetorian legate of the emperor and Sextus Caelius Tuscus was legate of the emperor'.

The Sixth remained in Germania Inferior at Novaesium, Neuss. Twenty years later, under the Emperor Domitian, they were sent to quell a rebellion in Germania Superior and were awarded the title *Pia Fidelis Domitiana*, Dutiful and Loyal of Domitian. This title was dropped after Domitian's assassination in 96. The legion moved again, this time to Xanten the site of the Roman victory years before. They may have taken part in the Dacian Wars of Trajan, 101–106 but they were back in Germania Inferior when Hadrian ordered the construction of the Lower Rhine Limes.

Their arrival in Britain is well documented and many inscriptions attest to their presence in the construction of both Hadrian's and the Antonine Wall. By the time Pertinax arrived the latter frontier had been abandoned some years and the Sixth was one of three legions left in Britain, along with *legio II Augusta* at Caerleon and *legio XX Valeria Victrix* at Chester. The Sixth was based at York, seventy miles south of Hadrian's Wall. Supporting the legions were several dozen auxiliary units, many of which were concentrated in northern Britain.

We see detachments of the legion present at various northern forts most notably at the major supply base at Corbridge. However by this time the legion's main base had become York.[9] It is to here Pertinax would have travelled when he was posted from the eastern war.

As we shall see the Sixth would be involved in significant unrest after Pertinax departed. A major incursion in 182 was followed by mutinies, one of which almost resulted in the death of Pertinax himself when he returned as Governor of Britannia. Their role in the rebellion of Clodius Albinus and the Caledonian campaign of Severus Septimius will be covered in this and the next chapter. It was under the latter campaign they were awarded the title *Victrix Britannica pia Fidelis* implying a level of loyalty. Little is heard of the legion in the third century and it may at one point have been the last remaining legion in Britain.[10]

It may have succumbed to the military reorganisation under Diocletian or Constantine when many legions were split up and reduced in size. Nothing is heard in the fourth century but it may have survived to be removed by the general Stilicho in 402 or Constantine III in 407. A fifth century manuscript, *Notitia Dignitatum*, may refer to a remnant of the Sixth still at York, a point that will be covered towards the end of the book.

Back in the second century Pertinax would have arrived at York to serve as a A *tribunus angusticlavius*, 'tribune with the narrow stripe'. As one of the five equestrian tribunes his role was to support the legionary legate and the *tribunus laticlavius*, 'tribune of the broad stripe'. Both of these men would have been off the senatorial order. Next in line in this command structure was the *praefectus castrorum*, camp commander. Along with the leading centurion, the *primus pilus*, these men made up the command staff for the ten cohorts of over 5,000 men.

Pertinax, early career

The normal career progression for an equestrian was via the *tres militiae*. Normally this would start with an auxiliary quingenary infantry cohort. Next would be his current post at York, *tribunus laticlavius*. The last of the 'three posts' would be as commander of an auxiliary cavalry unit, *ala*. Pertinax had turned this on its head, most likely due to his mentor Pompeianus pulling strings. His first significant post seems to have been as *praefectus cohorts IV Gallorum ala*, a cavalry unit of 500, in Syria. Having performed well in the Parthian War he was posted to be legionary tribune of the Sixth. His third posting was as commander of a double sized (approximately 800) infantry cohort of Tungrians.

Fort Housesteads and the *cohors I Tungrorum milliaria*

We met the first cohort of Tungrians earlier in this book at Vindolanda, at the end of the first century, a little over two decades before Emperor Hadrian's visit. We recall the details from one of the 'Vindolanda Tablets' which gave us the only known example of a strength report of an auxiliary *cohors milliaria peditata* (tablet 154). Pertinax's predecessor, Iulius Verecundus (c.92–7), gave the unit strength as 752 of which only 296 were fit and present. Of course we don't know the situation in the late 160s under Pertinax.

It was a very different posting from his previous one at York. There he had been one of five equestrian tribunes assisting the senatorial tribune and legate. The cohorts and centuries tend to be led by the centurions. As a praefectus of an auxiliary unit he was now in sole command with a support staff. The unit was divided in a similar way to the legions, with, on paper, ten centuries of 80 men each led by a centurion.

The regiment had originally been raised in Gallia Belgica and military diplomas have been found for several individuals dated to the first half of the second century. Under Hadrian they were moved to Birdoswald. Under Antoninus they moved north to Castlecary on the Antonine Wall. By approximately 160 they were back on the southern wall at Housesteads, a couple of miles north-east of their earlier base at Vindolanda.[11] There they remained until the fourth century.

In figure 27 we can see an aerial view of the fort at Housesteads. Hadrian's Wall forms the northern wall of the fort and we can see a Roman *vicus* to the south and east. The original fort had a high curtain wall 1.4 metres wide, backed by an earthen rampart, and 4.25 metres up to the walkway. Corner towers allowed a view along the entire length of each wall and further towers protected the four main access gates. The principal gate was in the east through which the road ran to the centre of the camp, the *principia*, headquarters. The largest single building was the *praetorium* where Pertinax resided.

We know more details about Pertinax' career from an inscription that was found in Bruhl, near Cologne, dated c. 169–170 which lists his posts: prefect of the Fourth Regiment of Mounted Gauls; tribune of the Sixth Legion Victrix; prefect of the First Tungrian Regiment; procurator of the food supply; prefect of the German Fleet; imperial procurator in the Three Dacian Provinces and in Moesia Superior. This would suggest he only spent a brief time in Britain, perhaps a year or two in each post.

Figure 27. Aerial view of Housesteads Roman Fort, Vercovicium. (*Wikimedia Commons*)

After his postings in Britain he led a cavalry regiment in Moesia and commanded the *Classis Germanica*, the naval forces guarding Germania inferior and superior.[12] He next obtained a procuratorship in Dacia before falling foul of palace intrigues. The influence of his patron once again came to the rescue. Pompeianus appointed him as his aide and he was placed in charge of detachments fighting in the first Marcomanni War against various Germanic tribes that had made serious incursions across the Rhine and Danube. At some point in the early 170s he was promoted to the senate achieving a suffect consulship by 175. It was that same year dramatic events were taking place in Britain. Very likely involving his old legion, the Sixth at York.

The nearly emperor – Priscus

As the Second Marcommanic War drew to a close in 180 Commodus was with his father on the Danube when the emperor fell ill. Contrary to the famous 2000 film *Gladiator* Commodus did not kill his father with his own hands and there was no plan to return the empire back to a republic. The cause of death is thought to have been the Antonine plague. This was brought west by victorious Roman soldiers after the Parthian War and ravaged the empire. The new emperor was only 18 years old. The sources are generally unkind to Commodus claiming he ran back to Rome as soon as he could.

However others suggest the evidence points to him conducting a successful continuation of the war on the northern frontier for the first year or two of his reign.[13] The assassination attempt by a senator, spurred on by his own sister, may have been the turning point early in his reign. He also had to deal with two major conflicts in the first two years of his rise to power, first in Dacia and then Britain. It is from this latter province we see the events that lead up to our 'nearly emperor'.

Cassius Dio records wars in Dacia but that his 'greatest struggle' was in fact in Britain early in his career.

> When the tribes in that island, crossing the wall that separated them from the Roman legions, proceeded to do much mischief and cut down a general together with his troops, Commodus became alarmed but sent Ulpius Marcellus against them … and he ruthlessly put down the barbarians of Britain.
>
> Cassius Dio book 73.8

The word 'general' may simply mean a commander. Some have suggested it was a legionary commander, most likely from VI Victrix at York. However it could just as likely mean one of the auxiliary commanders of a unit stationed along the wall. This would be an equestrian praefectus commanding a unit of 500 to 1,000 men, a far more likely scenario perhaps than elements of the Sixth at York, 70 miles to the south. Another alternative is the supply base at Corbridge a couple of miles to the south. Vexillations of the Sixth are known to have been posted here and a commander of the fort would also have had various detachments of auxiliary units under his command.

The signs point to Corbridge as the most likely target. Archaeological evidence of destruction can be found along the eastern section of the Wall and at the following forts:[14] Halton Chesters, Rudchester and Corbridge. Forts north of the wall appear to have been abandoned: Birrens, Newstead, High Rochester and Risingham. A plausible scenario presents itself: Major unrest north of the wall culminated in an incursion between the forts at Halton Chesters and Rudchester. The outposts north of the wall were destroyed as part of this uprising or abandoned as a consequence after. The route of attack

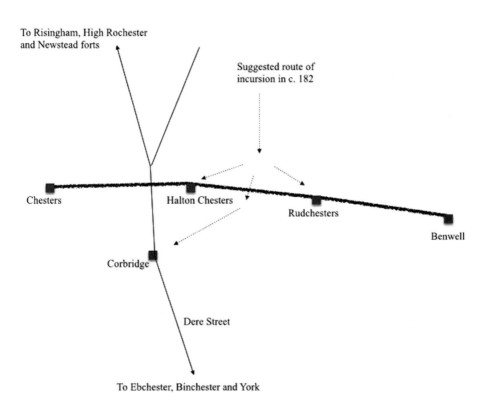

Figure 28. Map of the incursion of 182.

down eastern Northumberland and the lower Tweed Valley used the Roman road to the west as a guide.

The supply base at Corbridge at the time was unprotected by walls. The vicus, warehouses and other buildings had all sprung up around the fort over the preceding decades. It was a tempting and lucrative target. In order to get access and protect their escape route the first at Halton Chesters and Rudchester had to be taken. From there it was only a short distance to Corbridge and Dere Street. This allowed them easy access to forts further south although there's no indication they reached anywhere near the legionary base at York. Figure 28 shows one possible scenario for this event.

There is also a question of whether this was the first or second governorships of Ulpius Marcellus. He is known to have been governor in 178 and such a long posting is unusual. Some have suggested he was sent back a second time to deal with the incursion. However, on balance Birley finds it likely the general killed was the legionary legate of VI Victrix and Marcellus served from 178–84 and was sent from London rather than elsewhere.[15] Whatever the case the war was finished by 184 as the title Britannicus starts to appear on coins. We can thus date this major incursion to the first years of Commodus's reign, c. 182.

It was in this same year that the first major assassination attempt occurred directed at the young emperor. Commodus was entering the 'hunting-theatre' where a certain Claudius Pompeianus (not Lucilla's husband of the same name) was waiting. Cassius Dio places the blame on Lucilla, the eldest sister of Commodus. A senator hid en route to the hunting theatre. As Commodus approached he jumped out into the narrow passage thrusting out his sword: 'See! This is what the senate has sent you'.[16] The senator was betrothed to Lucilla's daughter and, according to Dio, 'had intimate relations both with the girl herself and with her mother'. Commodus held him off until his guards arrested him.

This event was soon to affect Britain. Commodus, now unsurprisingly wary of the senate, began to promote, and rely on, freedmen and equestrians rather than senators. The freedman Saoterus, hated by the senate, was the first to be caught up in the plot that led to Lucilla's execution. The next to rise to prominence was the praetorian prefect Perennis and it is his actions that are connected with events in Britain. By 184 Ulpius Marcellus had restored order but he was 'strict, arrogant and unpleasant' and the army mutinied.[17]

The *Historia Augusta* claims that because of the war in Britain Prennis had dismissed 'certain senators' and placed equestrians 'in command of the soldiers'. We are left to wonder if this means the senatorial tribunes or legates? And if so of which legions? The more contemporary accounts of Cassius Dio and Herodian fail to mention this aspect and give an alternative account of a plot by Perennis. Yet all three record the ultimate outcome in 185 when he was 'delivered up to the soldiers to be torn to pieces' as soon as the matter was reported to Commodus.[18] We can thus date our 'nearly emperor' to somewhere between the defeat of the northern incursion and death of Perennis, c. 184–5.

It would appear that as the young emperor avoided senators and concentrated on more physical pursuits such as chariot racing, Perennis had been acting as de facto head of state, managing both military and civil affairs. The army in Britain grew restless and no doubt resented Ulpius Marcellus and his regime of strict discipline. They soon rebelled but, we are told, they placed the blame on Perennis rather than the emperor.

Cassius Dio states they choose 'Priscus, a lieutenant' as their emperor.[19] Their chosen emperor declined stating: 'I am no more an emperor than you are soldiers.' This did not satisfy the soldiers in Britain. Still rebellious they chose 'out of their number fifteen hundred javelin men and sent them into Italy'. Commodus met them on the road to be informed 'Perennis is plotting against you and plans to make his son emperor'. No mention of equestrian legates here and the near contemporary Herodian agrees with Cassius Dio. This resulted in the death of Perennis along with his wife, sister, and two sons. But unrest in Britain continued until 'Pertinax quelled them' a couple of years later.

Before we return to Pertinax who was this Priscus? This 'lieutenant' is not of course the same Statius Priscus of the AD 160s.[20] He could be Junius Priscus, a later legate of V Macedonia. In Britain he was most likely the legate of VI Victrix. Birley has suggested his full name was Junius Priscus Gargilius Quintilianus. From an inscription in Rome some of his posts may be as follows: '…propraetorian legate of the Emperor of the Second Legion Italica, commander of vexillations of the three British legions, legate of the Fifth Legion Macedonica, legate of the Sixth Legion Victrix Pia Fidelis…'.[21]

If this is correct then we have a senatorial legate of the Sixth Legion being touted as a potential emperor in c. 184–5. Ulpius Marcellus was recalled to Rome around the same time although it's impossible to know which event came first. Birley goes on to suggest the next governor was Marcus Antius Crescens Calpurnianus, the senatorial iuridicus in Britain.[22] His inscription reads: 'vice legati legato pro praetore, acting legate, propraetorian legate'. His reasoning includes the possibility the *Historia Augusta* contains a grain of truth and senatorial legates had been recalled by Perennis. If a subsequent revolt resulted in Marcellus also being recalled it is plausible Crescens, now one of the few of senatorial rank in Britain, served as acting-governor until Pertinax arrived in 185. One possible scenario would have our 'nearly emperor' Priscus being transferred to the Rhine after 184–5, possibly with vexillations of rebellious British legions'. Commodus now turned to a tried and trusted commander to stamp his authority back on the province.

The revolt under Pertinax

After a promising early military career, partly in Britain in the 160s, Pertinax served as an equestrian procurator in Dacia before falling foul of palace intrigue and being recalled to Rome. His new patron, Pompeianus, resurrected his career, and he served with distinction on the Danube during the First Marcommanic War. He was promoted to the senate by Commodus and by 175 had received a suffect consulship, a remarkable achievement on its own for a son of a former slave. His experience as an equestrian procurator served him in good stead when he was appointed as governor of several provinces in succession: Moesia, Dacia and Syria. He once again fell briefly out of favour with Commodus mainly due to the machinations of the emperors praetorian prefect, Perennis.

The revolt of the army in Britain led to the recall of Ulpius Marcelllus and the attempted proclamation of a new emperor, Priscus. These events contributed to the downfall of Perennis placing Pertinax back in favour. Cassius Dio tells us that even after these events the soldiers in Britain remained restless 'until Pertinax quelled them'. The *Historia Augusta* gives a little more information. After the death of Perennis, Commodus sent a letter asking him to be governor of Britain. The soldiers,'… wished to set up some other man as emperor, preferably Pertinax himself'.[23] Like Priscus before him Pertinax refused and suppressed the mutiny, '…but in so doing he came into great danger; for in a mutiny of a legion he was almost killed, and indeed was left among the slain'. Pertinax punished the mutineers severely but petitioned Commodus to be excused from his governorship. The reason he gave was '…. the legions were hostile to him because he had been strict in his discipline'.

Reading between the lines this is a remarkable scenario. Pertinax, governor of Britain, rules from the governor's palace in London. No doubt he wished to inspect the troops and hear from his legionary commanders. Perhaps he travelled in turn to the legionary bases at Caerleon, Chester and York. He is likely to have prioritised the northern frontier as well. he would have remembered York well, having served there 20 years before. It is possible some of the older hands had served with him when he was an equestrian tribune. Perhaps they didn't all remember him with fondness.

There is no clue as to where this mutiny occurred and what scenario resulted him being left 'among the slain'. If the identification of Priscus is correct this would suggest the Sixth was a major source of unrest in the province. Doubly so if they were involved in the incursion of c. 182 and the subsequent imposition of strict discipline by Ulpius Marcellus.

Pertinax was governor for just two years, leaving in 187. Despite the apparent failure of his tenure he remained in favour with Commodus. He went on to be appointed proconsul of Africa and served as consul for a second time alongside the emperor himself. During his two years as governor of Britain he would have spent some time at least at the provincial capital and it is to that we will now turn.

Londinium

Londinium was built by the Romans near a ford close to modern day Westminster. It began life as a fort on one of the three hills overlooking the surrounding marsh land: Cornhill, Ludgate Hill and Tower Hill. On the south bank, a further raised area allowed for the occupation of modern day Southwark. The first bridge was close to where London Bridge stands today. London grew into a centre of commerce and finance. It's population of mainly Roman immigrants enabled it to quickly surpass Camulodunum in importance. It's rapid expansion and easy links by sea with the continent ensured its eventual replacement of Camulodunum as the provincial capital.

Londonium had been destroyed in the Boudican revolt of 60, alongside Camulodunum and Verulamium (St Albans). A red ash layer can still be identified by archaeologists signifying the fire that destroyed the town. After the revolt was suppressed a large fort was built in the north west corner at Cornhill. Covering 15,000 square metres it was protected by double ditches and banks 3 metres in height and depth. Ten years after the town was destroyed a basilica was constructed. This was the civic centre housing law courts and offices.

Around the year 90 work started on a new basilica and forum. It took 30 years to complete and it is likely Hadrian had some input into it's finally stages.[24] The new forum was over four times as large at 300 feet in length. The large square, often full of market stalls and traders, was surrounded by a colonnaded veranda which protected shops and offices. The basilica now covered two hectares and rose to three storeys in height making it one the largest of it's kind outside Rome. This majestic building could be seen from most parts of the city. Together with two known Roman bath houses and an amphitheatre this shows both the importance of Roman London and the extent to which the Roman way of life had embedded itself. Many of the new buildings used stone quarried in the Maidstone area of Kent and transported by barge up the River Medway and down the thames.

Another site uncovered beneath Cannon Street railway station has been identified by some as a potential governor's palace.[25] An enormous building covering 3.5 acres it housed an 80 feet long hall with wings on either side. An equally impressive ornamental pond, 100 feet long, fronted the building. It sat on a raft of concrete 6 feet thick. A similar sized building sat on the opposite bank at Southwark. One interesting point about early London was there were no walls, even after its destruction by Boudica. An earth bank and ditch marked the boundary making the fort the only truly defendable place in the city.

It wasn't until the late second to early third century that a wall was constructed out of over a million blocks of Kentish ragstone transported from quarries in the Maidstone area of Kent.[26] This wall was over 2 miles long, 20 feet high and 8 feet thick. It enclosed 350 acres of the city. Webb, in *Life in Roman London*, dates its construction to between c. 190–210. Not only did it serve as a defensive barrier it also allowed the authorities to control and tax goods coming into and out of the city and port.

Some have suggested London was abandoned soon after c. 410 AD.[27] Others claim Romano-British activity within London may have lasted as late as 450 after which time Anglo-Saxon settlements appear outside at nearby Lundenwic a mile to the west.[28] No evidence of Anglo-Saxons have been found within the city walls for the fifth century.[29] The ninth century Anglo-Saxon Chronicle claims that in 457 there was a battle at Crecganford (Crayford in Kent) after which the Britons 'forsook the land of Kent and fled to their stronghold at London'. The archaeological record suggests the Roman city was deserted by 500 AD and not reoccupied until Alfred the Great in 886 AD. Bede however references the nearby growing Saxon town when he mentions a bishopric in 604 and describe sit as an important market.[30]

Estimates of its population suggest it peaked between 30–60,000 in the mid-second century. It seems to have declined, partly perhaps by the Antonine plague which swept the empire after the Parthian War of 161–6. Pertinax might have seen this reduction with his own eyes when he arrived twenty years after his posting as tribune. In 185 the new governor arrived to a bustling port and unwalled town. It was every inch a Roman city and he may well have resided at the magnificent building now lying beneath the platforms at Cannon Street. The gates of the later walled city are echoed in the names today: Ludgate, Newgate, Cripplegate, Bishopsgate and Aldgate. The distance between Aldgate in the east and Ludgate in the west is just a little over a mile. From the north at Bishopsgate to the water's edge on the thames it is an even shorter distance. Pertinax could have strolled from the palace at Cannon Street to the basilica and forum (underneath Leadenhall Street) in five minutes. He would have no doubt inspected the fort in the north west corner and sat in the best seat at the amphitheatre watching a beast hunt or gladiatorial contest.

London's amphitheatre was discovered in 1988 below Guildhall Yard. The initial structure would have been constructed in wood built around the same time as the first basilica in c. 70. A stone structure was built in the early second century able to entertain 6,000 spectators. It was about 105 m long and 85 m wide. This is roughly the same size as a premiership football pitch but as it

Pertinax and Clodius Albinus 95

Figure 29. Aerial view of London. (*Wikimedia Commons*)

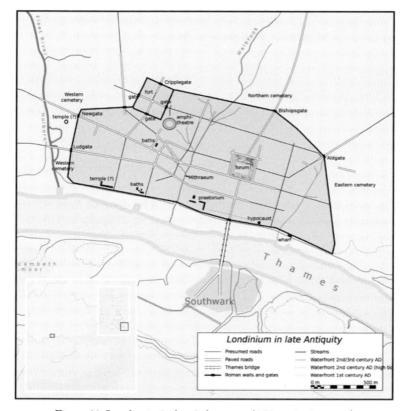

Figure 30. London in 2nd to 3rd century. (*Wikimedia Commons*)

includes the seating area the arena floor would have been a bit smaller than an average playing field. By comparison the London Palladium theatre holds just under 4,000 and my local football club, Bromley, FC holds just over 5,000. The smallest division two football ground is Salford which holds 5,100.

Figures 29 and 30 give us an indication of what London might have looked like when Pertinax arrived. We can see the fort and amphitheatre in the north-west corner. The forum and basilica sits directly in line with the bridge.

Provincial government

As provincial governor Pertinax had authority over the military units in the province. Although it is worth noting the legion commanders owed their appointments, and in theory loyalty, to the emperor. The three legionary legates in Britain were all of senatorial rank and no doubt hoped they too would one day be appointed to the lucrative post of provincial governor. Their second in command, *tribunus laticlavius*, were also of senatorial rank, usually in their early twenties. Pertinax we recall had served as a *tribunus angusticlavii* in the sixth whilst still an equestrian. Pertinax also had authority over several thousand men in the *classis Britannica*, which patrolled the coastline. More significant were the several dozen auxiliary units which numbered over 30,000 troops, far out numbering the 15,000 men of the three legions.

He also had a senatorial *iuridicus* in charge of legal matters and who could step up in the event of illness, death or recall of a governor. We get some idea of

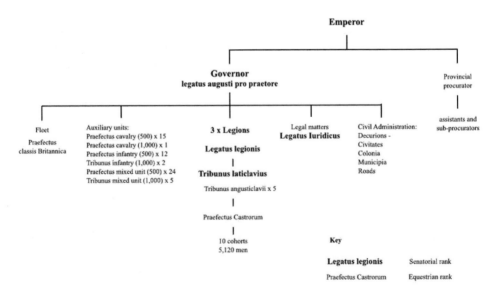

Figure 31. Civil and military administrative structure of Britannia in the second century.

the personal staff a governor might have had in London from the much later *Notitia Dignitatum*: 'a chief of staff from the school of confidential agents the first class, a chief deputy, two receivers of taxes, a chief clerk, a custodian, a chief assistant, a keeper of the records, assistants, secretaries, notaries, a curator of correspondence and the rest of the staff'. The province itself was divided into civitates. These tended to have been based on previous tribal areas, each with its own town capital. Other towns, *municipium*, sprang up, some of which were settled by retired soldiers. These latter were called *Colonia*. Such urban centres were usually administered by a town council. Separate from the

Figure 32. Bust of Pertinax. (*Wikimedia Commons*)

governor's jurisdiction was the imperial procurator. This man was of equestrian an rank and was appointed by, and reported directly to, the emperor.

Pertinax as emperor

Pertinax left Britain in 187 and never returned. The subsequent events had a major impact on our story. The relationship between Commodus and the senate deteriorated further. After the death of Perennis in 185 the freedman Cleander rose to prominence. He soon became widely hated, especially by the senate who resented a mere freedman having power over them. We are told he 'sold senatorships, military commands, procuratorships, governorships, and, in a word, everything', appointing an unheard of twenty-five consuls in one year. This allowed him to amass 'more wealth than any who had ever been named cubicularii'.[31]

In the spring of 190 Cleander eventually went one step too far. Commodus placed him in charge of the grain supply and Cleander took full advantage. Buying up and storing the surplus he trie to manipulate prices and win support through later generous donations. Many Romans however 'hated the man and blamed him for all their difficulties; they especially despised him for his greed.'[32] Dio takes up the story at horse race at the Circus Maximus where a mob, incited by 'bitter words' about Cleander, marched to the palace where Commodus lay blissfully unaware. the situation may have been saved but Cleander made a fateful decision.

He sent soldiers against the crowd most likely the 1,000 strong *equites singulares augusti*. Dio tells us the Praetorian Guard turned out in support of the people after many had had been killed. The sources differ as to exactly what happened next but either the emperor's sister, Fadilla, or lover, Marcia, rushed in to warn Commodus. Terrified the people would turn on him and urged on by his sister and lover he had Cleander killed and his body thrown to the mob. The corpse was dragged away, abused and they 'carried his head all about the city on a pole' while many who had 'enjoyed great power' under Cleander were also killed.[33] Herodian has a terrified Commodus ordering the unsuspecting Cleander to his presence where he was 'seized and beheaded, and, impaling his head on a long spear, sent it out to the mob'.[34]

With another advisor gone Commodus gave in to 'licentious pleasures'. Men of 'intelligence and … even a smattering of learning' were driven out and replaced by 'the filthy skits of comedians and actors'. He turned his attention to the games, taking lessons in driving the chariot and training for beast fights.[35] There is a another reason for the sources hostility. They tell us Commodus was attempting to raise revenue through fair means and foul.[36] Not only were taxes raised but he brought charges against senators only to drop them for a price. Some were even accused simply for not naming Commodus as the heir in their will.

In addition there was a marked increase in executions and despotic behaviour. He ordered Rome be renamed Commodiana, the legions Commodian, and a day of Commodiana to celebrate this 'elevation'. He named himself the grand title of: Emperor Caesar Lucius Aelius Aurelius Commodus Augustus Pius Felix Sarmaticus Germanicus Maximus Britannicus, Pacifier of the Whole Earth, Invincible, the Roman Hercules, Pontifex Maximus, Holder of the Tribunician Authority for the eighteenth time, Imperator for the eighth time, Consul for the seventh time, Father of his Country. Even the months of the year were renamed: Amazonius, Invictus, Felix, Pius Lucius, Aelius, Aurelius, Commodus, Augustus, Herculeus, Romanus, Exsuperatorius. Dio sums up the general feeling: 'so superlatively mad had the abandoned wretch become'.

It was in this post-Cleander period that Decimus Clodius Albinus is first attested to be governor of Britain in c. 191. It is possible he was there much earlier and may have succeeded Pertinax soon after 187. As we shall see Albinus was to be our next emperor in Britain after Pertinax and he played a pivotal role in the ascension of Septimius Severus. By 192 Commodus was identifying as Hercules and received deification from the senate, most likely through gritted teeth. The *Historia Augusta* lists a number of senators killed suggesting another plot.[37]

It was towards the end of 192 that Commodus proposed something extraordinary. Up to this point many of his gladiatorial bouts had been in private and with blunted or wooden swords. Now he decided he wished to fight in the arena against hardened gladiators. The senators were scandalised but the people seem to have loved it and came from far and wide to witness an emperor fighting in the arena. He took part in beast hunts and was apparently extremely skilled, never missing with either bow or javelin.[38] This was bad enough for his advisors but he then planned a ceremony for the festival of Saturnalia in mid- to late December. He wished to stay over night at the gladiator barracks and arrive at the arena dressed as a secutor leading the other fighters. Marcia pleaded with him to not debase himself but he angrily threw her out. Next his praetorian prefect Laetus and his freedman Eclectus also advised against it only to receive the same treatment.

Commodus then went to sleep but not before writing a list on a wax tablet of all those he wished to kill.[39] Top of the list was Marcia, Eclectus and Laetus, as well as various senators and advisors. As it turned out it was to prove his own death warrant. Finding the list Marcia understandably panicked no doubt recalling the fate of previous close advisors. Commodus was poisoned and when that failed, strangled in his bath by his wrestling partner Narcissus.

With the deed done the conspirators rushed to the house of Pertinax who initially thought they had been sent to kill him. Reassured he recalled the senate who gratefully acclaimed Pertinax as emperor. A remarkable achievement for the son of a freedman. There is some suggestion that the story in the sources masks a deeper plot. The timelines don't exactly fit for a rushed affair. The argument with his advisors would have been before Saturnalia whereas he was killed on 31st December. There is sone suggestion that Pertinax, popular with the sources, may have at least known in advance. The presence of important senators in Rome and the ready acquiescence of Narcissus do suggest something deeper. This is covered in more detail in my previous book, *The Real Gladiator*.[40]

The sources claim the people were overjoyed. No doubt many senators breathed a huge sigh of relief, although some owed their appointment to Commodus and the story that he died of apoplexy was not universally believed. Pertinax gave a rousing speech and promised to be more like the esteemed Marcus Aurelius and less like Commodus. The sources are very positive about Pertinax with Cassius Dio calling him an 'excellent and upright man'. The praetorians however, loyal to Commodus, felt very differently and only the promise of 12,000 sesterces placated them. But not for long.

It did not take long for the first attempt of regime change to be uncovered. While he was in nearby Ostia in early AD 193 he was informed of a plot by a group of praetorian officers to replace him with the consul Quintus Sosius Falco. Pertinax rushed back to Rome and the senate declared Falco a public enemy. The emperor kept his promise not to execute a senator and merely banished Falco to his estates. On 28 March he heard of further unrest in the praetorian camp and sent his father-in-law and Urban Prefect, Sulpicianus to placate them. The praetorians held Sulpicianus against his will and 300 armed soldiers marched on the palace.

Many of the staff fled but Eclectus and Pertinax bravely stood their ground, meeting their assailants face to face. At first Pertinax shamed them into sheathing their swords. But a Gaul named Tausius could not be dissuaded and he struck the emperor down. Eclectus bravely stepped in but he too was killed. The praetorians then marched back to camp with the emperor's head on a spear but with no clear plan as to what to do next. One wonders how Sulpicianus felt when he saw his son's head bobbing up and down on a spear as the soldiers returned through the gates of the praetorian camp.

It appears he soon got over any initial grief over his son-in-laws demise when he saw an opportunity in the chaos. He quickly offered them a sum of money for their support. Those senators who had been loyal to Commodus and suspected foul play may have allowed themselves a wry smile. Many others fled the city fearing further reprisals. But another man also spied an opening. Senator Didius Severus Julianus had been at dinner and, urged on by his guests, rushed to the praetorian camp. He arrive just in time to find them mulling over whether to proclaim Sulpicianus emperor.

The praetorians wouldn't let Julianus in but they soon found themselves in the middle of a bidding war between the two would-be emperors. Inside the camp Sulpicianus got to 20.000 sesterces but Julianus, shouting counter offers through the locked gates, finally offered 25,000 cash immediately and hinted that the father-in-law of the man they just murdered might not be their best choice. That swung it and Didius Severus Julianus was marched to the senate and acclaimed by the senators, no doubt again through gritted teeth, encouraged by the presence of armed praetorian guards.

When news spread across the empire three other claimants declared themselves emperor. Each had something Julianus lacked, powerful military support: Prsecennius Niger in Syria had the eastern legions, Septimius Severus had the legions on the Danube and Clodius Albinus with the three legions in Britain. Severus was closer and moved first. He secured his western flank by making the governor of Britain Caesar in return for support. Julianus spent the next two months trying to shore up support and offering increasingly desperate deals, first to the senate and then to the advancing Severus. Just sixty seven days after his proclamation he was found alone in his palace by a single tribune. His last words were 'But what evil have I done? Whom have I killed?'.

Severus quickly hunted down and executed all the conspirators in the murders of both Pertinax and Commodus. Narcissus the wrestler was thrown to the beasts in the arena. The praetorian guards were assembled in ceremonial dress without armour or weapons, harangued by the new emperor and disbanded and dismissed. Within a year one rival was defeated an killed. Niger was beheaded following the battle of Issus in 194. Clodius Albinus was still in Britain and perhaps dreaming of his own eventual elevation to augustus. When Severus declared his son Caracalla as his heir, Clodius Albinus realised he'd been duped.

Clodius Albinus

Decimus Clodius Septimius Albinus was born c. 145 and came from a wealthy family in Hadrumetum in North Africa. He served with distinction in the Marcommanic Wars and was elevated to the senate by Marcus Aurelius. He fought in Dacia under Commodus went on to govern one of the German provinces before receiving a consulship c. 190. Caracalla was only 5 years old when his father promised Albinus the title Caesar. In 194 he was offered a second consulship alongside the emperor. This arrangement was not to last. Within a year Severus had declared his son as heir and Albinus duly proclaimed himself Augustus in Britain.

Dio tells us Albinus had 'aspired even to the pre-eminence of emperor'.[41] Herodian makes it clear Severus deceived him and Albinus was 'conceited and somewhat naive in his judgment, really believed the many things which Severus swore on oath in his letters'.[42] His reputation is tainted by his enemies such as Severus who called him 'drunken, effeminate, crafty, shameless, dishonourable, greedy and extravagant, a man better suited to the stage… than for the battlefield'.[43] Yet the sources also tell us the senate preferred him 'because he belonged to a noble family and was reputed to have a mild nature'.[44]

The *Historia Augusta* states he was 'greatly beloved by the senate', more than any other emperor. Although this was in part because of 'their hatred of Severus, who was greatly detested by the senate because of his cruelty'. It describes him as 'tall of stature, with unkempt curly hair and a broad expanse of brow'. His skin was 'wonderfully white' and he 'had a womanish voice, almost as shrill as a eunuch's'. He had a terrible temper 'easily roused' and 'relentless'.[45] Marcus Aurelius described him as 'a man of experience, strict in his mode of life, respected for his character'. He also commended him for his loyalty during the revolt of Avidius Cassius in 175.

Herodian places the blame for the next sequence of events on Severus. Albinus was in Britain, residing in the governor's palace that likely lies today beneath Cannon Street railway station. No doubt he followed the footsteps of Pertinax the short distance to the forum and basilica and enjoyed the pleasures of the amphitheatre. Word reached Severus was 'acting more and more like an emperor' and worse still was reaching letters of support from 'the most distinguished senators'.[46] It would appear the senate preferred Albinus and some even urged him to come to Rome while Severus was still occupied in the east. The Augustus decided to use trickery first.

Figure 33. Bust of Clodius Albinus. (*Wikimedia Commons*)

The battle of Lugdunum

Severus sent messengers to Albinus on the pretext of secret orders. They were to request a meeting in private. If successful in seeing him without his body guards they were to cut him down like some mafioso hit from the film *The Godfather*. Plan B was to administer 'deadly poisons' to his food or drink.[47] The *Historia Augusta* tells us 'five sturdy fellows were to slay him with daggers hidden in their garments.' However Albinus was already on his guard. Severus had behaved cruelly towards the supporters of the defeated Niger. Not only had he executed rank and file soldiers but he had slaughtered various governors. He even held their children to ensure good will and once achieved executed them anyway, even the children. Herodian describes the character of Severus as despicable. Dio Cassius states that he was ruthless in extracting huge sums from anyone who was perceived as supporting Niger whether they did so voluntarily or not.

Albinus was in no mood to trust such a man and so the messengers were seized and tortured revealing the plot. A cold-war situation now developed as both sides prepared for war. Herodian quotes a rousing speech given by Severus to his legions.[48] Albinus, he claimed, had 'violated his pledges and broken his oaths, and … chosen to be hostile rather than friendly and belligerent instead of peaceful … so let us now punish him with our arms for his treachery and cowardice.' The legions of Britain are described as 'small and island-bred, will not stand against your might'. He reminded them of their great victories, superior numbers and experience and, of course, they alone had a 'brave and competent general' to lead them. Albinus is lambasted as having an 'effeminate nature' more suited to 'the chorus than for the battlefield'. Crucially, we also read of 'generous gifts to the soldiers' which may have played a bigger part than his words. Conflict was now inevitable and Severus publicly announced the expedition against Albinus and seized the Alpine passes.

Albinus responded by crossing to Gaul with much of the army from Britain. How much of a skeleton force was left to defend the province is unknown. However given the size of the armies at the final battle it is reasonable to suggest the bulk of the three legions and many of the auxiliary units were present. Cassius Dio tells us that there were 150,000.[49] He must mean combined which would suggest Severus may have outnumbered his foe perhaps three to two. Whilst the emperor had not personally been present at a major battle Cassius Dio describes him as 'superior in warfare and a skilful commander'.

We then read a curious tale of a certain Numerianus, 'a schoolmaster', who pretended to be a Roman senator. He set out from Rome to Gaul, collected a small force and preceded to attack Albinus' troops. He killed a few of the enemy's cavalry and 'other daring exploits in Severus' interest'. Albinus set up his headquarters in Gaul and requested aid from local governors in the form of supplies, food and money. This decision was to prove fatal for those who backed the wrong emperor. A few minor skirmishes occurred in late 196 and Albinus won an initial victory against the Severan general Lupus, killing many of his soldiers. The final battle occurred outside the city of Lugdunum in south east Gaul on 19th February 197.

The shortest route from Italy would be from the south east across the Alps. However it is possible Severus headed from the Rhine and Danube first before heading west and coming towards the city from the north. In fact an initial battle took place at Tinurtium, modern Tournous, sixty miles north of Lugdunum. The final engagement occurred outside the city which makes a northern route seem more likely. The conflict was evenly balanced and we get our first hint of the British legions being present from Herodian: 'in courage and ruthlessness the soldiers from Britain were in no way inferior to the soldiers from Illyria'.[50] The battle first swayed in the emperor's favour when the left wing of Albinus was driven back. They fled to their camp, pursued by the Severan right, which suggests the camp was outside the city.

On the opposite flank the situation was the reverse. The British troops had dug trenches and pits covering them with branches and earth. Advancing to the edge of these hidden defences they hurled their javelins and other missiles

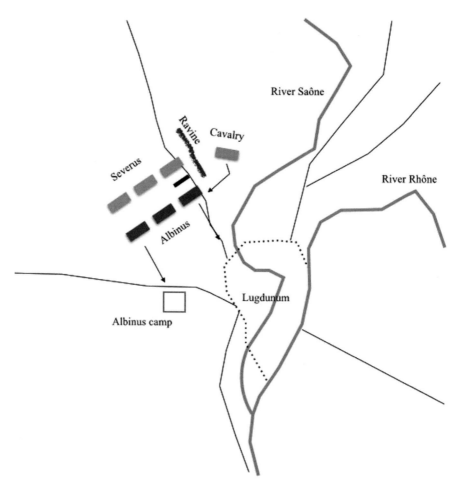

Figure 34. Battle of Lugdunum 197.

luring the Severan army on to them. The Severans attacked and the defenders quickly retreated. Buoyed with the hope of a quick victory the front ranks of the Several army plunged into the traps. Those behind stumbled and fell over their comrades. The rear ranks panicked and a shower of missiles and arrows caused enormous losses in men and horses. Part of the army was pushed into a deep ravine, an example of which is indeed north of the city.

Severus saw the danger and rushed into the breach with his praetorian guards to stop the retreat turning into a rout. The empire hung in the balance: We read, 'the emperor slipped from his horse and fled, managing to escape by throwing off the imperial cloak'.[51] Shades of Richard III at Bosworth as we get an image of a desperate emperor trying too escape a confused melee surrounded by enemy. Cassius Dio gives a slightly more heroic narrative. Seeing his left wing disintegrate he tore off his riding cloak, draw his sword, and rushed in to shame his men or die in a valiant attempt to stem the tide.[52] Whatever the case the Severan army turned and fought.

Meanwhile the Severan cavalry commander Laetus was waiting and watching. Sources were later to accuse Laetus of hedging his bets and waiting to see who was winning. Notably Severus was to reward all his generals except Laetus who was later executed. At Lugdunum he chose his moment well. The Severan left flank took heart, found a new horse for their emperor, wrapped him in his imperial cloak and charged. Then Laetus slammed into the flank with his cavalry. The Britons offered a brief resistance before breaking and fled towards the city. The fugitives were pursued and slaughtered and driven into Lugdunum.

Even the victors deplored the devastating aftermath. The plain was covered in the corpses of men and horses, mutilated by sword and spear. Bodies piled in heaps and weapons scattered across the fields. Blood flowed into streams and rivers. Albinus took refuge in a house in the city beside the River Rhone. Cassius Dio has him committing suicide whilst Herodian says the victorious army burned the city, found Albinus and beheaded him. The *Historia Augusta* has the more grisly tale. The attempted suicide failed and Severus had his rival beheaded. This wasn't to be the last emperor of the western provinces to die at Lugdunum as we shall see.

All the sources tell of the emperor's disrespect over his fallen enemy's body. Severus verbally abused the corpse then the body was cast away and the head sent to Rome on a spike. Again the *Historia Augusta* is more vivid. The headless-body of Albinus was laid out so that Severus could ride his horse over the corpse and when it shied away calmed it down so it could trample the body even more. There it remained for some time before being cast into the Rhone along with the bodies of his wife and children.

This wasn't the only sign of the emperor's cruelty. He ordered the bodies of senators slain in the battle to be mutilated. Significant numbers of others were also executed, especially in Gaul and Spain. Unluckily for some, private letters offering support to Albinus were discovered. Some senators who had openly supported Albinus were spared although he confiscated huge sums to swell imperial coffers. But any who were now found to have tried to play both sides were killed. One notable death was Sulpicianus, father-in-law to Pertinax, who we recall lost the auction for the imperial throne to Didius Julianus just six years earlier.

The defeated legions returned to Britain no doubt under new leadership. Some appeared to have stayed loyal to Albinus even after his death but were defeated by Severus who went on to 'settling affairs in Britain'. There's no indication he came in person. However he is our next emperor to visit just over ten years later. In fact we have three current and future emperors coming at the same time. Britain received a new governor, Virius Lupus and we see an inscription at Corbridge dedicated to him: 'A detachment of the Sixth Legion, Victorious, Dutiful and Faithful, [built this], under the charge of Virius Lupus, senator of consular rank.'[53] Still 'dutiful and faithful' the legions were now Severus' men.

Chapter Six

The Severans

Lucius Septimius Severus was born in 145 at Lepcis Magna in modern day Libya. His father, Publius Septimius Geta, was 'obscure' but he had two cousins who had risen to senatorial status.[1] Severus followed them into the senate in 173 and governed Gallia Lugdunensis and Sicily. In the last years of Commodus he was governor of Upper Pannonia. The later *Historia Augusta* describes his ancestors as equestrians.

In 175 he married his first wife, Pacia Marciana. A year after her death in 186 Severus married the daughter of a Syrian high priest, Julius Bassianus. His daughter, Julia Domna, was to have two famous sons, Caracalla and Geta, both of who will be pivotal to our story. Julia's older sister, Julia Maesa, was to be the grandmother of another two future emperors Elagabalus and Alexander Severus. The marriage took place in Lugdunum in 187 where Severus was governor. Little did Julia know that six years later she would be empress and four years after that the bloodiest battles in Roman history would be fought outside the very city in which they now celebrated their marriage.

Twenty years later Julia would find herself in northern Britain along with her two grown sons. Interestingly it is possible her nieces, Julia Soaemias and Julia Mamaea, may also have travelled with the court. If so then it's very likely two further future emperors may have also visited Britain. For these were the mothers of Elagabalus and Alexander Severus respectively. The latter was born after the campaign started so this might be unlikely. However the father of Elagabalus was Sextus Varius Marcellus, who was made Procurator of Britain in 208. It is thus likely his four year old son accompanied him along with the boy's mother and empress's niece Julia Soaemias.

During the reign of Commodus, Severus came very close to being executed. The *Historia* tells us he was accused of 'consulting about the imperial dignity with seers and astrologers'. Commodus had encouraged a culture of accusations as a means of extracting wealth allowing successful accusers to retain a proportion. This was not an entirely risk free means of taking down a rival as false accusations often resulted in the accuser being punished. A twist of fate would have ended the Severan dynasty before it began. But Severus was acquitted and his accuser was crucified.

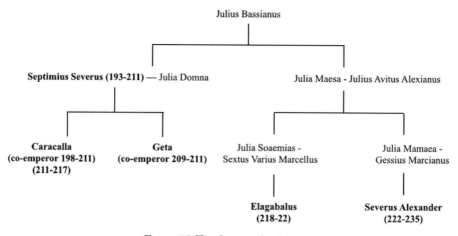

Figure 35. The Severan family tree.

In the previous chapter we read how Severus was acclaimed emperor by the legions on the Danube when news of the murder of Pertinax reached them. As he marched on Rome the brief reign of Didus Julianus came to an equally murderous end. The praetorian guard who had behaved so disloyally towards Pertinax were disbanded and replaced by men from the new emperor's own legions. The subsequent civil wars against Pescennius Niger and Clodius Albinus portrayed his brutal nature.

His physical appearance was 'small of stature, but strong and energetic' with a small nose, turned up at the tip.[2] Later historians mistakenly described him being African and depicting him with black skin. In fact being North African he would have had a Mediterranean complexion. The *Historia Augusta* claims he retained a north African accent throughout his life. He increased the number of legions to thirty three and double the pay. His attitude to the army can be summed up by his alleged death bed last words to his sons: 'Keep on good terms with each other.. be generous to the soldiers and take no heed of anyone else'.

Severus copied Pertinax in promising to never put a senator to death. He even swore an oath that if either he, or any working on his behalf, did so they and their children would become public enemies. This was to prove a false promise. He killed many of Niger's men and extracted huge sums of cash from those senators who had supported him. When Byzantium fell after a long siege all the defending soldiers and magistrates were put to death. The *Historia Augusta* tells of 'cruel punishments' to Niger's followers. He allowed senators who had sided with Niger to live but senatorial legates and tribunes who took an active part in military operations were put to death.

We have already noted how he allegedly rode over the corpse of Albinus at Lugdunum and executed his supporters. Perhaps more telling is his speech to the senate on his return: 'he praised the severity and cruelty of Sulla, Marius and Augustus as the safer course and deprecated the mildness of Pompey and Caesar as having proved the ruin of those very men'.[3] Herodian tells us he 'put to death all the eminent senators of that day' along with many others noted for their wealth. All 'driven by an insatiable lust for money; no other emperor was ever so greedy for gold'.[4] The *Historia* tells us 'countless persons who had sided with Albinus were put to death', men and women. The confiscated goods swelled the public coffers allowing him to leave a fortune to his sons 'greater than any other emperor'.

Figure 36. Bust of Septimius Severus. (*Wikimedia Commons*)

Early in his reign we get reports of trouble from Britain. The Caledonians 'broke their promises' and aided the Meaetae, a tribe near the former Antonine Wall. Quite what this means we are not told. Its likely the removal of troops by Albinus created an opportunity exploited by northern tribes. The new governor, Virius Lupus, appointed by Severus, was forced to make peace for 'a large sum' and took captives. He served as governor from 197 to c. 201 so this appears to have occurred just a decade before the emperor himself came to Britain.

Described by the sources as cruel, after his death much was forgiven mainly due to the chaos that followed. He was frugal and wore plain clothes, rarely wore the imperial purple and often had a simple 'shaggy cloak'. His eating habits were equally conservative and he often went without meat. His appearance was handsome with a long beard and curly hair that had greyed in old age.

The invasion of Caledonia 208–11

The campaign in Britain came towards the end of his reign. His first son, Lucius Septimius Bassianus, later known as Caracalla, was born in 188 at Lugdunum. His reign was to prove every bit as bloody as the battle fought outside the city between his father and Clodius Albinus, His second son, Publius Septimius Geta, was born less than a year later in Rome. The sources describe them growing in to rebellious and badly behaved teenagers. However the most serious problem was they had developed a deep hatred for each other. This was especially true of Caracalla who detested his younger brother. Severus tried to reconcile his sons and warned them of the dangers of division. This was to prove to be in vain. The emperor determined to remove them from Rome and a life of shows, games and debauchery.

Events were to give him the opportunity. Despatches reached the emperor's hand from the governor of Britain, likely Alfenus Senecio.[5] The Britons were in revolt 'overrunning the country, looting and destroying virtually everything on the island'.[6] He requested a larger army or even the presence of the emperor himself. Given there were three legions in Britain and a similar number of auxiliary troops the situation must have been serious. It is possible the emergency was exaggerated and this was a literary device used to justify the subsequent actions and praise the achievements of Severus.

Cassius Dio makes no mention of the revolt and makes the reason for the campaign more personal.[7] Tired of his sons' behaviour and not wishing the legions to become idle he decided to lead a campaign. It's likely this may have been the main reason as Herodian also tells of him wishing to get his sons away from Rome and under some military discipline. Cassius Dio also claims Severus was frustrated that others were winning wars in Britain. This would suggest the situation wasn't as dire as Herodian claimed.

The year was 208 and it was to be the emperor's last war. Prophecies and seers had predicted teh emperor would not return and the superstitious Severus believed it. One wonders how he felt when he looked back at the city on his way to the port at Ostia to make the long journey north.

The enemies Severus was marching to confront are named as the Caledonians and the Maeatae. It is likely some of the tribal groups named by Ptolemy had merged into confederations. The Maeatae were located in central to southern Scotland 'next to the cross-wall which cuts the island in half' and the Caledonians are said to live 'beyond them'.[8] We read in Cassius Dio that the Romans held a little less than half the island which suggests the Maeatae were close to Hadrian's Wall rather than the Antonine Wall. It is left frustratingly unclear. Birley interprets Dio as meaning the Antonine Wall which runs between the Firth of Forth and the Firth of Clyde.[9] This is where most scholars place the Maeatae rather than further south. The Caledonians seem to be the same as those placed by Ptolemy north of the Antonine Wall.

Cassius Dio goes on the describe the Britons: They inhabit 'wild and waterless mountains and desolate and swampy plains'; they had no cities or wall; they did not till their fields; and lived on 'flocks, wild game and certain fruits'. We have to take this with a large pinch of salt especially when we read the Britons lived in tents, 'naked and unshod'. Reading that the barbarians 'shared' their women and children in common would have flirter scandalised civilised Roman readers.

We learn a little of military matters: Raiding was endemic and they had a love of plunder choosing the boldest to lead them implying a warrior culture. They used chariots pulled by 'small, swift horses'. The infantry were fast but could stand their ground, although the battle at Mons Graupius would suggest they could not match the Romans in a pitched battle. As we shall see this no doubt remained the case as the Caledonians and Maeatae resorted to guerrilla tactics.

Armed with shields, daggers and short spears they had one specific tactic that is of interest. At the end of their spears they had a 'bronze apple' which they bashed against their shields to terrify their enemies. We can imagine the reaction of Roman soldiers unused to the sound, marching or camped in hostile territory. Short cold days often surrounded by mists. Freezing dark nights huddled inside earth banks and wooden ramparts. Herodian describes the country as always gloomy with thick mists arising from the marshes. Suddenly out of the mists or surrounding forests comes the rhythmic drumming of hundreds or even thousands warriors smashing metal onto wood. Cassius Dio may well be exaggerating the Briton's martial abilities when he states they could endure extremes of hunger and cold and plunged 'into the swamps and exist there for many days with only their heads above water'.

Herodian repeats Dio's account that the Britons are naked but gives us the alleged reason. They were covered in tattoos with coloured designs and drawings of animals which they wish too display. Both sources say the Britons were used to swimming or wading through waist-deep marsh pools, unconcerned about muddying their bodies.

These fearsome sounding warriors awaited the legions. Herodian tells us of the emperor's advance:[10] He was sixty three years old and 'crippled with arthritis' but when he announced the campaign 'in his heart he was more enthusiastic than any youth'. So bad were his ailments that he had to be carried in a litter most of the way. Whether arthritis or gout it gave him crippling pain in his legs or feet making walking difficult. Yet they made good time and arrived ahead of schedule with a 'powerful' army. Septimius would have had first hand reports of the Britons. He was friends with Pertinax who served in the province in the 160s. Closer to home his own brother Geta had been a tribune in the Second Augusta at Caerleon.

It's not certain which units Severus took with him. As one of the praetorian prefects, Aemilius Papinianus was present, so it's likely a significant proportion of that force accompanied him. In addition some scholars have speculated the Romans pulled troops from a number of different sources:[11] the imperial guard cavalry, *equites singulares Augusti*, one of the urban cohorts from Rome; units from legio II Parthica stationed in Italy; vexillations from several legions on the Rhine and Danube; and auxiliary units from the same regions.

These were added to the three legions already stationed in Britain: legio VI Victrix at York; legio II Augusta at Caerleon; legio XX Valeria Victrix at Chester; and a similar number of auxiliary troops, many already posted to northern Britain. In total it is estimated Severus mustered an invasion force of 50,000 supported by a further 7,000 naval *milites* of the *Classis Britannica*.[12] He arrived at York in the late spring of 208 and made preparations for the invasion. Huge granaries dated to this time have been found at South Shields capable of holding enough grain for 50,000 troops to last two months.

The Britons sent envoys to sue for peace but Severus was in no mind to listen. He was motivated to avoid a quick return to Rome and wished to gain honour from a victory over the Britons. As well as teaching his two rebellious sons a lesson. Dykes were built in marshy regions creating 'earth causeways' allowing troops to move troops and fight on firm ground. Pontoons and bridges were built to traverse swamps and rivers. Coinage from 208 show a bridge which may reference this type of engineering activity.[13] We are reminded of Julius Caesar bridging the Rhine to conduct a punitive campaign across the Rhine.

There appears to have been two campaigns. The first was likely in 209. Septimius advanced with his eldest son, the twenty year old Caracalla. Geta was left at York with his mother to administer the province. The territory directly north of Hadrian's Wall may have been relatively subdued however the further north they travelled the more nervous the marching column would have got. No doubt flanked and supported by the *Classis Britannica* they still had the problem of crossing the Forth.

One suggestion is South Queensferry east of Edinburgh where a fort, supply base and harbour have been found.[14] A crossing here would have entailed a pontoon made up of approximately 500 boats lashed together. A massive undertaking considering the British fleet had 900 ships. Interestingly a marching camp just north of the Forth is in direct line between Queensferry and the base at Carpow.

Simon Elliott argues there were two lines of attack.[15] Caracalla lead about two thirds of the army north east along the Highland boundary fault building several marching camps of approximately fifty four hectares along the way. A system of watchtowers and signal stations were built along the Gask Ridge which provided protection from attacks from the Glens and valleys to the north west. The emperor lead the remaining forces north, through the territory of the Maeatae, where we find evidence of smaller twenty five hectare marching camps at Auchtermuchry and Edenwood. This advance may have resulted in Severus reaching Carpow on the River Tay, which became a major fort, supply base and harbour. If so then it is likely the praetorian and urban guard units and the emperor's own legio II Parthica accompanied Severus.

Herodian refers to frequent battles and skirmishes in which the Romans were always victorious. The Britons were 'extremely savage and warlike… armed only with a spear and a narrow shield, plus a sword that hangs suspended by a belt from their otherwise naked bodies. They do not use breastplates or helmets, considering them encumbrances in crossing the marshes'.[16] But perhaps Cassius Dio is more accurate when he states they fought no battles and couldn't even find a sizeable force 'in battle array'. Instead we read of a steady slog across an unforgiving terrain.

They 'experienced countless hardships in cutting down the forests, levelling the heights, filling up the swamps, and bridging the rivers'.

As the Romans advanced the Britons laid traps. Sheep and cattle were left out to be seized only for pursuing soldiers to be ambushed. The lack of clean drinking became a major problem. The retreating Britons no doubt poisoned sources with butchered animals or fallen legionaries as well as burning crops as they went. Whilst Dio's claim of 50,000 Roman dead may be an exaggeration the campaign sounds vicious. We read the Romans would kill their injured soldiers rather than leave them behind for the enemy. The clear implication is they did not have sufficient control or time to transport their injured back to camp. The fate of captives was so horrific a quick death was preferable.

But Severus ploughed on determined to subjugate the entire land indeed we read he reached the 'extremity of the island'. This too may be an exaggeration but we read he 'observed accurately the variation of the sun's motion and the length of the days and the nights in summer and winter respectively'. How ever far north he reached it was a remarkable feat for someone suffering so much he had to be carried in a litter most of the way. Eventually the Britons were forced to come to terms and abandon a 'large part of their territory'. Severus returned south to the 'friendly portion' of the island which presumably means south of Hadrian's Wall.

Regarding the negotiations Cassius Dio seems delighted by one particular anecdote. We learn of one chieftain's name, Argentocoxus of a Caledonian tribe. The Empress Julia was conversing with the wife of the British leader. Julia jestied with the Briton concerning the free intercourse the women of Britain had with their men. If accurate this portrays the words of a British woman from over 1,800 years ago: 'We fulfil the demands of nature in a much better way than do you Roman women; for we consort openly with the best men, whereas you let yourselves be debauched in secret by the vilest.'

The agreement with the tribes was to prove short-lived. The Maeatae rebelled again and the Caledonians soon followed. Severus had lost none of his decisive ruthlessness: 'Let no one escape sheer destruction … not even the babe in the womb of the mother, if it be male; let it nevertheless not escape

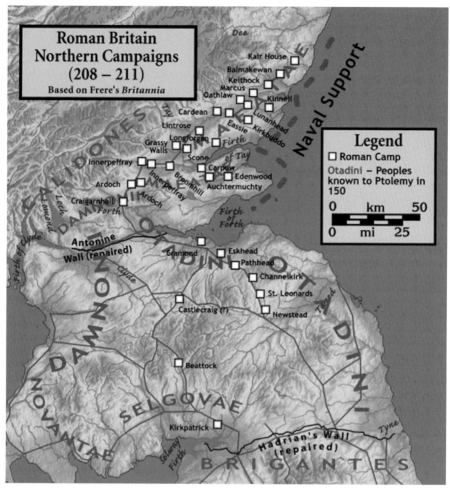

Figure 37. Map of northern campaign of Septimius Severus c. 208–11. (*Wikimedia Commons*)

sheer destruction'.¹⁷ Preparations for another campaign began but old age and illness finally caught up with the emperor. He fell ill at York and on 4th February 211 died. Cassius Dio tells us his advise to his sons from his deathbed was: 'Be harmonious, enrich the soldiers, and scorn all other men'.

The first of these requests was to prove a forlorn hope. Caracalla's murderous nature was already known. He had been placed in command of the army at one point during the first campaign during one of his father's many deliberating periods of illness. Herodian tells us he tried to persuade the soldiers to back him as sole leader. He allegedly even tried to bribe his father's doctors to poison the emperor. A more alarming plot was reported by Cassius Dio.

During the northern campaign we are told Caracalla accompanied his father to discuss terms with the Caledonians. It is likely this was in 210 if it signalled the end of the initial war. Caracalla suddenly reigned his horse and draw his sword. Those around the emperor cried out in alarm fearing the son was to strike his father down. This caused Caracalla to hesitate and re-sheath his sword. Severus though had turned just in time and witnessed it. The subsequent events suggest he guessed what his son's intention had been.

One can only imagine what was going through Caracalla's mind as his father ignored the incident and carried on to the negotiations. It wasn't until the end of the day back in camp that Caracalla was summoned to his father's tent. Their Severus placed a sword within easy reach and harangued his son for daring such a 'monstrous crime' in front of army and the enemy. He then goaded his son to slay him stated he was old and prostrate whereas Caracalla was young strong.

Given both contemporary sources refer to Caracalla wanting to kill his father and brother we can only conclude there is some truth in it, especially given subsequent events. The son was to prove even more ruthless and bloody than his father. Ironically Cassius laments Severus would often complain that Marcus Aurelius should have killed Commodus. But he could not bring himself to do follow his own advice and thus his love for one son condemned the other. It is to Geta we will turn to next.

Publius Septimius Geta

Publius Septimius Geta was born on 7th March 189, possibly in Rome. The war in Britain was the not the first time he had accompanied his father and older brother on campaign. In 197 at the age of 8 years he had followed his father to Parthia. Following the victory at Ctesiphon in 198 Caracalla had been named Augustus alongside his father whilst Geta was titled Caesar. The family travelled extensively after the victory, first in the east, then Thrace, Moesia and Pannonia and finally North Africa in c. 204. The following year the brothers shared the consulship by which time their relationship was already hostile. The praetorian prefect, Plautianus, had done his best to placate the two young men but after his execution in 205 there was no-one to to keep them in check.

As men they had both obtained the *toga virilis* (toga of manhood). They were 17 and 16 when Plautianus was killed and Cassius Dio paints a vivid picture of two young men unrestrained by any discipline: They abused many women and boys alike; embezzled money; and made gladiators and charioteers their companions. Their enmity grew and seems to have been a driving force in their lives. On one occasion this was so competitive and dangerous that a chariot race ended with a broken leg for the older brother. Their father tried to reconcile them, dragging them off to Campania in southern Italy with him between 205–7 and appointing them joint consuls for the second time in 208.

As his father and brother campaigned in the north of Britain in late 208 he stayed with his mother at Eboracum and administered the province, receiving the title of Augustus giving him equal rank to his brother. By 210 he was titled Imperator Caesar Publius Septimius Geta Pius Augustus Britannicus.

There's very little known about Geta's time in Britain. He had just turned nineteen years old when he arrived in Britain and a month short of his twenty second birthday when his father died at York in 2011. One tantalising piece of evidence links him to Britain's first Christian martyr.[18] The earliest reference to St Alban's martyrdom states the following: 'Without an order from the emperors the most impious Caesar ordered the persecution to cease, reporting to them that slaughtering the saints was causing Christianity to flourish, rather than suppressing it'.

There are only two possible times when there were multiple emperors and a Caesar present in Britain to issue such an order. The 'Great Persecution' under Diocletian in the early fourth century may seem an obvious choice. Constantius Chlorus was appointed Caesar in 293 when Diocletan created the Tetrarchy. There were thus two *augusti*, each with a caesar to support him. Constantius, Caesar in the west, was in Britain in 296 when he defeated the usurper Allectus, as we shall read in the next chapter. However there is no evidence for martyrdoms in Britain at this time and Constantius Chlorus offered some protection being reportedly well disposed to the Christians. When he returned in 305 it was as Augustus. The future Constantine I accompanied him but at this point was neither caesar or augustus.

It would thus appear the second, earlier option is possible. With the two augusti, Severus and Caracalla, on campaign in the north, Geta, titled caesar prior to 210, was in charge of provincial affairs from York. It would therefore appear this event occurred in 208–9. The story of St Alban is recorded by the sixth century Briton, Gildas, and also later by Bede. Both agree with the main aspects of the tale.

A christian was fleeing persecution and Alban hid him in his house, changing clothes with him so he could escape. He then took his place but before his execution performed 'wonderful miracles' including parting the waters of the Thames allowing a path across. St Germanus reported visiting his shrine at Verulamium, St Albans, in 429. Bede in the eighth century tells us he was beheaded along with one of his would-be executioners who dropped his sword and fell to his knees on witnessing the miracles. The 'judge' ordered the persecutions to stop after the events. Bede dates it to the 22nd June but frustratingly does not give the year.

One further piece of evidence comes from an inscription at Aenus in Thrace. On 12th September (again frustratingly the year is unknown) an embassy arrived at Eboracum. They were were lead by a certain Diogenes, son of Theocaris, and the *defensores* of the people of Aenus. The decision must have been favourable to warrant an inscription and Birley dates this as likely 208.[19]

The Historia Augusta describes him as handsome in his youth and 'brusque in his manners though not disrespectful'.[20] He loved food and wine to the point of gluttony. he was more studious than is brother and less blood thirsty. When his father talked of destroying rival factions he reportedly asked if they too did not have families. Caracalla ominously remarked he

Figure 38. Bust of Publius Septimius Geta c. 208 (*Wikimedia Commons*)

would like to kill their children too and must have thought his younger brother naive and foolish. He is described as more affectionate than Caracalla and closer to their mother. He had a stammer and a love of colourful clothes. It seems he was well liked especially among the soldiers.

Herodian makes an interesting comparison between the brothers.[21] Back in Rome open hostility followed the funeral of their father. The two emperors privately solicited support, sending letters with lavish promises. The majority favoured Geta due to his 'reasonable disposition' and his mild and moderate behaviour. He is describe as kind and courteous with an excellent reputation which included a respect for learning and 'serious pursuits'. Caracalla though was 'harsh and savage' and scorned intellectual interests for a military and martial life. He was motivated by anger and used threats instead of persuasion. Even his friends were bound to him more by fear than affection.

With the death of their father a significant restraint on their behaviour disappeared. Some senior commanders and advisors tried to maintain a semblance of a working relationship urged on them by Severus on his deathbed. But their own mother could not placate the apparent implacable hostility especially from Caracalla. Some started to choose sides, know doubt aware of the potential consequences of the wrong decision. Perhaps few realised just how bloody the future was to be and how quickly the horror would fall on the empire.

York

A generation after the invasion of 43, and less than a decade after Boudicca's revolt, the Romans had extended their authority northwards reaching a line roughly between the Rivers Humber and Mersey. To the north of this was the Brigantes, possibly a confederation of tribes. In the main they lived in small villages and farms spread across the north, up to the lowlands of Scotland. One significant site is found at Stanwick which lies roughly midway between York and Hadrian's Wall. This impressive iron-age hill fort covered 741 acres and was protected by a bank and ditch. Evidence of trade links with the Roman world suggests it was a centre of Brigantian power.

The Brigantes had been friendly to Rome. Queen Cartimandua, wishing to foster good relations, captured and handed over the British rebel leader, Caratacus in 51. Tacitus relates a tale of marital strife which leads up to the Roman advance into the region. The Queen's estranged husband, Venutius, led an anti-Roman faction. Internal frictions increased when the queen took her former husband's armour-bearer as her lover. The subsequent political in-fighting resulted in Venutius getting the upper handy the year 69. Whether out of necessity or opportunism the Romans moved in and secure the Queen's position.

It seems the Romans chose, or perhaps were given, an area on which there is no evidence of previous native settlement.[22] The first archaeological evidence comes from Roman military activity before the construction of the fortress.[23] It was the Ninth legion which pushed north and founded a fort on the site of where modern York sits today. It had a number of benefits:[24] It was on the boundary between the Parisi in the old East Riding of Yorkshire and the Brigantes to the west and north; it had good communications by road to Lincoln to the south and Tadcaster to the south-west; it also had good links via the River Ouse to the Humber and thus the sea; it was well placed on a piece of high ground providing access through the marshy Vale of York; and it was protected on two sides by the rivers Ouse and Foss.

The fort was laid out in the traditional 'playing-card' plan. The longer side ran north-east to south-west for 1,600 Roman feet (slightly smaller than an imperial foot). The width, south-east to north-west, measured 1,360 Roman feet. This meant the diagonal was 2,100 Roman feet, suggesting that the surveyors were well aware of Pythagoras and thus could ensure reasonably accurate right angles at the corners.

This first fort consisted of a ditch and a rampart, approximately nine-feet high and nineteen-feet wide, strengthened by timbers and turf. A timber palisade protected an eight-feet-wide timber walkway. The towers and four gates were also made of timber.

The earliest written reference to York, c. 100, comes from one of the famous Vindolanda tablets. York also appears in the Antonine Itinerary and the Ravenna Cosmography as well as the works of Ptolemy, the second-century Greek geographer. In c. 122 the Sixth arrived in Britain and took over York as their

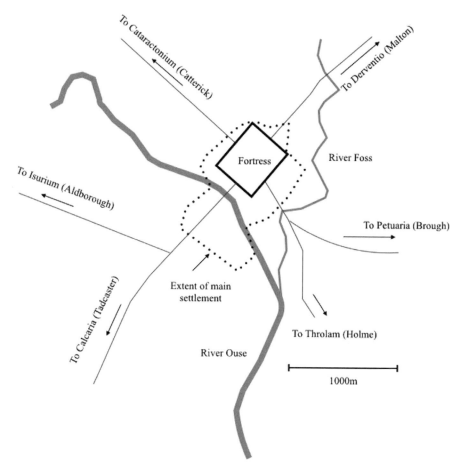

Figure 39. Map of Roman York.

legionary headquarters replacing the Ninth. The fate of the Ninth has been covered previously. Over the next few decades a major urban settlement developed around the town. When the province was split in two in early third century York became the provincial capital of Britannia Inferior. This dual role of major military and civilian centre of authority was unique in Roman Britain.

Two emperors died at York: the first was Septimius Severus in 211; nearly a century later Constantius I passed away after a similar northern campaign in 306. It was there Constantine the Great was proclaimed emperor by the troops after his father's death. Figure 39 places York with the main roads and rivers and within the main settlement that grew outside the original fort. The next map shows the layout of the fort along with the later large stone towers added to the southern side in the third century. Returning to the death of Severus we recall that Geta was at York when his father fell ill. Caracalla was likely in the

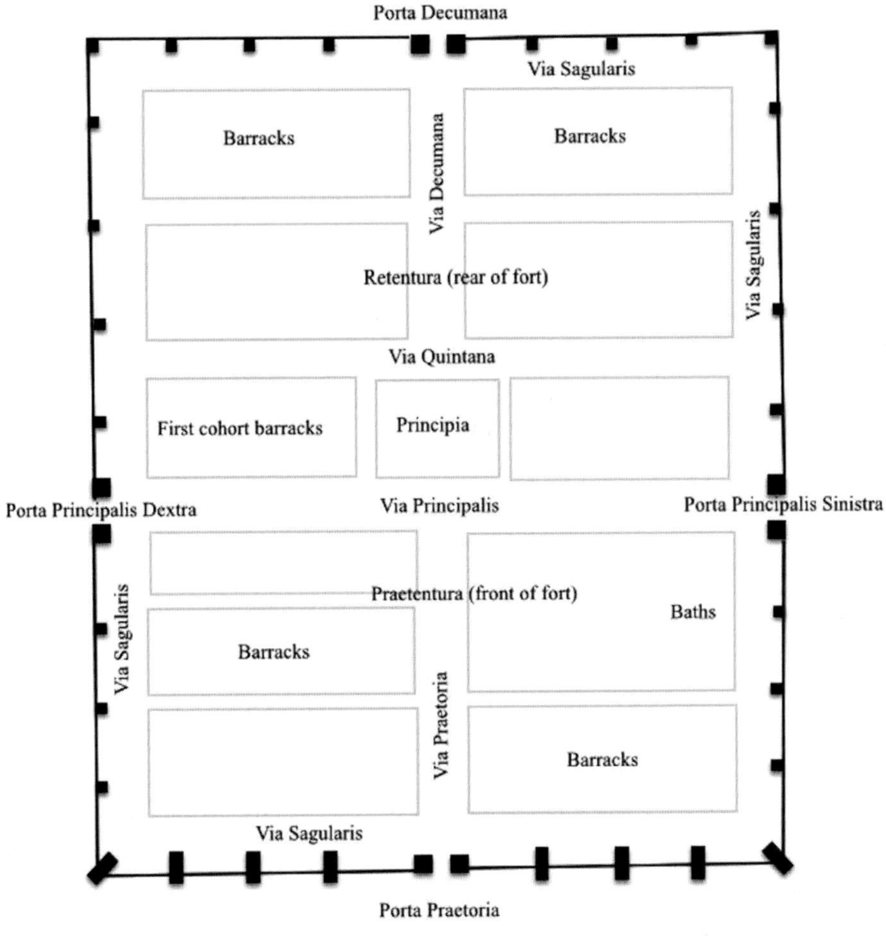

Figure 40. Layout of Roman Fortress of Eboracum.

north with much of the army. If so he would have raced south at the news. The brothers were 22 and 21 respectively and hated each other. Whatever promises they may have made on their father's death bed about 'living harmoniously' were quickly forgotten.

The reign of Caracalla

The sources record the immediate aftermath of the emperor's death at York.[25] Caracalla seized control and began a murder spree. Among the victims were: the physicians who had refused to poison his father; those who had raised both his brother and himself because they urged him to live in peace with Geta; and all those who attended his father 'or were held in esteem by him'.

One of his first acts was an attempt to bribe the army commanders to support him as sole emperor. This failed mainly because there was a general respect for the wishes of Severus, who was popular with the army. This, coupled with a genuine affection for Geta (who also resembled his father in appearance), prevented Caracalla moving against his brother straight away. However whilst in theory the brothers ruled jointly in reality Caracalla controlled the army.

It seems Caracalla was still in the north with the bulk of the army when Severus died because we read he immediately signed a treaty with the Britons and headed south to his mother and brother. Cassius Dio repeats much of what Herodian tells us:[26] Caracalla 'withdrew from their territory, and abandoned the forts'. Much of the army returned south of Hadrian's Wall. His failure to get overwhelming support caused him to promise to live 'in peace and friendship' with his brother although Herodian doubts his sincerity.

The co-emperors left Britain with their mother early in 211 and landed in Gaul with the army. If the 50,000 casualties are to be believed they left behind the bodies of many of their comrades north of the Antonine Wall. We can only guess at the death and destruction of the indigenous population. The new co-emperors returned to Rome with their father's remains.

The journey must have been arduous, especially for their grieving mother. They quarrelled continually and even used separate lodgings. They refused to eat together and both reportedly feared poisoning. Back in Rome they each took up residence in one half of the palace, barricading the inner doors that connected the two parts. Guards were placed by each brother in the palace and an uneasy 'cold-war' gripped the city.

An agreement was eventually reached whereby the empire would be split in two with Caracalla having 'the whole of Europe' and north west Africa with his brother given Asia and Egypt. The former was to have his capital at Byzantium with Geta taking residence in Antioch or Alexandria. But this was abandoned before it could be finalised. The meeting was adjourned when their mother pleading with them to reconcile. The brothers returned to their separate quarters. The enmity and plots continued.

Perhaps unsurprisingly Caracalla was to prove the more determined and ruthless one. He tricked his mother into arranging a private meeting with Geta, in her apartment without guards present.[27] Caracalla had placed centurions hiding nearby ready to rush in and attack Geta. Julia was wounded on the hand as she tried to protect her son as he 'clung to her bosom'. He was only 22 years old. The architect of the murder rushed out of the room shouting that he had been the victim of a plot and ordered the guards to escort him to the praetorian camp. Unaware of the true events this was duly done.

Once at the camp he presented his version of events and offered increased rations and the significant sum of 2,500 denarii. The praetorians again allowed self-interest to trump their vows. They proclaimed Caracalla emperor and marched to the senate. Geta was declared a public enemy and Julia wasn't even allowed to mourn her son.

Caracalla's true nature then came out. Unencumbered by the restrains of his father or existence of a co-emperor he ordered a massacre of all Geta's friends and supporters. Even his attendants and servants living in his half of the palace. No one was spared, not even the infants.

Figure 41. Bust of Caracalla c. 212. (*Wikimedia Commons*)

Even acquaintances were killed: athletes, charioteers, singers and dancers of every type were killed. Senatorial rank was no protection. Evidence was not required. A mere accusation was all that was needed. The bodies of the victims in Rome were dragged out of the city and dumped in piles, burnt or thrown into ditches. The elderly daughter of Marcus Aurelius, Cornifica, was killed for merely crying over Geta's death.

She wasn't the only member of the imperial family to die: his own cousin, Severus; the son of Pertinax; the son of Lucilla, grandson of Marcus Aurelius; and Caracalla's own wife Plautilla. The killing wasn't confined to Rome or the first days of his reign. Caracalla's assassins spread out across the empire and procurators and governors alike suffered the same fate. Anybody who had been remotely favourable to Geta was killed. Cassius Dio puts the number of dead at 20,000.

At some point Caracalla turned his attention back to Britain. We recall the troops there had not agreed to make him sole emperor when Severus died. It is unlikely any senior commanders perceived friendly to Geta or even neutral were left in place. Britain was a significant province with three legions a significant force of auxiliaries. This may be why the new emperor decide to split it into two. Before we examine that we will leave the last word as to Caracalla's character to the *Historia Augusta*: 'Evil and more brutal than his cruel father…gluttonous in his use of food and addicted to wine, hated by his household and detested in every camp save that of the praetorian guard; and between him and his brother there was no resemblance whatever'.[28]

The first division of Britain

There has been some debate about when exactly Britannia was divided into two provinces. Herodian seems to place it during the reign of Severus. However there is some evidence to suggest he was mistaken, perhaps confusing the attested division of Syria at the time. Herodian himself refers to a single governor and province in the events leading up to the campaign of 208–11. In addition we have a reference to a single procurator of a seemingly single province dated to 208–11. This is father of the future emperor, Elagabalus, previously mentioned. In addition we have a number of governors, also of a single province, attested throughout the reign of Severus.[29]

Figure 42. Map of the first division of Britannia from c. 213.

The first reference to two distinct provinces of Britannia comes under the reign of Caracalla. Cassius Dio refers to Lower Britain, in the north, as possessing one legion, the Sixth. Upper Britain, in the south and west, were home to the Second Augusta at Caerleon and the Twentieth Valeria Victrix at Chester. A similar change occurred in Pannonia, dividing it into Upper and Lower Pannonia between 212 and 217. It is likely these divisions formed part of a general re-organisation and happened around the same time.

Birley suggests 214 is a likely date for the division of Britannia.[30] It certainly occurred before 216 as there is epigraphical evidence for a governor of northern Britain by this time. We also have a dedication slab which may refer to Gaius Marcus Julius, governor of Britannia Inferior as early as 213.[31] There is thus still some debate as to the exact year the change was made. Leaving that to one side we do have a reasonable idea as to where the dividing line was: running just north of Chester, east towards the Humber, then looping south of Lincoln. To the north of this line was Britannia Inferior with it's capital at Eboracum where the Sixth Legion was based. To the south was Britannia Superior with Londonium as the capital. The second and Twentieth Legions remained at Caerleon and Chester respectively.

Aftermath

Caracalla's reign was known for one major change: The Antonine Constitution of AD 212 declared all free men in the Roman Empire to be given full Roman citizenship. This may have had more to do with expanding the tax base rather than any noble motive. His cruelty continued during his reign and proved to be this undoing. In 215 he seized the Armenian king and when the Armenians revolted sent a Roman army against them. The following year he made war on the Parthians. It was in the spring of 217, on a journey from Edessa, he humiliated his praetorian prefect, Macrinus one time too many. Fearing his own imminent execution and aggrieved by his treatment he arranged for the emperor to be killed. Caracalla stopped by the roadside to urinate and was stabbed to death.

Macrinus, the first equestrian to be declared emperor, and his 10-year-old son, Diadumenianus ruled for just a year. They too were killed and his successor was the 14-year-old Elagabalus. We recall he may have accompanied his father Sextus Varius Marcellus to Britain in 208 as a child. His reign lasted just four years and he was replaced by his cousin Severus Alexander. He was to prove the last of the Severans. The sources however are rather kind to him: 'he left the state strengthened on every side'.[32] He too was murdered by his troops, in 235.

The academic consensus is he was assassinated at Mainz on the River Rhine. However an interesting reference in the Historia Augusta suggests he may have been in Britain: 'And finally, while he was in quarters with a few men in Britain, or, according to some, in Gaul, in a village named Sicilia, some soldiers murdered him'.[33] Aurelius Victor copies this apparent mistake stating he was killed at Sicilia, a *vicus Britanniae*.[34] It is worth noting historians generally dismiss this. His death proved a turning point for the empire. Events were set in motion that would cause Britain to break away not once, but twice, over the next decades.

Chapter Seven

The Gallic Empire and the Pirate King of Britain

The death of Alexander Severus heralded what became known as 'The crisis of the Third Century'. Maximinus, proclaimed by the Germanic legions after Alexander's execution was himself murdered by his own men three years later during the siege of Aquileia. A succession of emperors and bloody civil wars followed. The political upheavals weakened the empire allowing their enemies to take full advantage. Perhaps most notable was the victory of Persia and capture of Emperor Valerian in 260. The humiliation of defeat was compounded by rumours of Valerian's fate: Either forced to swallow molten gold or kept as a slave before being skinned, stuffed and left on display. Back in Rome his son, Gallienus, was notable for replacing senators with equestrians as commanders of legions or governors of provinces.

Little is known of events in Britain. The campaign of 208–11 seems to have stabilised the northern frontier for several decades. However the death of Valerian caused the empire to fragment into three separate pieces. In the east Egypt, Syria, Arabia and Palestine formed the Palmyrene Empire. In the west Postumus was declared emperor by the army on the Rhine. Gaul, Spain, Britain and two German provinces supported him forming a new Gallic Empire. Gallienus was too weakened to bring either region back under Rome's control.

Postumus

Little is known of Postumus. the *Historia Augusta* describes him as 'valiant in war and most steadfast in peace… respected for his whole manner of life'.[1] Yet he broke faith with Gallienus murdering the emperor's son Saloninus. Nevertheless he is credited with restoring the provinces of Gaul and pushing back invading Germanic tribes. Before his capture by the Persians, the Emperor Valerian praised Postumus as: 'a man most worthy of the stern discipline of the Gauls… able to safeguard the soldiers in the camp, civil rights in the forum, law-suits at the bar of judgement, and the dignity of the council-chamber, and he will preserve for each one his own personal possessions'.

We get little information concerning the Gallic Empire in Britain. An inscription from Lancaster dated 262–6 references the governor of Britannia Inferior: praeses

Octavius Sabinus. A bath-house and basilica was rebuilt, 'collapsed through age, restored from ground level, for the cavalrymen of the Ala Sebosiana, Postumus' own…'.[2] It would appear Postumus still appointed senators to such positions whilst elsewhere Gallienus had replaced them with equestrians. A number of milestones have the inscription Marcus Cassianius Latinius Postumus Augustus (for example RIB 2255 and 2232).

A new *civitas Carvetiorum* is recorded at Carlisle from c. 260: 'For the Emperor Caesar Marcus Cassianius Latinius Postumus Augustus Pius Felix, the Community of the *civitas* of the Carvetii' (RIB 3524). It is thought some of the forts later attributed to the Saxon Shore command, such as Reculver and Brancaster, were also constructed in the mid-third century.[3] British towns started to build defences, including stone walls in this period. This may be in response to Frankish and Saxon raids which appeared c. 250. Birley lists epigraphical evidence, such as milestones, for some of the other 'Gallic Emperors' as well as for Aurelian after Britain returned under central authority.[4]

Figure 43. Gold aureus of Postumus in a pendant. (*Wikimedia Commons*)

It is likely in Britain civil and military administrations carried on as before. Before the decade was over both Postumus and Gallienus was dead, both killed by their own men. After the death of Postumus Britain returned to central control.[5] The Gallic empire was to last fourteen years and have just four emperors, listed in table five. The last, Tetricus, surrendered to Aurelian in 274. Perhaps surprisingly Aurelian allowed Tetricus to live and even awarded him a high-ranking position. With the Palmyrene Empire defeated the year Aurelian had united thwe empire once more. However any hopes of stability were dashed when he was murdered by his praetorian guard just a year after. The table below lists the known emperors of the short-lived Gallic Empire. It is not known if they all set foot in Britain, although Grant is certain at least Postumus did.[6]

Table 5. Emperors of the Gallic Empire.

Emperor	Date	Comments
Postumus	260–8	Established after death of Valerian in response to barbarian invasions and instability in Rome. Initially included Britain, Spain and Gaul. Killed by own troops.
Marius	268	Reigned a couple of months. Killed by troops.
Victorinus	269–71	Killed by one of his officers
Tetricus	271–4	Defeated at battle of Châlons and surrendered to Aurelian

After Aurelian's murder two emperors, Tacitus and Florian, followed him to the grave within a year. Their successor, Probus, managed to last a year longer than Aurelian before he too was murdered by his own troops. We get an interesting snippet of information about Britain regarding captured Burgundians and Vandals sent to Britain, c. 276–82: 'Living in the island they were useful to the Emperor when someone rebelled'.[7] It is worth noting this early reference to Germanic troops coming to Britain. Three emperors followed in quick succession: Carus, 282–3, Probus's praetorian prefect, and his two sons Carinus, 283–5 and Numerian, 283–4.

Carinus adopted the title *Britannicus Maximus* in 284, suggesting a successful campaign. However there is no suggestion any of these short-lived emperors came to Britain personally. The posting of barbarian troops, hints of rebellions and victorious campaigns suggest the long period of peace and stability imposed by Severus and Caracalla decades before, was under pressure towards the end of the third century.

It is only with hindsight that the elevation of Diocletian to the throne is credited with ending 'The Crisis of the Third Century'. A witness in the first years of his reign would be forgiven in being sceptical of anyone claiming a new period of stability had begun. His reforms were certainly substantial and far-reaching as we shall see later. Within two years of the beginning of his reign the empire was plunged into civil war again. Once more Britain was involved. This time the province was central to events. An enigmatic figure emerged who made Britain an island fortress. A fortress that held off the empire for over a decade. It was lead by a man the historian Simon Elliott calls 'Roman Britain's Pirate King'.[8] His name was Carausius.

Carausius

As Diocletian consolidated power Maximian was named his Caesar and soon after declared Augustus and co-emperor. In the west several problems plagued the empire. In Gaul rebels and deserters known as *bagaudae* roamed the countryside. Many may have simply been the dispossessed fleeing raiders, invading barbarians and Roman corruption. The sources describe them as 'rural insurgents' or 'bandits'. However historians suggest the term can mean anyone outside of of mainstream society: escaped slaves, disaffected peasants or deserters from the army.[9]

Not only had people experienced major political upheavals but raids across the Rhine from the Alemanni had sacked 60 towns in 276. Many survivors of these raids were left destitute and it's possible they formed a significant proportion of the *bagaudae*. In addition tax was seen by many as punitive, an issue that was to have major ramifications in the fifth century and events leading up to the end of the western empire. Around 285 Maximian put down the rebellions and beat back raids by Alemanni and Burgundians in the Upper Rhine. One of his decisions was to appoint a certain Carausius to command the channel fleet.

Carausius was born in Menapia. The Manapii were a Belgic tribe located on the northern coast of Gaul. Their tribal territories stretched from Boulogne-Sur-Mer in northern France to the Rhine delta, centred roughly on modern Belgium. He was of humble origin, a helmsman in his youth. He gained grudging respect from the sources: 'distinguished himself in this war, an uprising of the bacaudae'; and 'he gained a great reputation in a command on active service with the army'.[10] While his military skills are acknowledged, he was regarded in hindsight as 'nothing but a barbarian'.[11] It seems clear Carausius played a significant role in the campaigns of Maximian and his later actions caused Roman historians to paint him in a bad light.

We don't know his age but it might be reasonable to suggest he spent much of his childhood living under the Gallic Empire 260–74. To be given a major command in c. 285 one might estimate his age very roughly at 35. This would place his birth in the year c. 250. He was certainly of fighting age by 284 and very likely experienced enough to get a command. We could of course be a decade or more out and tribal identity doesn't prove that's where he spent his early years. However it does show we cannot assume where his loyalties may have been. Whatever the case he must have been a talented commander to rise to prominence as he was appointed to command the fleet based at Gesoriacum, Boulogne, and successfully cleared the area of Frankish pirates. All these events must have occurred in the two years between Diocletian's ascension to the throne and the events we shall soon turn to.

Before we do it is worth remembering two things. Firstly the Gallic Empire had only ended a decade before and had lasted fifteen years. Many officials and commanders had lived through these times. No doubt there were a range of political views and loyalties just as there are in Britain today. Secondly Carinus had adopted the title *Britannicus Maximus* in 284 suggesting the provinces of Britannia had experienced unrest very recently, although we cannot know if this was driven by internal or external enemies. What these events suggest is the political and military situation was not stable. Unsurprising after five decades of civil wars and a long line of murdered emperors.

It is worth noting what the sources say about his appointment:[12] He was a successful military commander fighting in Gaul under Maximian and an experienced sailor.[13] He'd earned his living that way as a young man (implying at this point he was no longer a 'young man'). He was ordered to 'put together a fleet' and fight of the German raiders who were infesting the coasts. The question arises why did he have to 'put together' a fleet. Where was the *classis britannica*? Eutropius names the enemy as Franks and Saxons and places his posting to Gesoriacum, Boulogne, in northern Gaul.[14]

Carausius proved to be as effective on sea as he'd been on land. However he quickly lost the favour of the western Augustus. The sources allege corruption:[15] Rather than prevent raids it was claimed he allowed safe passage and then intercepted them afterwards. This may well have made strategic sense as the raiders were weighed down by captured slaves and goods. Perhaps more tellingly the other allegations was he kept all the stolen booty for himself. Maximian ordered his arrest and death *in* absentia. Dramatically Carausius was tipped off as his executioners rushed to arrest him.

Carausius usurped and took the fleet to Britain. It has been suggested he was proclaimed emperor not at Boulogne but at Rouen on the River Seine in Normandy about 100 miles to the south.[16] It may be this is where he sited a mint. Coins from apparently minted in London commemorate a number of specific legions which supported the break-away provinces:[17] Legio XX Valeria Victrix and Legio II Augusta from Britannia Superior; Legio VI Victrix, Britannia Inferior; Legio I Flavia Minervia pia fidelis and Legio XXX Ulpia Victrix from Germania Inferior; Legio XXII Primigenia pia fidelis and Legio VIII Augusta from Germani Superior; Legio IIII Flavia Felix and Legio VII Claudia pia fidelis from Moesia Superior; and Legio II Parthica from Italy. Taken at face value these ten legions would have given Carausius over 50,000 men as well as a similar number of auxiliaries. However it is likely some of these were vexillations rather than the entire legion. Still it shows the usurpation was had perhaps wider support than many of the contemporary sources wished to admit.

After the events a panegyric (a text or speech in praise of someone) lists the forces under the 'usurper':[18] First the fleet used to protect Gaul was 'stolen by the pirate' and many others built 'in our style'; a 'Roman legion was seized, several units of non-Roman soldiers were secured, Gallic merchants were recruited' and 'considerable forces of barbarians'. We are told all these were 'trained in seamanship' and contrasted with the Roman's 'lack of naval experience'. Here we get a different picture. The Menapian usurper was mainly assisted by barbarians. We can take this perhaps with a pinch of salt as the one Roman Legion seized must surely have been in addition to the three in Britain. As he held out for many years Carausius clearly had support.

Around the time Carausius was escaping Maximian's clutches the western Augustus was campaigning on the Rhine. It is here we first meet another future emperor, Constantius Chorus, 'a vigorous man in his 30's'.[19] At this point in time he was Maximian's praetorian prefect. His victory over the Franks created a client kingdom acting as a buffer state on the frontier. The Romans then turned to deal with Carausius. It would appear an initial attempt to end the new breakaway regime failed. If one accepts Carausius broke away in late 286 it is likely this attempt occurred in the campaigning season of 287. This seems to be what a panegyric dated to 289 alludes to. At the very least it suggests the Romans were in control of part of the coast and were preparing further inroads or even an invasion.

Yet Carausius still had a foothold on the continent: a redoubt around Boulogne-sur-Mer, the western part of Galia Belgica and much of Germania Inferior. The sources all then focus on Britain as being the centre of the rebellion with the consensus being he 'usurped the purple and seized the British provinces'.[20] He took many of the auxiliary units and barbarian mercenaries, along with the fleet, to Britain. There's no evidence to suggest he took any of the continental legions with him so it's likely these, or their vexillations, were left behind to guard the coast in northern Gaul.

Evidence of new building work has been uncovered in London and at some forts on the Saxon Shore, such as Pevensey. Some of this seems to have been constructed in haste.[21] One example is a river wall running alongside the Severan land wall around London. One notable addition was Roman Britain's first ever official mint.[22] Coins with the mark RSR has been interpreted as meaning *Reduent Saturnia Regna* (the kingdom of Saturn returns). A medallion, now in the British Museum, displays the words *Iam nova progenies caelo demittitur alto* (now a new generation comes down from heaven above).

If the panegyric of c. 289 suggested Maximian was winning, a panegyric dated to 291 hints at an abandoned invasion attempt. A year was spent preparing a fleet and then we read a reference to a 'war abandoned in despair'.[23] In addition we read in Eutropius that peace was arranged with Carausius after a failed military operation. Reluctantly, the two emperors, Maximian and Diocletian,

Figure 44. Gold aureus of Carausius, minted at London. (*Wikimedia Commons*)

had to accept the situation for a time. In Britain Carausius tried to ingratiate himself with the *augusti*. He took their names, Aurelius and Valerius, and issued coins with the inscription 'Carausius and his brothers'. These London-minted *aurei*, dated to c. 290s displayed the triple image of Diocletian, Maximian and Carausius. Importantly Carausius was titled *caesar* and not *augustus*.[24] Aurelius Victor stated: 'Carausius was allowed to retain his sovereignty over the island, after he had been judged quite competent to command and defend its inhabitants against warlike tribes'.[25]

An uneasy peace ensued but clearly the goal remained to remove Carausius and take the break away regions back under Roman authority. The usurper was now at the height of his powers. It is worth, at this point, introducing another 'emperor' of Roman Britain. Little is now about Allectus some have suggested he was Carauius's praetorian prefect, a point we will return to. Another suggestion is he was the leader of Frankish or other Germanic mercenaries brought over to Britain with Carausius in 286. We have already mentioned another important figure in our narrative, as well as a future emperor, Constantius Chlorus.

The pace in events quickened. On 1st March 293 Diocletian formed the Tetrarchy. Each Augustus now had a caesar to help him. In the west Maximian was assisted by the new Caesar Constantius, the co-emperor's former praetorian prefect. In the east Diocletian appointed Galerius as his caesar. Constantius was tasked with retaking Britain. His first priority was to retake the northern coastal strip of Gaul. Expanding the fleet he used small naval units strategically positioned to drive enemy ships away from supporting troops in Gaul. Shipping to and from Britain was disrupted severely.

We can create a rough timeline of events: Diocletian came to power in 284. By 285 Carausius is commanding forces under Maximian in Gaul against raiders and *bacaudae*. In 286 he is appointed to a major command on the Gaulish coast. Before the year was out he was accused of corruption and in response declared himself emperor of a breakaway region. This included northern Gaul, parts of Germania Inferior and the provinces of Britannia. An initial campaign in 287 and attempted invasion, likely in 290, failed. A level of stability lasted two or three years. By 293 the Romans were ready to strike.

Constantius cleared the coastal strip of rebels and was able to box the remaining troops in at Boulogne-sur-Mer. Elliott suggests the one remaining legion loyal to Carausius on the continent was legio XXX Ulpia Victrix. The sources say they were blockaded by land and sea. Carausius was prevented from resupplying the port by Constantius making the harbour 'inaccessible to ships by driving piles into the entrance and dumping stones over them'.[26] The same panegyric, *Panegyrici Latini*, tells us the siege eventually ended when the defenders opened the gates trusting on the mercy of Constantius. A subsequent land campaign between the Rivers Scheldt and Rhine, in modern Netherlands, drove barbarians out of the 'treacherous swamps' forcing them to migrate and some to be conscripted.

It seems likely the loss of the foothold on the continent, and the harbour at Boulogne in particular, was the catalyst that brought the reign of Carausius to an end. The sources seem clear this occurred in 293. The 'pirate king' had lost his continental possessions and forces. He had lost access to further Germanic mercenaries. Perhaps more importantly he had lost control of the seas. However he still retained considerable forces in Britain. Three full legions, several thousand auxiliaries and whatever Germanic troops he had taken with him to Britain. We will never know if Carausius might have been able to turn events around because his henchman, Allectus, killed him. It is to him we will now turn.

Allectus

Very little is known about Allectus. His name may mean something like 'chosen' or 'promoted' similar to when someone was addicted to the senate. Aurelius Victor states Carausius made him his 'chief minister of finance.'[27] This would make him akin to the fourth century *Comes Sacrarum Largitionium*, who levied taxes to pay for imperial donatives. Birley suggests he was the praetorian prefect or some other senior military figure.[28] Victor makes no mention of this whilst naming Constantius as the prefect of Maximian. Terms such as ally, henchman or co-conspirator offer no help. A 'senior military figure' could mean a commander of an auxiliary or mercenary force. The later sources paint his supporters as mainly barbarian but this could simply be propaganda to erase any 'Roman' support he had.

If we accept Victor that he held a senior administrative post this would not exclude a former military or even current command alongside those duties. Nor can we assume ethnicity. The impression one gets is of a hasty decision to murder Carausius once defeat seemed certain. However this clearly didn't prevent the later invasion. There's no suggestion Allectus attempted to sue for peace or step down. The evidence rather points to the transfer of power going smoothly suggesting Allectus had significant support in Britain, enough to last a further three years.

Additionally further evidence points to a confident regime:[29] Coin production continued, and unlike with Carausius, none display Diocletian and Maximian. Building work dated to his reign show two monumental buildings with massive foundations in London. Evidence of building work at several of the Saxon Shore Forts, coastal defences and at York may also have been from this period. In the north there appears to have been a reduction of garrison strength on Hadrian's

Figure 45. Roman copper coin of Allectus c. 293–6. Reverse with Galley. (*Wikimedia Commons*)

Wall in the last quarter of the third century, along with deterioration in buildings leaving some forts, such as Birdoswald and Housesteads, were in need of repair. Epigraphical evidence, along with the late-fourth or early-fifth century *Notitia Dignitatum*, point to considerable continuity regarding military postings.

There is no evidence the British legions were utilised in the subsequent battles and we left to conclude Allectus relied heavily on the very troops Carausius had brought across in 286. Many of the Saxon Shore forts are thought to pre-date Carausius but there is clear evidence from coin deposits that they were extensively garrisoned during his rule. Whilst some date it to Probus, Pevensey at least seems to have been built under Allectus.[30]

In a review of the sources and contemporary accounts Casey summarises the invasion on 296 as follows:[31] Constantius split his fleet in two: one from Boulogne and one from the mouth of the River Seine. Constantius set sail first from Bolougne but encountered rough weather. His praetorian prefect, Julius Asclepiodotus, lead the southern fleet which sailed just after that of Constantius. Asclepiodotus headed for the Isle of Wight where a British fleet lay in wait. However thick fog enabled the Romans to slip past and they landed near Southampton Water. As a sign of intent Asclepiodotus burnt his boats and marched inland.

The panegyric to Constantius gives us more details: Allectus, 'the standard bearer of the criminal rebellion', left the fleet and harbour and rushed to confront Asclepiodotus. It would be logical to assume Allectus had strategically placed himself somewhere along the southern coast. Julius Caesar and Claudius had both landed in east Kent and it's likely he suspected that was the most likely landing place. Clearly he was aware of a threat elsewhere as he had a fleet positioned off the Isle of Wight.

The Gallic Empire and the Pirate King of Britain   135

Was Allectus with the fleet off the Isle of Wight? Or was he with a second fleet positioned near one of the Saxon Shore Forts? Pevensey has been suggested as a likely candidate. Silchester is about two days march from Southampton Water, London a further day. Pevensey though is three days away. Given it would have taken sometime for Allectus to receive news of the landing it's likely he would have been closer to the landing point. A scenario where Asclepiodotus lands near Southampton and Allectus marches from east Kent is therefore unlikely. Either Asclepiodotus landed further east than suspected or Allectus was positioned further west.

The panegyric referenced previously gives us more information: Allectus 'did not even form a battle-line or draw up all the forces he was leading, but, forgetting all his great preparations, charged headlong with the old ringleaders of that conspiracy and the units of barbarian mercenaries'.[32] Taken at face value it's possible Allectus left the troops stationed on the Saxon Shore Forts anticipating a second landing by Constantius. He then rushed to head off Asclepiodotus before he reached London. Somewhere between the south coast landing site and the provincial capital the usurper intercepted the Roman invasion force. They were

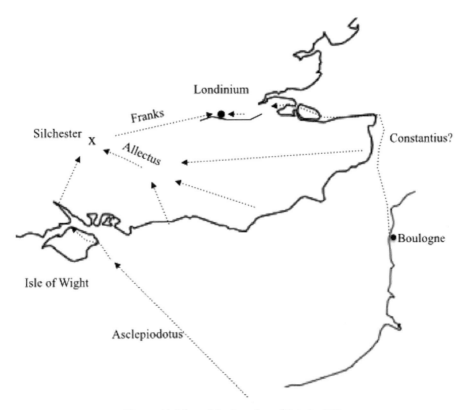

Figure 46. Map of the invasion of Britain, 296.

likely marching along the Roman road between Clausentum (now a suburb of Southampton), and Calleva (Silchester). From there the Portway Road heads east to London.

The source claims 'hardly a single Roman died' but goes onto to describe the bodies that covered the battlefield as 'barbarian, or imitating barbarian in the clothes they wore and their long, reddened hair'. Even Allectus is described as having 'cast off the costume that he had dishonoured when alive, with hardly a single garment by which he could be identified'. No mere 'financial officer' then, but a man leading his troops into battle. The Franks were especially singled out as a significant part of his force.

Surviving remnants of the defeated army fled to London where 'that horde of barbarian mercenaries' attempted to loot the city. Contingents of the Roman army lost in the sea-fog finally arrived just in time. This could be Constantius himself, with his second fleet from Bolougne. The Franks were destroyed, the province saved and grateful Britons jumped for joy and thanked the gods, and Constantius, for their deliverance. So say the panegyrics to Constantius.

Figure 47. Gold coin of Constantius I. Reverse with Galley outside London. (*Wikimedia Commons*)

More reliable sources suggest the victory belonged to Asclepiodotus alone and Constantius may have only arrived in London much later to claim the glory and be hailed as 'liberator' and the 'true light of the empire'. By 301 all four tetrarchs had taken the title *Britannicus Maximus* and coins appear commemorating Constantius as 'restorer of the eternal light'. The western Caesar is seen mounted with a kneeling supplicant arms raised in welcome. Behind are the gates of a city with the letters LON below.

Diocletian reforms

We shall leave Constantius to focus on the reforms introduced by Diocletian. Some of these changes were subsequently built upon by Constantine the Great and its difficult to date them precisely. We have already noted the start of the Tetrarchy in 293. The intention was to ensure a smooth transition of power and avoid the disruptive civil wars and procession of usurping and murdered emperors of the mid-third century. In the east Diocletian was assisted by his

Caesar, Galerius. In the west Maximian had Constantius. All four men were from Illyria and bonded by marriage ties. Each Caesar married a daughter or step-daughter of their respective Augustus. Constantius had to divorce his wife Helena to do so. Their son, Constantine, was to go on to be one of the most influential emperors in Rome's history.

In the first century there had been around thirty six provinces but under Diocletian these more than double to over one hundred.[33] These new provinces were grouped together into twelve *dioceses*. In the case of Britain's case the diocese was effectively the same as the former province of Britannia in the first and second centuries. Caracalla had separated it into two provinces, Britannia Superior and Britannia Inferior, in c. 213. Now it was split into four provinces: Maxima Caesariensis (capital at London), Britannia Secunda (York), Flavia Caesariensis, (Lincoln), and Britannia Prima (Cirencester or Gloucester). The former had a consular governor whilst the other three were administered by a *praesides*. All four reported to the *vicarus* in London.

The first division of Britannia into Superior and inferior was dated to c. 213 and we know there were still at least two provinces in 297 as a panegyrist thanked Constantius for supplying craftsmen to Autun from *Britanniae*.[34] The re-organisation was complete by the time of the compilation of the *Laterculus Veronensis*, the Verona List, between 303 to 314. In 314 three Bishops from York, London and Lincoln travelled to the Council of Arles, and it is thought these represented the capitals of three of the provinces. The remaining province, Prima, is thought to have had its capital at Cirencester, due to an inscription (RIB 103) found there referring to a governor. The face reads: 'To Jupiter, Best and Greatest, His Perfection Lucius Septimius …, governor of Britannia Prima, restored (this monument), being a citizen of the Remi tribe'. The rear and side reads: 'This statue and column erected under the ancient religion Septimius restores, ruler of Britannia Prima'. However, this does not make it certain. As York and Lincoln were both coloniae it has been suggested that a third colonia, Gloucester, may have been capital of Britannia Prima.

We can therefore date this drastic re-organisation fairly tightly to 296–313, but suggest it occurred closer to 296 than than 213. Unfortunately, no document or source survives showing the provincial boundaries, let alone those of the *civitates*.[35] In addition, our understanding of political structures also remains poor.[36] A common version for the location of the provinces is as follows:[37]

- Britannia Prima covering the west country and modern-day Wales with the provincial capital at Cirencester
- Flavia Caesariensis covering the Midlands and Lincolnshire, the capital at Leicester and possibly later Lincoln.

- Britannia Secunda covering north of Hadrian's Wall up to Hadrian's Wall and at times beyond, the capital at York.
- Maxima Caesariensis covering the South East with London being both the capital of the Province and the Diocese.

Other options are possible and one example places Flavia Caesariensis and Britannia Secunda the other way round.[38] As Maxima Caesariensis was the only province at this point with a consular governor it is very likely that this was centred on the diocesan capital, and largest city, London. Birley

Figure 48. Map of the second division of Britannia.

suggests the re-organisation, starting under Diocletian, was completed under Constantine. This may have coincided with major changes in military structure. The introduction of a potential fifth province, Valentia, in the mid-fourth century will be discussed later.

The first known *vicarius* of Britain is dated to 319, Lucius Papius Pacatianus. The evidence comes from a rescript of Constantine dated precisely to 20th November of that year. Other sources present an interesting career.[39] First as governor (*vir perfectissimus praeses*) of Sardinia in 308 or 309. This was under the usurper L. Domitius Alexander but as it was against Maxentius rather than Constantine did not affect his career. He was a praetorian prefect between 329 and 337, by then the senior of five prefects and also *consul ordinarius* in 332. He was attached to Constantine's son, Constans I, in the last years of his career and disappears from the record after 341.

A governor of Britannia Secunda can be dated accurately to between 296 and 305 as it clearly names the Augustus and Caesars:[40] 'For our Lords Diocletianus and Maximianus, unconquered Augusti, and Constantius and Maximianus, most noble Caesars, under the most perfect man Aurelius Arpagius, governor…'. Found at Birdoswald on Hadrian's Wall we read the commanding officer's residence 'had been covered with earth and had collapsed'. This was rebuilt along with the headquarters building and the bath-house. All under the watchful eye of centurion Flavius Martinus. The name of his cohort or legion is unfortunately illegible.

The Vicarius of Britannia reported to the praetorian prefect. Civilian and military commands were separated. The army, which we will turn to next, was now headed by *comes* and *duces*. The latter were generally placed on border areas and often commanded regions that crossed provincial borders.

Diocletian had begun redeploying vexillations of 1,000 to 1,200 men from legions from the beginning of his reign. Hughes argues by the start of the fourth century this became the norm. This new system of 'defence in depth' consisted of 'defensive belts' of smaller-sized legions. Thus the number of legions was increased, almost doubled, but their size reduced drastically from the old-fashioned large legions of over 5,000 men to perhaps only 1,000. Later Constantine was to create central mobile forces, *comitatenses*, formed away from border areas. These became the main field army units while the *limitanei* literally meant soldiers in the frontier districts. There was no particular difference in equipment or training.[41] However a *comitatus* had in effect already been around since the 'The Crisis of the Third Central' when successive emperors needed to retain a permanent, large, loyal force on campaign. The loyalty sometimes proved to be elusive but by the time of Diocletian the *comitatus* 'had acquired a permanent status'.[42]

We leave the third century with Britannia back in the bosom of the Roman Empire. Its citizen's may have started to believe the decades of war and upheaval had come to an end. The two Augusti and their Caesars had imposed stability. This was perhaps re-enforced when Diocletian and Maximianus stepped down in 305. Constantius and Galerius were both promoted to Augustus and each appointed a Caesar as their subordinate, Flavius Valerius Severus in the west and Maximinus II in the east. Constantine, the son of Constantius, was now 33 years old and remained at the court of the eastern Augustus Galerius, possibly as an unofficial hostage.

The scene was now set for the appearance of Constantius in Britain and another major invasion of the north. It was also to prove the catalyst in elevating his son Constantine to the throne. The path would not be smooth, and as ever in Roman history, would be paved with civil war and covered in blood.

Chapter Eight

The House of Constantine

Constantius I

Flavius Valerius Constantius was born c. 250 on the Danubian frontier of humble origins. His nickname, Chorus, meaning 'pale', was added by later Byzantine sources. The fourth century historian Eutropius says this about him: 'He was an excellent man, of extreme benevolence, who studied to increase the resources of the provinces and of private persons, cared but little for the improvement of the public treasury... by the Gauls... not only beloved but venerated'.[1] He was described as a 'powerful, stout, rough and red-faced man'.[2]

He came from very humble origins despite pronouncements by later flatterers. He was the son of a goat-herder and freedman's daughter. He rose through the ranks to become an officer and must have been talented to reach the heights of praetorian prefect. In many ways his rise was as spectacular as that of Pertinax, son of a freedman, over a century before. We can see how the figures in the first Tetrarchy were connected in figure 50.

Figure 49. Bust of Constantius Chorus. (*Wikimedia Commons*)

His first marriage was to Helena, an innkeeper's daughter from Naissus, modern Serbia.[3] Their son Constantine was born in c. 272. He had been Maximian's praetorian prefect before being elevated to Caesar in 293. He may have already set Helena aside to marry Maximian's step-daughter, Theodora, by 289. Constantine was already a young man in his twenties when his father's forces, lead by his prefect Asclepiodotus, defeated Allectus in 296. Orosius describes Consatntius as having a 'mild disposition'. After Diocletian and Maximian stood down (1st May 305) he took control over Italy, Africa and the Gallic province, which included Britain.[4] In the east Galerius was also promoted to Augustus.

There had been an agreement that Maximian's son Maxentius would become Caesar in the west whilst Constantine would hold that post in the east. However

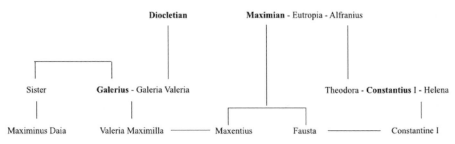

Figure 50. Family tree of the Tetrarchy.

Galerius manoeuvred his preferred choices in to position. His friend Flavius Valerius Severus became Caesar in the west whilst his nephew, Maximinus Daia, became Caesar in the east. Constantine remained at the court of Galerius, possibly as a means of providing leverage for Galerius over his fellow Augustus.

Little is known of the campaign to Britain in 305–6. Like Septimius Severus a hundred years before he made York is base of operations. The sources suggest he reached the furthest edge of the known world. Archaeological evidence, such as pottery from Carpow and Cramond, dates to this period. He received the title *Britannicus Maximus* by January 306.[5] On 25th July 306 Constantius died at York just as Severus had nearly a century before. In theory the succession was clear. The Caesar in the west, Flavius Valerius Severus, would be elevated to Augustus. The army in Britain however had other ideas. For Constantine was not with Galerius when his father died. Instead he was in Britain.

Constantine I

Flavius Valerius Constantius, later known as Constantine I or Constantine the Great, was born at Naissus in Dacia Ripensis, Upper Moesia. There is some debate about the exact year, estimates range between 272–82. The earliest date is considered more likely.[6] He remained with Diocletian in the east eventually serving as a tribune in the emperor's bodyguard. He fought against the Persians in 297–8, which if the early date of birth is accepted, would make him 25 years old. When Diocletian stood down in 305 his successor Galerius kept Constantine at court. This was perhaps as leverage over his perceived rival, Constantine's father, Constantius, Augustus in the west.

The sources suggest Constantine was expected to be appointed Caesar. he was popular with the army and described by one source as 'a young man of very great worth, and well meriting the high station of Caesar. The distinguished comeliness of his figure, his strict attention to all military duties, his virtuous demeanour and singular affability'.[7] However the machinations of Galerius conspired to place two of his supporters in position instead: his nephew Maximinus Daia as eastern Caesar and his friend, Flavius Valerius Severus, in the west. Constantius was now politically isolated in the west with his son effectively 'hostage' in the east, serving under Galerius.

The Christian author Lactantius, was tutor to Constantine's son Crispus. He describes Constantine's dramatic escape in *De mortibus persecutorum*, 'On the Deaths of the Persecutors'.[8] Constantius pleaded ill-health and wrote to Galerius requesting his son be sent to him. The eastern emperor was reluctant to let such a valuable, and potentially dangerous, man go. He was equally fearful of appearing openly hostile or causing a rift. He made repeated excuses putting off the decision.

Lactantius claims Galerius had attempted various traps and 'snares for the life of that young man' in order to remove the potential threat. Eventually he ran out of excuses and was forced to allow his departure. He gave him a warrant to depart with the imperial despatches the following morning. Secretly the emperor planned for his arrest, either the next morning, or on the road to Britain by Severus, the Caesar in the west.

Constantine saw through the plan and waited until Galerius retired to bed. He then left that very evening and 'carried off from the principal stages all the horses maintained at the public expense, and escaped'. The *cursus publicus* was the state supported courier service which provided horses at stage-posts at regular intervals. Constantine rushed ahead, changing horses whilst at the same time leaving none behind to facilitate his pursuers. The next morning Galerius awoke and ordered Constantine to his presence. When he heard he had already left he was furious and sent guards after him. Hearing that 'all the horses had been carried off from the great road, he could hardly refrain from tears'.

The Stanford Geospatial Network Model of the Roman World, Orbis, allows us to calculate travel times in the Roman world.[9] If Constantine traveled the 1,820 miles from Constantinople to Gesoriacum entirely by road at approximately 36 miles a day he would have taken about 53 days. An extra 10 days would have allowed him to land on the south coast of Britannia and reach York. The quickest route would involve journey by boat and take only 46 days. However using the horse relay system Orbis allows 155 miles a day. By this calculation he could have reached Eboracum within a fortnight.

It's not certain if he joined his father at Gesoriacum or Eboracum. Lactantius claimed Constantius died soon after his son arrived but this is very likely propaganda. Fourth-century chroniclers are not entirely consistent but the common theme is Constantine did make a rapid escape, killing 'post-horse' as he went. The most likely route taking him through Italy and across the Alps then by road to Gesoriacum where he met his father. From there they travelled together by boat the short distance to Britain.

We can create a reasonable timeline knowing that Diocletian abdicated on 1st May 305 and Constantius received the title of *Britannicus Maximus* by January 306. Constantius may have requested the presence of his son straight away. If we allow a couple of months for Galerius to receive and refuse requests to leave we can tentatively suggest Constantine left the court in July or August, reaching northern Gaul by late summer, 305. Just in time to travel and campaign in the far north before winter prevented large scale movement. The enemy are named as the Picts.

Constantius may have already been in ill-health but he lived long enough to complete this campaign and enlarge the fortifications at York.[10] On 25 July 306 the western Augustus died and York claimed another emperor. By rights the western Caesar, Severus, should have automatically taken his place. However the army in Britain had other ideas. The legion, most likely the Sixth still based at York, hailed him emperor egged on by Crocus, 'king of the Alamanni, who had accompanied Constantius for the sake of military assistance'.[11] Taking the earlier date for his birth, Constantine was now 34 years of age.

One contemporary writer describes him as follows: '… handsome physique and bodily height no other could bear comparison with him; in physical strength he so exceeded his contemporaries as even to put them in fear; he took pride in moral qualities rather than physical superiority, ennobling his soul first and foremost with self-control… fine, sturdy and tall, full of good sense'.[12]

Constantine formally sought recognition from Galerius. Lactantius writes that a 'portrait of Constantine, adorned with laurels' was sent to the east. Galerius's first instinct was to 'commit both the portrait and its bearer to the flames' as he had wanted to appoint Licinius as Caesar. Cooler heads prevailed acknowledging Constantine had wide support in the army. However instead of Augustus, Galerius appointed him Caesar and promoted Severus in the west. Constantine diplomatically accepted and bided his time. The Tetrarchy in the summer of 306 became as follows:

Table 6. The Tetrarchy c. 306–8.

	Augustus	Caesar
East	Galerius	Maximinus Daia
West	Severus	Constantine

The political situation was further complicated when, in October of the same year, the praetorian guard in Rome proclaimed Maxentius, the son of the former Augustus Maximian I, emperor. A complex series of shifting alliances and battles ensued. Severus marched on Maxentius. The usurper offered his father the role of co-emperor, making him Augustus for a second time. The presence of their old commander caused many of Severus's troops to desert. Severus fled but was later captured at Ravenna in the spring of 307 and killed, or forced to commit suicide, later that year.

In 308 Maximian broke with his son in Rome and sided with Constantine. This instability forced Diocletian to temporarily come out of retirement. The resulting meeting at Carnuntum on the Danube forced Maximian to abdicate again. Galerius got his way and elevated his ally Licinius to western Augustus over the head of Constantine. Diocletain went back into retirement and lived long enough to see the system he had put in place fall apart. In 310 his old friend and fellow Augustus Maximian rebelled against Constantine in the west and was forced to commit suicide. A year later his former Caesar, Galerius died, likely of cancer. Maximinus Daia stepped up to eastern Augustus but the position of Caesar remained vacant when Diocletian died in late 311.

The provinces of Britannia were largely untouched by these events although its likely Constantine withdrew troops to the continent to assist his campaigns. Constantine defeated Maxentius at the battle of the Milvian Bridge in 312 whilst Licinius destroyed Maxinimus Daia in 313. One notable result of Constantine's victory was the final disbanding of the praetorian guard. Both men were now undisputed Augusti of west and east respectively. Whilst the Tetrarchy was now effectively dead each man appointed their own Caesar. Another civil war erupted almost immediately followed by an uneasy truce for several years. This broke down c. 321 and by 324 Licinius was defeated leaving Constantine the undisputed sole Augustus.

The impression one gets from these momentous events is that Constantine left Britain in 306 never to return. However evidence suggests he may have come back on more than one occasion in his early years as western Caesar:[13]

- A coin dated to 307 states: FL VAL CONSTANTINVS NOB rev. ADVENTVS AVGG.
- Further coins issues 310–312 and 313–314
- References in Eusebius's *Vita Constantini*.
- He received the title Britannicus Maximus in 315.

Birley suggests that it is during one of these visits that he possibly created a fifth province, Valentia.[14] This is a point we will come back to later as some suggest it was created as the result of the Roman response to the 'barbarian conspiracy' of 367. The contemporary writer Eusebius in *Vita Constantini*, the Life of Constantine, tells us: 'With mild and sober injunctions to godliness he equipped his troops, then campaigned against the land of the Britons and those who dwell at the very Ocean where the sun sets'.[15]

It is a little ambiguous when exactly this occurred and could be mistaken for the campaign with his father. Later the source is more clear. After the death of Constantius he dealt with rebellious tribes on the Rhine. The next line is placed after these events and points to campaigns on the continent. The following then implies a second campaign in Britain: 'When these matters were settled to his satisfaction, he turned his attention to the other parts of the inhabited world, and first crossed to the Britains, which lie enclosed by the edge of Ocean; he brought them to terms, and then surveyed the other parts of the world, so that he might bring healing where help was needed.[16]

When the emperor finally left Britain it was considered a rich and prosperous province. His reign was to see many significant changes. Not least was the Edict of Milan in 313 which allowed for the recovery of loses some Christian communities had suffered under Diocletian. Not only did it recognise certain rights and 'freedom of worship' but it also allowed certain privileges and positive advantages.[17] The Council of Nicaea in 325 resulted in a codified doctrine known as the Nicene Creed. It would be wrong to thing this settled religious matters. Forms of Christianity considered heretical continued: Notably Donatism and Arianism, and later Pelagianism. However it wasn't until the reign of Theodosius I, another of our emperors who visited Britain, that Christianity became the official state religion. Other important reforms are worth noting.

Appearance and character

Constantine had long, shoulder-length hair, some of it false.[18] He wore elaborate jewellery, bracelets and robes with flowery designs. His a high-crested helmet, rich with gems, was replaced by a diadem, adorned with a double strand of pearls. He was a 'superb general… mastery, coldly intelligent organiser and leader an administrator, a man of action with an immense capacity for forming schemes and carrying them out'.[19]

He could be tolerant, patient and had an ironic humour. However he was also 'ruthlessly ambitious' and 'dedicated to his own personal success, and despotically determined at all costs to achieve it'.[20]

Eutropius writing a generation after Constantine died records just how murderous he could be: 'the pride of prosperity caused Constantine to depart his former agreeable mildness of temper. Falling first upon his own relatives, he put to death his son, an excellent man; his sister's son, a youth of amiable disposition; soon afterwards his wife, and subsequently many of his friends'.[21] His enduring image is perhaps that represented by the statue at York Minster.

Reforms

Whilst the praetorian guard was disbanded praetorian prefects were retained. By the end of his reign the number of prefects had been increased to five but their functions were now administrative, fiscal and juridical.[22] Two new military commands were created: *magister militum* and *magister equitum*, master of the infantry and cavalry respectively. It is thought that it was at this point he introduced the title of *Comes*, or Count. The post of *dux* had also evolved. From the first century this had been simply a descriptive terms meaning commander. By the third century it was being used to describe a permanent command in a geographical area, often along a border, but subordinate to the provincial governor. By the time of Constantine it had become a the supreme military commander of a region separate from the civilian governor. The *comitatenses* were posted back from the frontier areas and troops began to be billeted in towns. The frontier *alae* and *cohortes* units became *limitanei*, from the Latin *limes*, or frontier. He continued Diocletian's policy of in creating more numerous but smaller provinces. In Rome the *magister officiorum*, Master of Offices, controlled his personal bodyguard, *scholae*. The senate was increased from 600 to 2,000.

Figure 51. Statue of Constantine the Great in York. (*Wikimedia Commons*)

Constans

Flavius Julius Constans was the youngest son of Constantine, born c. 323. He was just 10 years of age when he was given the title Casear by his father. At 14 he became joint Augustus with his older brothers, Constantine II and Constantius II, on the death of their father. The relative stability of their father's reign did not last long. First a number of rivals were eliminated, among them family members. Constantine II, the eldest, held the western provinces including Britain. The young Constans held Italy, Africa and Illyricum. Constantius ruled in the east. Being still young Constans was very much the junior partner. When he reached adulthood he was in a position to exert his own authority.

Aggrieved at not receiving what he felt was a fair share, Constantine II invaded Italy in 340. Marching across the Alps he was ambushed and killed by Constans' troops outside Aquileia.

Constans took over his brother's part of the empire and travelled to Britain in 343.[23] This came soon after he had defeated a Frankish incursion and the fact that he travelled in January or February, when the crossing is dangerous, suggests there was a pressing reason. The sources aren't particularly clear. One writer makes it clear there was no revolt or rebellion taking place: 'as it was, affairs in Britain were stable, and there was no necessity to leave the land to enjoy the wonders of Ocean'.[24] Another states: 'In winter,

Figure 52. Bust of Constans I. (*Wikimedia Commons*)

which has never been done at any time, nor will be done, you pounded the swelling and raging waves of Ocean with your oars… the Briton was terrified at the unexpected face of the Emperor'.[25] Ammianus Marcellinus makes a passing reference that the emperor Julian (reigned 361–3), 'was afraid to go in person to help the Britains when they were ravaged by the Scots and Picts, as Constans had done'. It is likely there was a campaign in northern Britain beyond the frontier. Constans would have been 20 years old at this point and we can see his image in the bust in figure 52.

He was to be the last legitimate reigning emperor to visit Britain. As with his father the focus of his visit seems to have been in the north. The Picts were first mentioned under the reign of his grandfather, Constantius. The early fourth century *Laterculus Veronensis* referred to *gentes barbarae, quae pullulaverunt sub imperatoribus*, 'barbarian peoples which have sprouted under the emperors'. It begins with *Scoti, Picti* and *Calidoni*. We have already noted the rise of Saxon pirates from the time of Carausius. Irish, Pictish and Saxon raiders became a common threat from the mid-fourth century and beyond. However a young Romano-Briton waving Constans off in 343 may have felt confident he held citizenship in a stable, prosperous province within the empire. Little would he know his grandson might witness the end of Roman Britain and the last emperor leave with much of the garrison.

Chapter Nine

Usurpers and Tyrants

Constans's joint reign with his brother Constantius II lasted another seven years. By the year 350 he had lost the support of the army: 'The rule of Constans was for some time energetic and just, but afterwards, falling into ill-health, and being swayed by ill-designing friends, he indulged in great vices; and, becoming intolerable to the people of the provinces, and unpopular with the soldiery'.[1]

Figure 53. Gold Solidus of Magnentius from Trier. (*Wikimedia Commons*)

The troops on the Rhine frontier declared for Magnentius at Autun, a successful general who had fought in Gaul under Constans. The emperor fled, attempting to reach Hispania, but he was caught at a fortress on the Pyrenees and killed.

Britain once more sided with a western usurper just as it had done under Postumus and Carausius the century before. Constantius II, the last remaining son of Constantine and Augustus in the east, refused to acknowledge Magnentius. Civil war loomed, delayed first by conflict with Persia and then by overtures of peace. Talks failed and Constantius moved west. Magnentius was defeated at Mursa Major in 351 leaving over 50,000 dead on the battle-field. Magnentius retreated west and tried to bargain for peace. Constantius was in no mood to appease his brother's killer and crossed the Alps. At Mons Seleucus in south-eastern France in 353 Magnentius lost his final battle and fled to Lugdunum. Fifty six years earlier Clodius Albinus had been driven back into the city by Septimius Severus. The same fate awaited the new usurper. Magnentius fell on his sword leaving Constantius the sole emperor. His image survives on coins such as the gold solidus in figure 53.

Carausius II, a second Pirate King?

A number of coins have been found dating to c. 354–8 which intriguingly point to a second Carausius, this time confined to Britain. Some bear the words DOMNO CARAVSIVS CES, the latter word perhaps an attempt at CAESAR. Other coins have CENSERIS or GENSERIS. Some scholars suspect these may be forgeries.[2] We can say nothing more about this and so must leave it as a mystery.

Roman Britain in the mid-fourth century

Constantius cracked down on supporters of Magnentius. An imperial notary, Paulus Catena, notorious for his cruelty, was sent to Britain. Many were arrested, some on trumped up charges. The vicarious of the Diocese, Flavius Martinus, attempted to put a stop to the injustices and paid for it with accusations of treason and a threat of arrest. Taking matters into his own hands he tried to attack Catena and having failed was forced to commit suicide. Constantius II died in 361 and was succeeded by Julian, known to history as 'Julian the Apostate' for his pagan beliefs.

Fourth-century Britain was considered to be a prosperous diocese, described by some as 'very wealthy'.[3] It was productive enough for Julian to send 600 grain ships from Britain to supply troops on the Rhine. Archaeological evidence demonstrates that many luxurious and large villas were still being built.[4] It has been described as the 'heyday or Romano-British villas' within a 'wealth producing agricultural economy'.[5] The rural population that worked on these farms still accounted for the bulk of the population, around 90 per cent.[6]

At the same time there was a 'substantial urban population',[7] and evidence of maintenance and new construction exists within towns up to the mid-fourth century.[8] The population, especially in urban areas and the more romanised south-east, had a sense of Roman identity.[9] It is interesting to note at this point that it is these very areas that experienced an increase in Germanic material culture and settlement a century later. Equally it was the less urbanised and romanised areas of the west and north that developed (or maintained) a distinctive Romano-Brittonic cultural identity.

The second half of the fourth century showed a marked deterioration in urbanisation with towns becoming poorer and politically weaker.[10] Political power shifted away from urban centres to country estates. In addition to these changes raiding from outside the empire remained a significant problem. In c. 360 a major raid by 'the savage tribes of the Scots (Irish) and the Picts…had broken the peace that had been agreed upon, were laying waste the regions near the frontiers'.[11] This 'peace that had been agreed upon' may well have been a treaty negotiated, or imposed, when Constans came in 343. Unlike Constans, Julian was reluctant to leave Gaul with the threat of barbarian raids across the Rhine, notably from the Alemanni. He sent his 'master of arms', Lupicinus instead.

Julian died in 363 and was briefly succeeded by Jovian before, in 364, Valentinian I and his brother Valens became joint Augusti in the west and east respectively. Raiding continued and we read: 'the Alamanni were devastating Gaul and Raetia, the Sarmatae and Quadi Pannonia, while the Picts, Saxons, Scots and Attacotti were harassing the Britons with constant disasters'.[12] However the most serious raid was to follow and with it came a devastating Roman response. The campaign force was lead by an experienced, battle-hardened commander, Flavius Theodosius, known as Count Theodosius or Theodosius the Elder. With him was his 20 year old son, serving on his command staff. This young man would become one of the most famous of all late-Roman emperors, Theodosius the Great.

The Barbarian Conspiracy of 367

Most of our knowledge about the major incursion of 367 comes from Ammianus Marcellinus (c. 330–400).[13] Serious news reached Valentinian in northern Gaul. A *barbarica conspiratione* (barbarian conspiracy) had plunged Britain into 'a state of extreme need'. Nectraridus, *comes maritime tractus* (commander of the seacoast region) had been killed and Fullofaudes, a 'general', had been ambushed and taken prisoner. We can see the organisation of the late Roman Empire in the west in figure 54.

It is speculated that Fullofraudes was the *Dux Britanniarum* in northern Britain. However it is not certain when this rank came into existence. It may

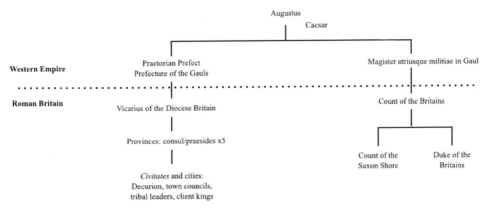

Figure 54. The Organisation of the late Roman Empire in the West.

have been introduced by Stilicho towards the end off the fourth century. Another possibility is the *comes Britanniarum* which made the holder the senior military commander in Britain. Regarding Nectraridus, the *comes maritime tractus* it is suggested that this post is synonymous with the later *comes litoris Saxonici*. This might be unlikely if the raids were in the north and thus it could be an as yet unknown command.[14] The word *tractus* suggests a region rather than *litoris* which implies a coastline. Irish raiders could easily target the south-west and modern Wales as well as Lancashire and Cumbria. The Picts could of course by-pass Hadrian's Wall by hugging either coastline.

Who then was this savage and ferocious enemy, capable of overrunning the empire's frontier troops? Ammianus isn't completely clear although in the subsequent passage he lists the following: the Picts (divided into two tribes: the Dicalydones and Verturiones); the Attacotti, 'a warlike race of men'; and the Scots (Irish). All of who were 'ranging widely and causing great devastation'. The phrase widely seems to mean in the north and west as he goes onto to describe the Franks and Saxons raiding the Gallic regions by land and sea 'with cruel robbery, fire, and the murder of all who were taken prisoners'.

It does sound like a complete break-down of authority. How organised it was is open to debate.

Whatever the case the emperor's initial response clearly didn't work. Severus, commander of the household troops, was sent but quickly recalled. A second commander, Jovinus, sent back a report full of alarm and requested reinforcements. Enter Theodosius, 'a man most favourably known for his services in war', who hastened to the coast with a powerful force.

He travelled from Bononia (previously called Gesoriacum, Bolougne) to Rutupiae, Richborough in Kent. He awaited with his legions for various Germanic units to join him: Batavi, Heruli, Jovii, and Victores and then marched to London, seemingly without incident. Interestingly we learn that Londinium had in 'later times' been called Augusta. A name change for which we have no further evidence. From the Diocese capital Theodosius planned his response and the young Theodosius was no doubt present in his command staff.

Dividing his troops into 'many parts' he scoured the countryside hunting down 'the predatory bands of the enemy'. We get the impression Theodosius spent some time in London as he mustered a force and then 'sallied forth', securing 'places suitable for ambushing the savages'. He routed and 'put to flight' the 'tribes' restoring the 'cities and strongholds'.

Ammianus makes it sound like the province was awash with small, wandering bands of lawless plunderers and raiders. There's no indication of a significant number or enemies or pitched battle. The Romans quickly routed them and recovered booty and captured slaves. One phrase stands out: The goods and captives were taken from 'the wretched tribute-paying people'. Is this merely clumsy language? Or could it refer to some formal arrangement? If so it would not be the last time the Romans paid off barbarians to avert attack.

Another interesting point arises after Theodosius intercepted the raiding parties and recovered the booty ('a small part which was allotted to the wearied soldiers'). He entered the city, 'which had previously been plunged into the greatest difficulties, but had been restored more quickly than rescue could have been expected'. But which city does this refer to? It isn't at all clear it means London. If not then perhaps a northern city such as York or Carlisle. We get more clues about the nature of the military collapse in 367: The Romans elicit confessions from their captives and, perhaps significantly, deserters. The next sentence too suggests a wide-scale mutiny or desertion: Theodosius issued proclamations and promises of pardon to persuade the deserters to return.

This seemed to have done the trick. His adversaries were described as a 'widely scattered enemy, a mob of various natives and frightfully savage' who could only be defeated by cunning and ambush. Theodosius, having subdued the island, then requested a certain Civilis be sent as a deputy-prefect and Dulcitius as as general, possibly to replace Fullofraudes, whose fate is unknown.

We also read of internal enemies. A certain Valentinus had been exiled to Britain because of a serious crime. We are not told what this was but he apparently held a grudge against Theodosius personally. He 'began to tempt exiles and soldiers by promising for bold deeds as enticing rewards' in an unspecified plot. This was uncovered and the ringleaders executed. At the same time the *arcani*, 'a class of men established in early times' had become corrupted. Their job seems to have been to travel through border areas and supply information to warn of possible revolt or attack. They were found to have betrayed their posts for the promise of a share of the booty from raiders.

It has been suggested the alleged incursion was exaggerated or masked an internal insurrection although this idea has not gained wide support.[15] One theory places the blame on the *arcani*, the Roman scouts mentioned above by Ammianus, who sided with the barbarians.[16] However Theodosius the Elder restored order and he, and his son, left Britain shortly after. Significantly we read of the restoration, or creation, of a new province: 'so completely did he recover a province which had passed into the enemy's hands and restore it to its former condition, that, in the words of his report, it had a legitimate governor; and it was henceforth called Valentia'.

Valentia, the fifth province

Locating this new province has proved difficult. Somehistorians have dismissed it and claim it merely represents the restoration and renaming of one of the existing four provinces. It may refer to a breakaway province or *civitas*.[17] However the later *Notitia Dignitatum* records it as a separate province leaving Britain with five provinces within one diocese. A fifth-century writer, Polemius Silvius, even added a sixth province, Orcades, or Orkneys. We recall there were four provinces listed in the *Laterculus Veronensis* between 303 to 314. This fifth province might have been added sometime between c. 314 to 367, perhaps under Constans in 343. If we take Ammianus at face value this seems to be the correct interpretation rather than Theodosius creating a new fifth province in 367.

If a province had indeed 'passed into the enemy's hands' during some sort of 'barbarian conspiracy' by northern tribes then we can speculate as to the most likely location. It may be that Constans had created a buffer province north of Hadrian's Wall. Alternatively the northern-most province, Britannia Secunda, may have earlier been divided. We remember that at the start of the incursion Nectraridus, *comes maritime tractus* (commander of the seacoast region) had been killed and Fullofaudes, another 'general', had been ambushed and taken prisoner. Additionally the enemy were Picts, Scots and Attacotti, all pointing to a northern location.

Our final clue comes from the *Notitia Dignitatum*. They list three of the provinces as being governed by *praeses*: Britannia Prima; Flavia Caesariensis; and Britannia Secunda. Only two governors are listed as being of consular rank: Maxima Caesariensis and Valentia. Arguably the second most important city in Roman Britain was York. York had been the capital of Britannia Secunda. It was the headquarters of the Sixth legion and later Dux Britanniarum. It was the city from which Septimius Severus and Constantius conducted their northern campaigns. Both emperors died there. Caracalla and Geta, and later Constantine were declared emperor within its walls.

One explanation is that Britannia Secunda had at some point been split in half, with one half being named Valentia. If so then York would be a reasonable suggestion for a consular governor's palace. Alternatively suggestions include Carlisle or even Chester. I suggest the three most likely locations for the province 'lost to the enemy' are as follows: The north-east, between the Humber and Hadrian's Wall; the north-west, between Chester and Carlisle; or the northern area either side of Hadrian's Wall. We can see just two of many possible scenarios for the locations of the fifth province in figure 55.

As to the enemy we are left to consider two options: Irish or Pictish raiders effectively destroyed a northern or western province; or the sources mask some

Figure 55. Valentia, the fifth province.

sort of internal revolt or usurpation of power. A combination of the two is also not impossible, with one event taking advantage of the other. The campaign of Theodosius in Britain may have quickly and efficiently destroyed both threats. But not for long. Major raids continued into the fifth century and the next usurper was to declare himself just fifteen years later. In fact he had very likely accompanied Theodosius the Elder to Britain in 367, fighting alongside the general's young son who would become Theodosius the Great.

Theodosius I

Theodosius was born on 11th January 347 in Cauca in the province of Gallaccia, Spain. His first appearance in the sources suggests he accompanied his father to Britain after the 'barbarian conspiracy' of 367.[18] However the first concrete evidence of his career places him as military commander in Moesia, *dux Moesiae Primae* in the year 373/4. After the successful campaign in 367 Valentinian I had appointed Theodosius the Elder *magister equitum*, commander of the cavalry. He soon added more victories, fighting against the Alammani and Sarmatians. Next the elder Theodosius was sent to North Africa to put down a revolt in 373. It is thought his son had built his own military reputation participating in his father's successful campaigns.[19]

Disaster befell the family when in 375–6 Theodosius the Elder was arrested and executed at Carthage, likely the victim of an internal power struggle. His son was able to survive and retreats to his estates in Spain. There he married Aelia

Flavia Flacilla. They were to have two sons, both future emperors, Arcadius (born 377) and Honorius (born 384). The disaster at Adrianople in 378 and death of the eastern Augustus, Valens, created a power vacuum in the east. Gratian, the emperor in the west and eldest son of Valentinian I (died 375), was just 19 years old. His half-brother and co-ruler, Valentinian II, was still a child of 8 or 9. Theodosius was 31 and an experienced battle-hardened commander.

Theodosius was appointed emperor in the east at Sirmium in January 379 a few months after Valens and his army had been destroyed. One significant development came when he awarded *foederati*, allied status, to Gothic tribes in 382. They were given lands and allowed to live under their own laws and rulers. He accepted baptism early in his reign and in 380 announced that the faith laid out in the Catholic Nicene Creed was the only true religion. Successive laws began to to attack beliefs considered heretical. In 391 he banned pagan worship leaving Catholic Christianity as the dominant religion across the empire.

In addition to these religious changes all property became taxable and tenants were not allowed freedom of travel without their landlord's consent. This was too would have a significant social impact and far reaching ramifications in the fifth century as Roman authority began to disintegrate in the west. The tax regime by central government became extremely oppressive. At one point even those responsible for collecting taxes suffered flogging with lead-weighted whips.[20]

Theodosius reigned for 16 years and briefly united the empire. How this came about will be discussed in more detail in the next section. Briefly Gratian was killed and replaced by Maximus who himself was killed in 388. Valentinian II died in 392 and was replaced by another usurper, Eugenius. His defeat and death in 394 left Theodosius under a sole ruler for the last time. He died on 17th January 395 at the age of 48.

Theodosius was described as blond, cutting an 'elegant figure' and possessing an aquiline nose.[21] He veered between opposites of 'febrile activity and indolent sluggishness'. Said by his enemies to be addicted to pleasure and luxury and untrustworthy as a friend or leader. Yet a decade after his death he was hailed as *Optimus ille divinum*, 'best of all the gods' and fifty years later was referred to as *megas*, the 'great'.[22]

His reign brought to the fore a number of people linked to elites of Hispanic and southern Gaul. One of these is our next

Figure 56. Gold solidus of Theodosius I minted in Constantinople, 379–383. (*Wikimedia Commons*)

Emperor of Britain, Magnus Maximus. It is thought both Theodosius and Maximus accompanied Theodosius the Elder to Britain in 367. If so they would certainly have known each other. Maximus would have been a little over ten years older than the twenty year old Theodosius. However Theodosius was also the son of the general who Maximus had to thank for his position. It is not known what sort of relationship they had although some sources hint that the elevation of Theodosius in 379 contributed to Maximus' decision. Whatever the case the two old comrades of 367 were to fight against each other twenty years later in a vicious civil war which would lend in defeat and execution.

Magnus Maximus to Constantine III

Magnus Maximus, born c. 335, came from a poor, Spanish family. It is thought he may have had connections to the family of Theodosius, with whom he had served in Britain after the invasion of 367.[23] He gained more experience fighting alongside Count Theodosius in Africa in 373–5 against the rebellion of Firmus. Sometime later he returned to Britain and became 'commander-in-chief', most likely *comes Britanniarum*. This would make him the senior Roman military commander in the diocese. Sources place him subduing another major raid against the Picts in c. 382.[24]

Valentinian had died in 375 and his brother Valens, co-emperor in the east, had fallen at the battle of Adrianople in 378, defeated by Fritigern's Gothic army. A disaster and pivotal moment for the Roman Empire. In the west Valentinian's son Gratian was the senior Augustus, controlling Britain, Spain and Gaul. His younger half-brother Valentinian II, aged only 7 in 378, ruled Italy, Illyricum and North Africa. The death of their uncle at Adrianople created a vacancy in the east. The family of Theodosius had fallen from grace His father was executed in 376, perhaps as a result of political manoeuvrings after Valentinian's death in 375. However by 377 the younger Theodosius was back in favour, leading a Roman army against the Sarmatians. On the death of Valens the nineteen year old Gratian could hardly rely on his young half-brother. Many experienced commanders had fallen at Adrianople and others had questionable loyalties. Theodosius was 31 and by now an experienced military commander.

It may not be a coincidence that Magnus Maximus was appointed *comes* in Britain shortly after Theodosius was appointed Augustus in the east in 379. The stage was now set for another usurper from Britain to sweep across the empire as Constantine had done eighty years before. In 383 the army in Britain grew restless. Dissatisfied with the rule of the western Augustus, Gratian, they declared Maximus emperor in 383.

Zosimus was writing a century and half later, and from the other side of the empire:[25] We are told Gratian elevated corrupt counsellors and disrespected his soldiers, an often fatal mistake for emperors. The final straw seems to have been when he allowed Alani 'fugitives' into his service and honoured them more than his own men. Maximus was described as a 'fellow-soldier of Theodosius in Britain' and seems to have had a better reputation in the army than their young emperor. Feeling jealous that his old friend Theodosius had been elevated to Augustus in the east Maximus was only too happy to exploit this discontent.

Having received 'the purple robe and diadem' in Britain he crossed to the continent taking much of the garrison with him. Landing at the mouth of the Rhine he found support amongst many of the troops there as well. Gratian marched against him. After five days of skirmishes the western emperor's troops started to desert him. A defecting unit of Mauritanian cavalry began a trickle that turned into a flood and the legitimate emperor was forced to flee with just 300 horsemen towards the south. Once again the road to Lugdunum ended with the grave of an emperor.

Maximus sent his *magister equitum*, Andragathius, after Gratian and he was quickly overtaken and killed. Maximus was now the undisputed ruler of the west up to the Alps. The twelve year old Valentinian II in his court in Milan had to look on impotently when news of his half-brother's murder reached him. In the east Theodosius was forced to accept the fait accompli and accept Maximus as joint emperor.

Maximus set up his headquarters and a mint at Trier. He was an orthodox Catholic and his reign is noted for the first Christian execution of a man for his religious beliefs.[26] In 387 he promoted his infant son, Flavius Victor, to co-Augustus. The stage was now set for a climatic battle between the two former comrades. The following year Maximus crossed the Alps and invaded Italy. Valentinian fled east seeking the protection of Theodosius. Maximus sent Andragathius to intercept but Valentinian managed to evade his ships and escape to Thessalonica. Theodosius determined his old comrade was now hell-bent on taking the whole empire. Maximus based himself at Aquileia whilst Andragathius led a force into Illyrium. The latter suffered a reverse near Siscia, modern Croatia. Theodosius advanced quickly and sent a substantial cavalry force towards Maximus's main forces near Poetovio on the River Save in Slovenia.

Much of Theodosius's army was made up of Gothic and Alanic troops. They were able to inflict heavy casualties and made a bridgehead on the northern bank in time for the main Theodosian army to arrive. The western usurper's army regrouped and attacked the next day. They were beaten again and Maximus was forced to flee back to Aquileia and seek refuge. Here he was besieged and eventually forced to fall on the mercy of Theodosius.

Usurpers and Tyrants

Figure 57. Roman Miliarensis of Magnus Maximus. (*Wikimedia Commons*)

Unfortunately for Maximus mercy was in short supply. After the treatment of Gratian and subsequent invasion of Italy and Illyricum, Theodosius was in no mind to let his former 'fellow-soldier' live. Maximus was executed outside the city walls. Meanwhile the eastern emperor had sent his Frankish general, Arbogastes, on a northern route towards Trier where Victor, Maximus's son, was resident. He was apparently still an infant when he was elevated to Augustus in 383 and must have been still a child when he followed his father to an early grave.

It is worth briefly describing the aftermath. Theodosius and Valentinian were now emperors of the east and west respectively. However, with the latter still a teenager in 388, Theodosius held the power and he appointed his general Arbogast as the western *magister militum*. Four years later the twenty one year old Valentinian was resident at Vienne, just over 20 miles south of Lugdunum. Arbogast claimed he found the young emperor hanging dead and claimed it was suicide. Others suspected foul play, especially when Arbogast elevated Eugenius, the *magister scrinorum* (master of scribes) to the throne. Theodosius didn't recognise this new usurper and once again marched west. The resultant conflict ended at the Battle of the Frigidus in 394 with Arbogast and Eugenius both killed in the battle. Theodosius was now sole ruler of a united empire. A year later Theodosius died from disease aged 48 and the empire once again was split in two, between the young sons of the late-emperor.

Constantine III

Our final three emperors from Britain occur a generation after Maximus was declared Augustus. It is impossible to date any of them although it is likely they were young men at the time. All three appear in the same year, 406, and if we speculate they were 30–40 years of age then they were born c. 370. Before we get to that we must first look at events directly following the death of Theodosius.

The empire was divided between the sons of Theodosius: The seventeen year old Arcadius in the east; and the ten year old Honorius in the west. Given their age their father had appointed two experienced generals to advise them: In the east the praetorian prefect Rufinus; and with Honorius, Stilicho, the *comes et magister utriusque militiae praesentalis*, the supreme military commander in the west.

Stilicho was soon busy, beating back incursions by Goths and Franks. Then around c. 398 northern Britain suffered another serious raid. Serious enough to warrant an intervention lead by Stilicho himself. A panegyric by the poet Claudian[27] in c. 402 refers to the 'Saxon conquered, the seas safe, the Picts defeated, and Britain secure'. Another specifically refers to Stilicho giving aid to Britain 'at the mercy of neighbouring tribes'. The Britons are described as 'clothed in the skin of some Caledonian beast, her cheeks tattooed, and an azure cloak'. The Scots (Irish) had 'roused all Hibernia against me and the sea foamed to the beat of hostile oars'. Thanks to his intervention they no longer feared 'the Scottish arms or tremble at the Pict, or keep watch along all my coasts for the Saxon who would come whatever wind might blow'. Evidence suggests parts of Hadrian's Wall was repaired. By 402 Stilicho had returned to the continent taking significant numbers of troops with him and, perhaps more importantly, much of the coinage.

The last mint was closed in the reign of Maximus and no new coins seem to have reached Britain after 402.[28] Delivery of coins was vital for the payment of soldiers as well as the wider economy. It is notable that we start to see signs of a drastic deterioration in both urban and economic life before the end of the fourth century. Low-value coins fell out of circulation around 410–430, suggesting higher-value coins may have lasted a little later, c. 450–470.[29] Money continued to be be available but the economic cycle and urbanisation that contributed so much to 'Roman life' was severely impacted.[30]

On the continent Stilicho held back barbarian raids on the Danube and in Italy. The most notable enemy was Alaric, king of the Goths. The Gothic victory over Valens in 378 had resulted in a treaty with Theodosius in 382 giving the Goths *foederati* status. This was the first of it's kind and allowed them to settle, free from direct Roman administrative control, in exchange for troops. Alaric had served under Theodosius in the battle of Frigidus in 394 but was left dissatisfied with the arrangement. The death of Theodosius meant the empire was now effectively in the hands of his two young sons, but controlled by two powerful men, Rufinus and Stilicho. Much political intrigue followed resulting in a number of important developments: the death of Rufinus in the east, killed by Gothic troops loyal to Stilicho; Stilicho being declared a public enemy by the eastern emperor Arcadius; and Alaric being appointed *magister militum per Illyricum*.

By 402 Alaric had entered Italy in search of provisions and plunder forcing Stilicho to confront and defeat him twice. The fact he chose not to destroy the Gothic army completely has lead historians to consider Stilicho's motives. Perhaps he wished to use Alaric's powerful army against the eastern emperor who had declared him a public enemy. However events were about to turn against the general. These were to lead to the elevation of our last Roman emperor in Britain.

In the winter of 406 the Rhine froze over. With Stilicho still busy holding back Alaric in northern Italy several tribes took the opportunity and streamed into into a weakened Roman Gaul: Vandals, Burgundians, Alemanni, Alans, Saxons and Gepids among them. The Britons, weakened by Stilicho's withdrawal of troops and coins, looked across the channel in horror. Or perhaps they simply saw it as an opportunity. Already with a long history of usurpers, from Carausius to Maximus, they rebelled again. Three leaders were appointed in quick succession: Mark, Gratian and Constantine. Three contemporary sources, Orosius, Olympiodorus, and Sozomen, described the events.

First Orosius:[31] The invading tribes plundered their way across Gaul all the way to the Pyrenees. Checked by this natural barrier they swept back, 'roaming wildly through Gaul'. In Britain Gratian, described as a 'townsman' was set up as usurper. He was killed and in his place Constantine 'a man from the lowest ranks of the soldiery, was chosen simply from confidence inspired by his name and without any other qualifications to recommend him'. He seized 'the imperial dignity' and crossed over to Gaul. He sent his son Constans, 'shamefully transformed from a monk into a Caesar', to Spain.

From Sozomen we learn that the Britons were the first to rise in sedition and that they proclaimed first Marcus, then Gratian.[32] Within four months he too was killed and replaced by Constantine. He repeats Orosius' claim that it was solely on account of his name. This seems an odd reason and perhaps it was a popular insult thrown at Constantine by his enemies.

Like Stilicho Constantine also took significant numbers of troops from Britain and became 'master of Gaul as far as the Alps'.[33] These dramatic events took place in c. 407. The following year the eastern emperor died and was succeeded by his 7 year old son Theodosius II. Stilicho sent a force against Constantine. After some initial success he was forced back into Italy and under pressure from several sides made peace with Alaric who was still in northern Italy. This was an unpopular move and Stilicho's enemies began to circle. An army mutiny proved his downfall and Stilicho was put to death in 408. Honorius, still only fifteen at this time, felt compelled to accept Constantine III as co-emperor.

Meanwhile back in Britain we get information from a near contemporary, and usually reliable, source. The *Gallic Chronicle* of 452 records a major raid on Britain for the following year, 409: Britain was 'devastated by an incursion of the Saxons'.[34] The Britons rebelled again, this time against the regime Constantine had left behind. Zosimus recorded the same events a little later:[35] The barbarian assaults caused 'Britain and some of the Celtic peoples to defect from the Roman rule … . independent from the Roman laws'. The Britons freed their cities from the barbarian threat and interestingly, together with 'all Armorica and the other Gallic provinces', expelled Roman officials and set up a constitution 'as they pleased'. Zosimus blamed the assaults squarely on Constantine and his 'carelessness in administration'.

The Britons, still under pressure from barbarian raids, and having revolted against Constantine, appealed directly to Honorius in Ravenna. The reply from Honorius, *The Rescript of Honorius,* is often cited as a turning point in history. He wrote telling them to look to their own defences. However it is important to note two points regarding this. Firstly it was only considered the end of Roman Britain in hindsight. As we have seen throughout this book there were multiple times when Britain broke away or part of political upheavals or usurpation. Secondly there is some debate as to if this letter really refers to Britain at all rather than Bruttium in Italy.[36]

If the letter was to authorities in Britain then it is interesting it is addressed to the *civitates* rather than the diocese or provinces. It is possible civil administration had broken down at provincial level but perhaps it is more likely Honorius simply couldn't trust those professing loyalty two years after siding with Constantine. Subsequent events make the debate rather academic. A citizen of Roman Britain might well have expected Roman rule to return. In reality this was to be the last revolt.

Honorius was to later send his general Constantius (Constantius III) to restore order in Gaul. Sozomen (c. 439) tells us a province, most likely Gaul, returned its allegiance to Honorius. He makes no mention of Britain. Procopius writing c. 540 states: 'However the Romans never succeeded in recovering Britain, but it remained from that time on under tyrants.'[37] The sources seem clear. The revolt under Constantine and subsequent rejection of aid by Honorius marked the end of Roman rule in Britain.

It is a little more difficult to precisely date the barbarian raid in Britain or Honorius' response. In 409 Alaric was in northern Italy putting pressure on Honorius. Constantine was duly accepted as co-emperor and given a consulship. Constantine also appointed his son Constans as co-emperor. Yet things began to rapidly unravel. Not only had Britain thrown out the regime he left behind but his general, Gerontius, had failed to secure Spain from barbarian incursions. Constantine sent his son, now Constans II, to take over. Gerontius refused to step down, rebelled and declared a *protector domesticus* (officer cadet), another Maximus, as emperor. Sources suggest Gerontius was a Briton and Maximus his son.[38] If so this would give us potentially another emperor who set foot in Britain.

Gerontius even minted coins commemorating three Augusti, presumably meaning Honorius Theodosius II and Maximus. In 410 Gerontius went on the offensive and advanced into Gaul. In Italy Honorius had his hands full with Alaric who famously sacked Rome that same year. The Visigoths ravaged the peninsula and would later be settled in south-western Gaul. Even though the western emperor had long resided at Ravenna the shock to the Roman world was profound.

In 411 Honorius was able to go on the attack. In Gaul Gerontius had taken the city of Vienne and executed Constans. He then moved to Arelate, Arles in southern France, besieging Constantine and his surviving son, Julian. Honorius ordered Constantius across the Alps forcing Gerontius back into Spain where he was killed. Constantine swapped one besieger for another and was eventually forced to surrender. He was promised safe passage but en route to Ravenna he and his son were killed.

Not much is known about Constantine's rule. Sources, biased though they likely are, described him as 'wayward and gluttonous'.[39] We have already noted he was regarded as a careless administrator and blamed for both barbarian incursions and the revolt of Britain and parts of Gaul.

In terms of dating Birley attempts to make sense of the, at times, conflicting sources:[40] Various Germanic tribes crossed the Rhine on 31st December 405 or 406. Another group, this time Goths from northern Italy, crossed the Alps into Gaul in the spring of 406. These were the survivors of a defeated army lead by Radagaisus which was beaten by Stilicho at Friesole (Florence). Alaric's Goths remained a threat in Italy. The sources seem clear that the rebellion in Britain can be dated to 406. We are thus left to choose which group of barbarians caused the rebellion in Britain. The earlier date for the first group across the Rhine makes more sense geographically and chronologically.

The consensus dates the elevation of Marcus to 406 and the cause seems to have been fear of attack from the same barbarian

Figure 58. Gold Solidus of Constantine III. (*Wikimedia Commons*)

invaders into Gaul with no help forthcoming from Rome, or more precisely Ravenna. Birley dates this more accurately to the summer of 406. Marcus is soon killed and Gratian acclaimed. Here Birley prefers the description 'a native of Britain' rather than 'civilian of Britain'. Gratian can be dated to October 406 as we are told he ruled for just four months. Word reached Honorius of Constantine's arrival in Gaul in March 407. This provides a reasonable explanation for the confusion in dating the rebellion precisely. Constantine's elevation was in early 407 giving a range of summer 406 to spring 407 for the three emperors.

Constantine consolidated his gains in 407 naming Constans Caesar in 408. With Stilicho's execution and the death of the eastern emperor Arcadius that same year Constantine no doubt felt confident and declared Constans Augustus in 409. This was perhaps his high-water mark. Gerontius in Spain rebelled and Britain suffered devastating Saxon raids in 409. It would seem it was at this point that some Gallic regions joined Britain in breaking away from Roman rule. Their subsequent appeal to Honorius received a hasty reply in 410 from Ravenna to look to their own defences. No wonder as Alaric was besieging Rome for the their time since 408. In the August of 410 his troops entered the city. This allows us to suggest the following timeline leading to the end of Roman rule in Britain.

Table 7. Timeline of the last years of Roman Britain.

Year	Month	
405	December	Germanic tribes cross a frozen Rhine into Gaul
406	Spring	Gothic tribes cross Alps from northern Italy
	Summer	Marcus declared emperor in Britain
	October	Marcus killed, Gratian declared emperor in Britain
407	February	Gratian killed, Constantine declared emperor in Britain
	March	Constantine III crosses over to Gaul
408	May	Eastern emperor Arcadius died, succeeded by his 7 year old son Theodosius II
	Summer	Constantine pushes forces loyal to Honorius back into Italy, garrisons Alpine passes and makes Arles his capital. Constantine names his son Constans Caesar and sends him with Gerontius to secure Spain.
	August	Stilicho executed
409		Constantine recognised by Honorius and received co-consulship with emperor Constans declared co-Augustus Gerontius rebelled against Constantine in Spain and declared Maximus emperor Saxon raids devastate Britain Britain and northern Gaul throw out Constantine's magistrates becoming independent of Roman rule

Year	Month	
410	Spring	Constantine invaded northern Italy but was repulsed.
	August	Alaric sacks Rome
411	Spring	Gerontius invades Gaul, kills Constans and besieges Constantine at Arelate
	Summer	Honorius sent Constantius into Gaul who defeated Gerontius who fled to Spain and later committed suicide. Constantine III besieged, surrendered and later executed.

Aftermath

Events had now been set in motion. In the east Theodosius II had succeeded his father Arcadius in 408 and was to rule for forty-two years. In the west, Rome had been sacked by the Gothic king Alaric in 410. The western empire was to suffer continued barbaric raids and a slow fragmentation of power and authority. Only Aetius was able to hold back the tide for a generation, culminating in his great victory over Attila the Hun at the Battle of the Catalaunian Plains in 451. His murder in 454 was followed by a succession of weak emperors and strong Germanic generals which ended when Odoacer deposed the last Roman emperor in the west, Romulus Augustulus, in 476.

What little we know of Britain from these last decades of Roman authority in the west will be covered in the last chapter. We have seen how Britain may have been denuded of troops by Maximus, Stilicho and, finally, Constantine III. This may not have been the last of the tyrants or visiting emperors as we shall see with some intriguing possibilities emerge.

Chapter Ten

The End of Empire

A popular narrative given to me at school over forty years ago is the Romans left in 410 leaving the Britons, or Romano-Britons, to fend for themselves against waves of Anglo-Saxon invaders. We now know this is inaccurate. Firstly we don't really know how much of the previous tribal cultures survived the four centuries of Roman rule. Before we look at changes to cultural identity we will first turn to military matters. It is estimated that, by the end of the fourth century, the army had dropped to between 12,000 and 20,000 men compared to a force of perhaps 50,000 in the second century.[1] One estimate places the army size as low as 6,000 by the year 400.[2] We must remember that this is before Constantine III crossed over to Gaul with a sizeable force. It is likely a skeleton force was left behind to defend the diocese and we see signs of continued occupation at various urban and military sites. One of the last documents comes from a manuscript known as the *Notitia Dignitatum*.

Notitia Dignitatum

The *Notitia omnium Dignitatum et administrationum tam civilium quam militarum*, more commonly known as the *Notitia Dignitatum*, is the earliest written source for the military and civil organisation of fifth-century Britain. It consists of two halves: a *Notitia Dignitatum Occidentis, Register of Offices in the West*, and N*otitia Dignitatum Orientis, Register of Offices in the West*. The earliest copy is from the now lost, eleventh-century, *Codex Spirensis*. Thought to be dated c. 390–425, it gives a snapshot of the structure of the late Roman Empire. It may be a copy of an earlier document and was possibly out of date when completed.[3] As such it may depict paper strength rather than the reality on the ground.

We recall that at the end of the fourth century the civilian and military authorities of Britain reported to the *Prefectis Praetorians per Gallias*, the Praetorian Prefect of the Gauls. The civilian authority was led by the *Vicarius Britanniae*, one of six vicars in the west. The staff of the vicarus included the following: a chief of staff, chief deputy, two receivers of taxes, chief clerk, custodian, chief assistant, keeper of the records, assistants, secretaries, notaries and 'the rest of the staff'.

The *Notitia Dignitatum* lists five governors in Britain reporting to him, one from each province: *Consularis per Maxima Caesariensis*; *Consularis per Valentia*; *Praesidis per Britannia prima*; *Praesidis per Britannia secunda*; and *Praesidis per Flavia Caesariensis*. The senior military authority was the *comes*, or count, who also reported to the praetorian prefect in Gaul. Britain had two: the *Comes Britanniarum* and *Comes Litoris Soxonicum per Britannias* with the former appearing to be the senior of the two. In the north the *Dux Britanniarum* reported to the *Comes Britanniarum*. The tables below list the units under each command.

Table 8. Units under the Comes Britanniarum.

Infantry units	Cavalry units
Secunda Britannica, legio comitatenses	Equites Catafractarii Iuniores, vexillatio comitatenses
Victores Iuniores Britanniciani auxilia palatinae	Equites Scutarii Aureliaci, vexillatio comitatenses
Primani Iuniores, legio comitatenses	Equites Honoriani Seniores, vexillatio comitatenses
Secundani Iuniores, legio comitatenses	Equites Stablesiani, vexillatio comitatenses
	Equites Syri, vexillatio comitatenses
	Equites Taifali, vexillatio comitatenses

Table 9. Troops and Offices of the Count of the Saxon Shore.

Name of unit	Location
Praepositus numeri Fortensium, Othonae	Bradwell
Praepositus militum Tungrecanorum, Dubris	Dover
Praepositus numeri Turnacensium, Lemannis	Lympne
Praepositus equitum Dalmatarum Branodunensium, Branoduno	Brancaster
Praepositus equitum stablesianorum Gariannonensium, Giariannonor	Burgh Castle
Tribunus cohortis primae Baetasiorum, Regulbio	Reculver
Praefectus legionis secundae Augustae, Rutupis	Richborough
Praepositus numeri Abulcorum, Anderidos	Pevensey
Praepositus numeri exploratorum, Portum Adurni	Portchester

Table 10. Troops and Offices of the Dux Britanniarum.

Name of unit, with location	Location
Praefectus legionis sextae	York
Praefectus equitum Dalmatarum, Praesidio	Newton Kyme
Praefectus equitum Crispianorum, Dano	Doncaster
Praefectus equitum catafractariorum, Morbio	Piercebridge

Name of unit, with location	Location
Praefectus numeri barcariorum Tigrisiensium, Arbeia	South Shields
Praefectus numeri Nerviorum Dictensium, Dicti	Wearmouth
Praefectus numeri uigilum, Concangios	Chester-le-Street
Praefectus numeri exploratorum, Lauatres	Bowes
Praefectus numeri directorum, Uerteris	Brough
Praefectus numeri defensorum, Braboniaco	Kirkby Thore
Praefectus numeri Solensium, Maglone	Old Carlisle
Praefectus numeri Pacensium, Magis	Burrow Walls
Praefectus numeri Longovicanorum, Longouico	Lanchester
Praefectus numeri superuenientium Petueriensium, Deruentione	Malton
Tribunus cohortis quartae Lingonum, Segeduno	Wallsend
Tribunus cohortis primae Cornouiorum, Ponte Aeli	Newcastle
Praefectus alae primae Asturum, Conderco	Benwell
Tribunus cohortis primae Frixagorum, Uindobala	Rudchester
Praefectus alae Sabinianae, Hunno	Halton Chesters
Praefectus alae secundae Asturum, Cilurno	Chesters
Tribunus cohortis primae Batauorum, Procolitia	Carrawburgh
Tribunus cohortis primae Tungrorum, Borcouicio	Housesteads
Tribunus cohortis quartae Gallorum, Uindolana	Chesterholm
Tribunus cohortis primae Asturum, Aesica	Great Chesters
Tribunus cohortis secundae Dalmatarum, Magnis	Carvoran
Tribunus cohortis primae Aeliae Dacorum, Amboglanna	Castlesteads
Praefectus alae Petrianae, Uxelodunum or Petrianis	Stanwix
Luguuallii	Carlisle
Praefectus numeri Maurorum Aurelianorum, Aballaba	Burgh-by-Sands
Tribunus cohortis secundae Lingonum, Congauata	Drumburgh
Tribunus cohortis primae Hispaniorum, Axeloduno	Bowness
Tribunus cohortis secundae Thracum, Gabrosenti	Moresby
Tribunus cohortus primae Aeliae classicae, Tunnocelo	Ravenglass
Tribunus cohortis primae Morinorum, Glannibanta	Ambleside
Tribunus cohortis tertiae Neruiorum, Alione	Lancaster
Cuneus Sarmatarum, Bremetenraco	Ribchester
Praefectus alae primae Herculeae, Olenaco	Ilkley
Tribunus cohortis sextae Neruiorum, Uirosido	Bainbridge

On paper at least there was still a significant military in Britain at when Constantine III was declared emperor. The three commands at the end of the Roman period could be summarised as follows.[4] The question is how many of these were left after the events of 407–11?

Table 11. Military commands of Roman Britain.

	Cavalry units (alae)	Infantry cohorts
Count of the Britains	6	4 (comitatenses)
Count of Saxon Shore	2	7 (limitanei)
Duke of the Britains (York)		
Along Hadrian's wall	5	18 (limitanei)
Reserves	3	11 (limitanei)
Overall total	16	40

Constantius III

Before considering Britain it is worth noting events in Gaul. In the first few decades of the fifth-century the Romans battled to control raiders and settlers. This was partially successful one example being the Gothic settlement in south-west Gaul. In the first quarter of the fifth-century Constantius, *the magister militum* and later Emperor, had defeated Constantine and regained control over much of the diocese. Sozomen, writing at the time, reported the province 'returning it's allegiance'. Most historians have accepted this simply means Gaul and Britain was left to its own devices. However there are intriguing later sources which suggest a possible Roman expedition after 410.

Firstly there is an entry in the Anglo-Saxon Chronicle for the year 418 which states:[5] 'Here the Romans assembled all the gold-hoards which were in Britain and hid some in the earth so that no-one afterwards could find them and took some with them into Gaul'. An earlier entry for 409 states: 'Here the Goths destroyed the stronghold of Rome, and afterwards the Romans never ruled in Britain…'. It follows by stating the Romans ruled for 470 after Julius Caesar first came. Interestingly this would bring us to 415, closer to the 418 'event' than the fall of Rome in 410.

Our second clue comes from the only contemporary witness for early sixth-century Britain. Gildas wrote *De Excidio et Conquestu Britanniae* (On the Ruin and Conquest of Britain) in teh second quarter of the Sixth century.[6] The narrative is frustratingly confused. However the style of Latin demonstrates a good level of training[7] and this suggests more of the fabric of Roman civilisation survived later than first thought.[8] Gildas does not mention Constantine III but importantly dates the events after the death of Maximus who we know was executed in 388. He states that the Britons suffered many years of raids from Picts and Scots (Irish). Twice they appealed and received military help. A third time they appealed to 'Agitius, thrice consul'. This is taken to be Aetius, *comes et magister utriusque militiae* in the west, who was consul for the third time between 445–454. It is not possible to determine if Gildas dated the first two military expeditions before our after 410. It is likely he did not have an exact timeline.

Nevertheless this leaves us with the suggestion Constantius campaigned in Britain c. 418. The argument for a Roman expedition after 410 is laid out in Edwin Pace's *The Long War for Britannia 367–664*.[9] It is not generally accepted by historians and there is nothing in contemporary or later sources that directly support the theory. His successful military campaigns in the west enabled his rise to power. In 417 he married Galla Placidia, the sister of Emperor Honorius. She persuaded her brother to elevate her hubsnd to co-Augustus in 421. In the east Theodosius II refused to recognise him. This proved academic as in a few short months Constantius died.

We hear next to nothing concerning Britain in these few years. Yet a military intervention should not seemed far fetched. Firstly there was likely many people in Britain who viewed Roman rule favourable. Many who had appealed for help to Honorius in 410 would have still been in positions of power when Constantius campaigned in northern Gaul. Secondly we do have an account of a Roman intervention less than a decade after Constantius reigned. This time it was not military but religious.

St Germanus of Auxerre

The importance of this visit is that it shows there was still considerable communication between Britain and the Western Empire. Also a religious delegation was able to travel to and across Britain. Lastly it points to a military force still existing in Britain nearly a generation after Roman authority ended. Constantius of Lyon writing in c. 480 tells of two visits. The first is dated to 429 and is in response to the Pelagian heresy.

Pelagius was a monk from Britain who favoured the concept of free will over that of original sin. Anti-Pelagian legislation appeared in 418 and subsequently Agricola, a Pelagian supporter, fled to Britain which appeared to be safe for followers.[10] Prosper, writing c. 455, states the following:[11]

> 'at the persuasion of the deacon Palladius, Pope Celestine sent Germanus, bishop of Auxerre, as his representative, and having rejected the heretics, directed the British to the catholic faith'. This seems to be connected with

another well-known papal delegation a year or two later: 'Palladius was sent by Pope Celestine to the Scots (Irish) who believed in Christ, and was ordained as their first bishop'.

Germanus travelled from his landing point to where there were crowds of people welcoming him, suggesting a vibrant christian and urban community. He wins a heated religious debate with the Pelagians. From there (possibly London) he travelled to the shrine of St Alban at Verulamium. We then read that an incursion of Saxons and Picts caused the Britons to request help from the hero of the tale. Naturally Germanus is appointed *Dux Proelii* (leader for battle). They win a great victory without spilling a drop of blood by repeatedly shouting 'Alleluia', scaring the enemy who fled, many drowning in a nearby river. If we accept this the Britons had a functioning army willing and able to fight in 429.

The 'most wealthy island' now secure Germanus returned to Gaul. The heresy returned and so did Germanus, possibly in 437. This time the Pelagians were condemned and exiled suggesting the church, and possibly Romans, still had some influence. In fact the contemporary writer Prosper makes the possibly significant comment: 'while he labours to keep the Roman island Catholic he has also made the barbarian island Christian'.[12] It is possible some still viewed Britain as Roman culturally if not politically.

Constantius of Lyon gives us few names. The Pelagians 'flaunt their wealth, in dazzling robes' followed by 'flatterers'. The contest is watched by 'vast crowds'. He meets a 'tribune' and his wife, curing their ten-year-old daughter of blindness. During the second visit he meets Elafius, one of 'the leading men in the country' and cures his son. We hear of no kings or Governors. Perhaps the first visit of Germanus was one of the Roman interventions Gildas referenced. The impression is one of a still functioning 'Roman' Diocese although operating outside central Roman authority.

St Patrick

The only other fifth-century source from Britain comes from two works of Saint Patrick: the *Confessio* and *Epistola*. From the first we learn he was born in *Bannavem Taburniae* (unknown location). His father, Calpornius, was a *decurio* (member of town council) and a deacon in the church and his grandfather, Potitus, a priest.[13] Given his likely timeframe this suggests a continuation of civic and religious life after direct Roman rule ended in c. 410. Whilst there is no provable date the Irish annals place his death in either c. 450–460s or c. 490s. The first may be a confusion for Palladius sent in 431 by Celestine and so the latter is considered more likely, with the Annals of Ulster giving 493.[14]

His capture by Irish raiders at the age of sixteen may have occurred around the same time as the raids mentioned by Gildas or the Romans hiding their gold in the Anglo-Saxon Chronicles. His escape and return to Ireland would then place him there in the mid-fifth century. His letter, *Epistola*, was in response to a raid by the soldiers of a certain King Coroticus where the 'newly baptised' were taken as slaves. It is not known who or where this king reigned, although some have suggested the Strathclyde area as the captured were sold to his allies the 'apostate Scots and Picts'.

A number of interesting points can be made. Firstly he made no appeal to a Roman *Vicarius*, Governor or *dux Britannarium*. Perhaps Coroticus is outside the former Diocese. However Patrick accuses him of being neither a christian nor a Roman citizen. Such an accusation would be felt keenly by someone who might have wished to be considered both. Lastly we have the appearance of a petty king. This is interesting because it suggests the breakdown of Roman rule and the emergence of a petty king in a area considered both Roman and Christian. We shall look at Gildas in more depth as he describes this fragmentation and mentions one last possible 'tyrant'. First we must look to Gaul.

Gaul

Shortly after the death of Constantius III the Roman General Aetius rose to become the senior military leader of the Western Empire. He successful played off the different tribal groups against each other: the Goths, Franks and Burgundians among them often using Hunnic mercenaries. It was to be this latter group, led by Attila, which was to prove the most dangerous. If we are to take Gildas at his word it was precisely at this point the Britons requested help to 'Agitus, thrice consul'. Indeed the later Anglo-Saxon Chronicles give this as the reason for rejecting the appeal: 'Here the Britons sent across the sea to Rome and asked for help against the Picts, but they had none there because they were campaigning against Attila, king of the Huns'.

We will cover the Britons' reaction to this rejection later. Aetius went on to defeat Attila in 451. Meanwhile significant cultural changes had been taking place in Gaul and we must wonder if similar events were playing out in Britain around the time Germanus visited. Groups of barbarians had been settled across the empire. Central authority became more corrupt and the tax regime more onerous. As Roman authority and central control broke down in the west a significant proportion of the people became disillusioned in Roman rule.

Salvian of Marseilles offers a vivid snapshot of life from the mid-fifth century: Romans began to reject Rome and vowed never to pass under Roman authority again:[15] The bulk of the Roman population were free but low-born Roman citizens and many now chose to escape Roman 'iniquity and cruelty' and live 'among the barbarians'. Salvian declared: 'the *Romana respublica* is now dead … strangled, as if by thugs, with the bonds of taxes.'[16] The blame is placed on the elites such as local town councillors, *principales* or *curiales*, who 'glory in this name of *tyrannus*'. Freeborn Roman citizens found themselves branded as *bacaudae*, outlaws, and subject to 'vicious campaigns of repression'.[17]

The turning point was perhaps the death of Aetius 454. He has been called by some the 'last Roman', an epitaph given to a certain Romano-Briton we shall meet later. His murderer, Emperor Valentinian III, died the following year. The Western Empire lurched from one crisis to another and went through a succession of short-lived emperors. The last emperor, Romulus Augustus was deposed by the Germanic general Odoacer and the western empire died. Out of its ashes emerged several new polities, notably the Frankish kingdom of Clovis, the Visigoth kingdom in southern Gaul and the Vandals in North Africa. Any pro-Roman Britons would have looked on in horror as any hope of a new *pax Romana* disappeared.

Britain

Despite the picture of Roman-culture continuing in the *Life of St Germanus* significant changes were taking place. Firstly the island had suffered a huge economic shock with the end of the coin supply and a process of de-urbanisation affected towns and cities across the diocese. Alongside evidence of decline and abandonment we also see significant pockets of continuation. Hill-forts in the north and west began to be re-occupied. Towns contracted and we see evidence of a change of building use and new fortifications. The amphitheater at Cirencester being one example.

When Constantine III crossed to Gaul in 407 he left behind a functioning administrative structure. The diocese was split between five provinces, within which were several *civitates*. The *civitas* was a significant 'socio-political unit' in the fifth-century and formed an important layer of Roman identity.[18] We see the survival of some of these names in the emerging petty kingdoms a century of two later, most notably the *Canti*, Kent. The question arises when and how did these provincial and military structures break down and how did petty kingdoms emerge?

By the year 600 we see many such kingdoms struggling for supremacy. Sources, as unreliable as they are for this period, point to these kingdoms already established by the mid-Sixth century. Some sort of Romano-British authority may have maintained power towards the the mid-fifth century. This gives a window of roughly 450–550 for the process of fragmentation and new polities forming.

One important point is the immigration of Germanic settlers. Firstly it is important to acknowledge Germanic soldiers from many tribes had served in the Roman army. Emperor Probus sent Vandals and Burgundians to Britain in the late third century. Crausius and Allectus used significant Germanic troops especially Franks in their rebellion. A Germanic commander of the Alemanni hailed Constantine I as emperor in 306. The title Count of the Saxon Shore suggests the presence of Saxon soldiers or settlers along the south and eastern coast. Alamanni troops based there in the 370s were said to be 'distinguished for their numbers and strength'.[19]

Archaeological evidence suggests a Germanic presence before 400.[20] But it is in the second quarter of the fifth century that we see a significant increase in Germanic material culture across southern Britain.[21] The initial evidence points to coastal areas and river valleys and suggests they were placed there by a surviving Romano-British authority. The important point is Germanic presence was growing two decades before the sources suggest a major transfer of power. It is noteworthy that this presence is predominantly in the south and east, areas that experienced the most Romanisation and urbanisation.

Three hundred years later Bede describes the arrival of 'three Germanic tribes': Saxons in Wessex, Sussex and Essex; Jutes in Kent and Hampshire; and Angles in East Anglia, Mercia and Northumbria. The archaeological evidence broadly supports this up to a point.[22] But Bede also lists several other peoples who settled in Britain: Frissians; Rugians; Danes; Huns; Old Saxons; and Bructeri.[23] It may be the cultural, political and military situation was far more complex and nuanced. What is certain is that there was no large scale one off invasion. Instead we get a broad consensus with the sources.

We recall Gildas dates these events to after appeal to Aetius in c. 445. Bede gives a more precise date of 449–56 for the *adventus saxonum*. The gallic Chronicles of 452 and 511 give 440/1 as the date Britain 'fell to the power of the saxons'. It is at this point we meet our 'last tyrant'.

The Last Tyrant

We have seen the contemporary account from early sixth century Britain. In *De Excidio et Conquestu Britanniae* Gildas delivers not history but a sermon full of fire and brimstone, lamenting the evil ways of his people. He gives a crucial snapshot into early sixth century Britain. Now there are kings who he calls 'tyrants' and their followers, 'bloody, proud and murderous men'. A war-band culture emerges in both Romano-British and Germanic cultures. The Roman

Villas of the fourth century give way to the mead-hall of the sixth century. Importantly he looks back and gives a narrative covering the period leading up to the time of his writing.

We read of a usurper having 'his evil head cut off at Aquileia'. This is one of the few events we can date (the death of Maximus in 388). Then the Britons 'groaned aghast for many years' due to 'two exceedingly savage and over-seas nations', the Scots (Irish) and Picts. Envoys are sent and Roman legions come to the rescue. Twice this occurs and Gildas wrongly attributed the building of the Antonine and Hadrian's Wall to this time. What he does not make clear is whether these raids are before of after Constantine III who he does not mention. The second time the Romans wave goodbye never to return.

The Scots and Picts return and seize 'the whole northern part of the land as far as the wall' causing the Britons to abandon 'their cities and lofty wall'. Massacres and famine follow which suggests this occurred either before of directly after Germanus visited in 429 and 437 as he witnesses neither. Then we get the famous letter: 'the groans of the Britons' to Agitius. If this is Aetius then we have second date, c. 445.

The appeal is rejected but the Britons manage to fight back driving the Picts and Scots out. There follows a period of abundance but the Britons turn to vice and 'falsehood'. Could this be a reference to Pelagianism? Kings are then anointed but some central authority must have remained for crucially we read of a council. At this point we also hear of a great plague killing so many that the 'living could not bury the dead'. We do have a record of pestilence in 442 that 'spread over almost the entire world'.[24] Worse followed as the council hears rumours of the Pict and Scots returning. Having been previously rejected by the Romans they turn to the tried and tested policy of hiring mercenaries.

The mercenaries arrive in three *cyulae* (keels), ships of war and they are led by Hengist and Horsa. The earliest Gildasian manuscripts state the council was led by a proud tyrant, *superbo tyranno*. It is Bede in the early eighth century who first names him: *Vurtigern, Uurtigern* or *Vertigernus*. The word itself is a compound of ver/wor/wer, meaning 'over', and -tigern, meaning 'lord'. Some suggest 'high-king' and 'supreme ruler' but a more accurate translation might be 'overlord'.

In my book, *The Early Anglo-Saxon Kings*, I argue that the Celtic word *tigernos* referred to a local lord or a king and was often equated with the Latin *tyrannus*.[25] It is also similar to how provincial people would refer to the local *decurion* or *curiale*.[26] As Roman rule disintegrated power became more localised. Local elites, such as town magistrates, villa owners, commanders of surviving military units, evolved into local lords. Yet in the mid-fifth century the Diocese of Britain still had a functioning central authority, a council, led by a 'proud tyrant' who could allocate land to mercenaries across the provinces.

Gildas states the mercenaries 'fixed their dreadful claws on the east side of the island'. Bede states they were given 'a place of settlement in the eastern part of the island' but after defeating the Picts 'the newcomers received from the Britons a grant of land in their midst'. The ninth century and unreliable *Historia Brittonum* says they were given Thanet and later Kent, plus land 'near the wall'. All agree they were fighting the Picts. The mercenaries proved successful and the Picts were defeated. The hosts and their guests then fell out. Whose fault it was depends which source one reads. Rather than an invasion the sources state it was the subsequent revolt that resulted in what Gildas called the 'disastrous division' or 'the unhappy partition with the barbarians'.

If we take these sources at face value then Vortigern was the last ruler of what remained of the Diocese of the Britains in the mid-fifth century. Nowhere is it suggested he was an emperor. Although interestingly there is an inscription linking Vortigern to both St Germanus and Magnus Maximus: The Pillar of Eliseg in Denbighshire, North Wales, was erected by Cyngen ap Cadell, a ninth-century king of Powys, to honour his great grandfather Elisedd ap Gwylog. The inscription includes: 'Britu son of Vortigern, whom Germanus blessed, and whom Sevira bore to him, daughter of Maximus the king, who killed the king of the Romans.' Magnus Maximus features in Welsh tradition and genealogies as *Macsen Wledig*, Emperor Maximus. This brings us to our last possible connection to Roman imperial power.

The last Roman, Ambrosius Aurelianus

The subsequent revolt of the mercenaries devastated Britain: 'it reached the other side of the island, and dipped its red and savage tongue in the western ocean'. The 'fierce and impious Saxons, a race hateful both to God and men' returned 'home' presumably to the land in the east allocated to them. Gildas claimed he could no longer visit 'the shrines of the martyrs' notably St Alban. The *Historia Brittonum* says Vortigern was forced to concede Middlesex, Essex, Sussex and 'other regions' to Hengest in Kent. This suggests much of the south-eastern former province of Maxima Caesariensis was under new masters.

The Britons fought back once more. They were led by Ambrosius Aurelianus, 'a modest man who, perhaps alone of the Romans had survived the shock of this storm'. We learn his parents had 'worn the purple' and been killed in the unrest. Gildas makes a distinction between Britons, barbarians and Romans and he clearly views Ambrosius as the latter. Bede dates him in his Chronica Majora to 'the time of Zeno (474–491). If so we can place these events a generation after Vortigern and the *adventus saxonum*.

In a much debated passage Gildas describes the subsequent war going back and forth: 'up to the siege of Badon Hill, pretty well the last defeat of the villains and certainly not the least. That was the year of my birth; … one month of the forty-fourth year since then has already past'. He seems to be writing forty four years after this famous victory. But the Roman world is now history despite Gildas displaying excellent Latin and rhetorical skills worthy of a Roman education.

Like Maximus, Ambrosius is also known in Welsh tradition: Emrys Wledig. The Histroia Bittonum calls him 'Emrys the overlord' and 'the great king among all the kings of the British nation', stating his father was a consul of the Roman people. We are left with legends to describe the next decades. The pseudo-historical twelfth century *History of the Kings of Britain* by Geoffrey of Monmouth takes up where the *Historia Brittonum* left off.

Ambrosius is succeeded by his brother Uther who in turn is followed by Arthur. I have covered the evidence for and against these figures in my other books. However historians tend to accept that Vortigern, Ambrosius and Badon are historical. What the sources seem to suggest is Britain limped on after Constantine III left for Gaul. Constantius III certainly reached the northern coast of Gaul even if he did not attempt to recover the former Diocese of Britannia. A decade later Germanus was able to travel to and across a province still culturally Roman. Some sort of central authority was able to hire and post mercenaries a few years later. Was Vortigern able to style himself emperor as Gratian, Mark and Constantine did in 406? Did enough of Roman Britain survive in the west and north for Ambrosius, 'the last Roman', to do likewise?

The emerging Brythonic kingdoms maintained a distinctive Romano-British culture. In the south-west Dumnonia survived for another few centuries. The Brythonic kingdom of Strathclyde lasted until the tenth century. In Armorica the Bretons fiercely maintained their independence against the Franks. But it is in what became Wales the descendants of the Romano-Britons maintained their distinct culture the longest, holding off the English until the middle-ages.

In the east an equally distinctive Germanic-Romano-British culture developed. Yet in the sixth century Gildas already saw the world in black and white. On one side the Britons, 'fellow citizens'. On the other the Saxons, a catch-all term for a range of Germanic peoples who, perhaps together with some of the indigenous Romano-Britons, forged new kingdoms out of the fragmenting provinces and *civitates* of Roman Britain. Later Anglo-Saxon kings would style themselves as the inheritors of Roman imperium. Indeed Bede himself listed seven kings as holding this imperium across much of southern Britain. The Anglo-Saxon Chronicles called them *Bretwalda*, 'wide-ruler'. It would take several centuries for one of these English kings to unite the former Roman provinces once more under one ruler.

Last words

We recall in Julius Caesar's first invasion the eagle-bearer of the Tenth Legion jumped into surf and turned the tide of battle. If the Romans had been pushed back into the sea that day history may have been very different. Caesar's second invasion secured an ill-defined treaty arrangement that perhaps changed little. Pre-Roman Britain was a patchwork of iron-age tribes with a warrior culture living in a world of scattered small farms and hill-forts. Nearly a hundred years later Claudius finally subjugated the mysterious island at the edge of the then-known Roman world. The future Emperor, Vespasian, played a major part in the invasion and nearly twenty years later his son Titus also served in Britain.

Under Roman rule towns and roads spread across the island. With it came new cultures and philosophies along with the *Pax Romana*. Hadrian left his mark with the famous wall that bears his name, settling the southern-most border of Roman authority that would last for three hundred years. Pertinax served twice, first as a tribune in the Sixth Legion and then as a praefectus of an auxiliary unit. He guarded the same frontier wall Hadrian had overseen being built forty years before. Pertinax returned as governor to an island beset by unrest and rebellion. Shortly after Clodius Albinus was made Caesar and later declared Augustus in Britain before his defeat and death at the hands of Severus. He wasn't to be the last to leave Britain as emperor only to die at the hands of a rival.

Our next emperors were the Severans. Septimius Severus, perhaps the first 'Hammer of the Scots', devastated the northern tribes pushing far into modern Scotland. Accompanied by his sons, the murderous Caracalla and the doomed Geta. We recall they may have been accompanied by their young cousins, the future Elagabalus and Severus Alexander. The first division of Britain occurred in the reign of Caracalla and Britannia experienced some stability as the wider empire lurched into 'The Crisis of the Third Century'.

The breakaway regimes of Postumus and Carausius and Allectus hinted at what was to come a century later. Constantius I brought Britain back under Roman rule and it was subsequently divided once more, this time into four provinces within a Diocese. In the early third century Constantine was declared emperor by the troops at York. The subsequent civil wars ended with this 'British usurper' as sole rule of a united empire. This was not to last. His son Constans was the last legitimate sitting-emperor to visit Britain and it is perhaps then that a fifth province was added.

The mid-fourth century saw two possible candidates for emperors in Britain: Magnentius and Carausius II. Raiding became endemic and a major incursion in 367 brought two future emperors to Britain, Magnus Maximus and Theodosius I.

Maximus made his son Victor co-emperor. Both were killed in 388. The year 406 saw three emperors declared in Britain in quick succession: Mark, Gratian and Constantine III. The latter elevated his son, Constans. Technically at this point Constantine had been acknowledged by Honorius. Thus Constans II might be the last legitimate emperor. The revolt by Gerontius, allegedly a Briton, resulted in the elevation of a second Maximus, possibly his son. If so this was perhaps the last known 'Emperor of Britain' to die. After his defeat in Gaul he fled 'amongst the barbarians in Hispania'.[27] He may be the same Maximus recorded as leading a later revolt and being executed c. 421.

We then saw the end of Roman Britain and three possible candidates to rival Maximus as our last emperor. First Constantius III who returned Gallic provinces to Roman authority. Did this extend across the Channel and allow St Germans to visit shortly after? We finished with Vortigern, 'the last tyrant' and Ambrosius, 'the last Roman'.

From Julius Caesar to Ambrosius Aurelianus covered over 500 years of history. The Romans left a significant mark on British history. New cultural identities emerged out of the ashes of the fragmented provincial structures. But these identities could not shake off their past. Brythonic and Anglo-Saxon kingdoms alike saw themselves as heirs to an imperial tradition. But Britain left its mark on Roman history too.

The first two centuries saw emperors arriving to conquer and impose Roman authority. The subsequent centuries witnessed repeated revolts, breakaway regimes and usurpers. More and more emperors were made in Britannia only to be destroyed by rivals. Only one of these was successful enough to secure the whole empire, Constantine the Great. Out of all the figures in this book it was perhaps his adoption of Christianity that had the most significant and long-lasting impact on the course of western history.

Britain may have began as a mysterious island on the edge of the known world. A magical, frightening place for the average Roman full of dark forests, cannibals and fierce savage-warriors who fought naked. By the end of our tale it was as Romanised and urbanised as anywhere else across the empire. It also contributed much to the course of Roman history. Despite the military might of Rome the Britons had a proud history of resistance from the time of Boudicca to the Picts of the fifth century. Perhaps Gildas had it right when he described his own people as 'of proud neck and mind, since it was first inhabited, is ungratefully rebelling, now against God, at other times against fellow citizens, sometimes even against the kings over the sea and their subjects'. A province that had always been 'fertile in tyrants'.

Sources for Images

Figure 5: Bust of Julius Caesar (Wikimedia Commons) By Ángel M. Felicísimo from Mérida, España – Retrato de Julio César, Public Domain, https://commons.wikimedia.org/w/index.php?curid=91281949

Figure 9: Bust of Claudius (Wikimedia Commons) By Marie-Lan Nguyen (2011), CC BY 2.5, https://commons.wikimedia.org/w/index.php?curid=23198004

Figure 12: Reproduction of Roman Ballista (Wikimedia Commons). By Rolf Krahl – dsc_3735, CC BY-SA 2.0, https://commons.wikimedia.org/w/index.php?curid=42587336

Figure 13: Drawing of a Roman onager (Wikimedia Commons). Author: Hermann Diels (1848–1922) – Antike Technik: Sechs Vorträge, Public Domain, https://commons.wikimedia.org/w/index.php?curid=37717934

Figure 14: Aerial view of Maiden Castle (Wikimedia Commons) https://commons.wikimedia.org/w/index.php?curid=12228040

Figure 15: Ramparts at Maiden Castle (Wikimedia Commons). By Nilfanion – Wikimedia UK, CC BY-SA 4.0, https://commons.wikimedia.org/w/index.php?curid=47632244

Figure 16: Roman *testudo* formation from Trajan's Column (Wikimedia Commons). By Cassius Ahenobarbus – Own work, CC BY-SA 3.0, https://commons.wikimedia.org/w/index.php?curid=104683968

Figure 18: Bust of Vespasian (Wikimedia Commons). By Heribert Pohl, CC BY-SA 2.0, https://commons.wikimedia.org/w/index.php?curid=34100478

Figure 19: Bust of Titus (Wikimedia Commons). DerHexer (Talk) – Own work, CC BY-SA 3.0, https://commons.wikimedia.org/w/index.php?curid=10494593

Figure 21: Map of Roman Britain c. 150 (Wikimedia Commons). By Andrei nacu at English Wikipedia – Transferred from en.wikipedia to Commons by Gpedro. Mason (2001), p. 128. Valeria Victrix was based at Deva Victrix., Public Domain, https://commons.wikimedia.org/w/index.php?curid=3575904

Figure 22: Bust of Emperor Hadrian (Wikimedia Commons). Author: Carole Raddato. From Hadrian's Mausoleum, possibly created following the emperor's death in 138 AD Vatican Museums, CC BY-SA 2.0, https://commons.wikimedia.org/w/index.php?curid=74822013

Figure 27: Ariel view of Housesteads Roman Fort, Vercovicium. (Wikimedia Commons). By Carole Raddato from FRANKFURT, Germany – Housesteads Roman Fort (Vercovicium), CC BY-SA 2.0, https://commons.wikimedia.org/w/index.php?curid=74317421

Sources for Images 181

Figure 29: Aerial view of London (Wikimedia Commons). Reconstruction drawing of Londinium in AD 120. Carole Raddato from FRANKFURT, Germany – Flickr, CC BY-SA 2.0, https://commons.wikimedia.org/w/index.php?curid=65370195

Figure 30: London in 2nd to 3rd century (Wikimedia Commons). By Fremantleboy, Drallim (translation) – http://upload.wikimedia.org/wikipedia/commons/5/59/Map_Londinium_400_AD-de.svg, CC BY 2.5, https://commons.wikimedia.org/w/index.php?curid=25150075

Figure 32: Bust of Pertinax (Wikimedia Commons). By L. Dyck (photo) – The Uffzi GalleryUffizi Digitalization Project (3D Model), Public Domain, https://commons.wikimedia.org/w/index.php?curid=122372578

Figure 33: Bust of Clodius Albinus (Wikimedia Commons). By © José Luiz Bernardes Ribeiro, CC BY-SA 4.0, https://commons.wikimedia.org/w/index.php?curid=53960363

Figure 36: Bust of Septimius Severus (Wikimedia Commons). By Yair Haklai – Own work, CC BY-SA 4.0, https://commons.wikimedia.org/w/index.php?curid=112504493

Figure 37: Map of northern campaign of Septimius Severus c. 208–11 (Wikimedia Commons). BY-SA 3.0, https://commons.wikimedia.org/w/index.php?curid=8496914

Figure 38: Bust of Publius Septimius Geta c. 208 (Wikimedia Commons). By Marie-Lan Nguyen (User:Jastrow), 2007, Public Domain, https://commons.wikimedia.org/w/index.php?curid=1756124

Figure 41: Bust of Caracalla c. 212 (Wikimedia Commons). By Marie-Lan Nguyen (2011), CC BY 2.5, https://commons.wikimedia.org/w/index.php?curid=17006023

Figure 43: Gold aureus of Postumus in a pendant (Wikimedia Commons). By PHGCOM – Own work by uploader, photographed at the Cabinet des Medailles, Public Domain, https://commons.wikimedia.org/w/index.php?curid=6227001

Figure 44: Gold aureus of Carausius, minted at London (Wikimedia Commons). Portable Antiquities Scheme from London, England – CC BY 2.0, https://commons.wikimedia.org/w/index.php?curid=10817339

Figure 45: Roman copper coin of Allectus c. 293–6. Reverse with Galley (Wikimedia Commons). By The Portable Antiquities Scheme/ The Trustees of the British Museum, CC BY-SA 4.0, https://commons.wikimedia.org/w/index.php?curid=55675712

Figure 47: Gold coin of Constantius I. Reverse with Galley outside London (Wikimedia Commons). Public Domain, https://commons.wikimedia.org/w/index.php?curid=6071025

Figure 49: Bust of Constantius Chorus (Wikimedia Commons). By Marie-Lan Nguyen – Own work, Public Domain, https://commons.wikimedia.org/w/index.php?curid=86235336

Figure 51: Statue of Constantine the Great in York (Wikimedia Commons). By Chabe01 – Own work, CC BY-SA 4.0, https://commons.wikimedia.org/w/index.php?curid=71214192

Figure 52: Bust of Constans I (Wikimedia Commons). Ladislav Luppa – Own work, CC BY-SA 4.0, https://commons.wikimedia.org/w/index.php?curid=58463017

Figure 53: Gold Solidus of Magnentius from Trier (Wikimedia Commons). By ANS – http://numismatics.org/collection/1944.100.20641, CC0, https://commons.wikimedia.org/w/index.php?curid=116383507

Figure 56: Gold solidus of Theodosius I minted in Constantinople, 379–383 (Wikimedia Commons). By Byzantium565 – Own work, CC BY-SA 4.0, https://commons.wikimedia.org/w/index.php?curid=112797030

Figure 57: Roman Miliarensis of Magnus Maximus (Wikimedia Commons). By The Portable Antiquities Scheme/ The Trustees of the British Museum, CC BY-SA 4.0, https://commons.wikimedia.org/w/index.php?curid=55867470

Figure 58: Gold Solidus of Constantine III (Wikimedia Commons). By ANS – http://numismatics.org/collection/1944.100.54848, CC0, https://commons.wikimedia.org/w/index.php?curid=116392879

Notes

Chapter 1
1. Beard, 2016: 373
2. Goldsworthy, 2009: 337
3. Julius Caesar, Gallic Wars, book 4.25
4. Elliott, 2021: 43–4
5. Goldsworthy, 2009: 347
6. Elliott, 2021: 57
7. Elliott, 2021: 61
8. Cunliffe, 2013
9. Cunliffe, 2013: 303–4
10. Cunliffe, 2013: 239–49
11. Strabo, *Geographica*, book 4 chapter 5
12. Julius Caesar, Gallic War books 4 and 5
13. Tacitus, *De vita Julii Agricolae*, The Life of Agricola
14. Suetonius, *De Vita Caesarum*, The Lives of the Twelve Caesars, Julius Caesar, 45

Chapter 2
1. Suetonius, *De Vita Caesarum*, The Lives of the Twelve Caesars, Caligula
2. Suetonius, *De Vita Caesarum*, The Lives of the Twelve Caesars, Claudius
3. Grant, 1997: 30
4. Elliott, 2021: 67
5. Cassius Dio, *Historia Romana*, Roman History, 53.22
6. Suetonius, *De Vita Caesarum*, The Lives of the Twelve Caesars, Life of Caligula, 46
7. Cassius Dio, *Historia Romana*, Roman History 54.25
8. Suetonius, *De Vita Caesarum*, The Lives of the Twelve Caesars, Claudius 17
9. Strabo, Geography, 5.8
10. Elliott, 2021: 75
11. Cassius Dio, book 60.19
12. Levick, 2013: 167
13. Elliott, 2021: 80
14. Webster, 1993: 101
15. Cassius Dio, book 60.21
16. Webster, 1993: 106
17. Strabo, Geography, Book 4, chapter 5.2
18. Caesar, Gallic Wars Book 5.9
19. Caesar, Gallic Wars Book 5.21
20. Collins, 2020: 23
21. Crummy, 1997: 11
22. Crummy, 1997: 15
23. Crummy, 1997: 13
24. Pliny the Elder, *Naturalis Historia*, Natural History, book 2.77

25. Tacitus Annals, 12.32
26. Tacitus, Annal, book 14.31
27. Wacher, 1995: 114–21
28. https://rogueclassicism.com/2010/07/28/first-elephant-in-britain/
29. https://en.wikipedia.org/wiki/History_of_elephants_in_Europe
30. Levick, 2013: 168
31. Cassius Dio, book 60.21
32. Polyaenus, Stratagems 8.23.5
33. Crummy, 1997: 32
34. Milner, 2011: 24 & 80–81
35. Milner, 2011: 10
36. Breeze, 208: 39
37. Webster, 1985: 119
38. Crummy, 1997: 35
39. Crummy, 1997: 37)
40. Crummy, 1997: 33–4
41. Webster, 1993: 106
42. RIB 91
43. Hopkins and Beard, 2011: 60

Chapter 3
1. Cassius Dio, book 60.19–23
2. Elliott, 2021: 80
3. Caesar, Gallic Wars book 4.17–20
4. Webster, 1993: 101
5. Webster, 1981: 109
6. Milner, 2011: 72
7. Milner, 2011: 44
8. Suetonius, The Life of Claudius, 25.1
9. McLynn, 2009: 325
10. Webster, 1981: 146
11. Webster, 1981: 150
12. Suetonius, The Life of Vespasian, 4.1
13. Wacher, 1995: 335
14. Wacher, 1995: 323
15. Webster, 1993: 108
16. Webster, 1993: 109–10
17. Ammianus Book 23.4
18. Goldsworthy, 2003: 244
19. Josephus, The Jewish War, Book III chapter 7
20. Procopius, Gothic war, chapter XXI
21. Procopius, Gothic war, chapter XXIII
22. Webster, 1993: 109
23. Cassius Dio, book 49.29–31
24. Suetonius, Life of Vespasian
25. Suetonius, The life of Titus
26. Grant, 1997: 55
27. Cassius Dio, book 66.26
28. Tacitus Annals, book 14, chapters 34–37

Chapter 4

1. McLynn, 2009: 27
2. Breeze and Dobson, 2000: 25
3. McLynn, 2009: 32
4. Grant, 1997: 77
5. Grant, 1997: 77
6. Grant, 1997: 79
7. Grant, 1997: 79
8. Breeze and Dobson, 2000: 25
9. Birley, 2002: 74–5
10. Symonds, 2021: 56
11. Breeze and Dobson, 2000: 23
12. Breeze and Dobson, 2000: 12
13. Breeze and Dobson, 2000: 13
14. Breeze and Dobson, 2000: 15
15. Birley, 2002: 76
16. Birley, 2002: 44–5
17. http://vindolanda.csad.ox.ac.uk
18. Birley, 2002: 95
19. Birley, 2002: 96
20. Birley, 2002: 80
21. Birley, 2002: 99
22. Birley, 2002: 116–7
23. Historia Augusta, Hadrian, 10.2
24. Birley, 2005: 123
25. Historia Augusta, Hadrian 11.4–7
26. Birley, 2005: 244
27. Birley, 2005: 122
28. Birley, 2005: 284
29. Birley, 2005: 122
30. Tomlin, 2018: 92
31. Tomlin, 2018: 94–6
32. Historia Augusta, Hadrian, 11.2
33. Breeze and Dobson, 2000: 47
34. Breeze and Dobson, 2000: 40
35. Breeze and Dobson, 2000: 42
36. Tomlin, 2018: 107
37. Tomlin, 2018: 114
38. Tomlin, 2018: 128
39. Tomlin, 2018: 311
40. Tomlin, 2018: 92–3
41. Breeze and Dobson, 2000: 53
42. Breeze and Dobson, 2000: 54
43. Birley, 2005: 250
44. Birley, 2005: 250–1
45. Elliott, 2021: 67
46. Elliott, 2021: 145–8
47. Birley, 2005: 228–30
48. Elliott, 2021: 64
49. Historia Augusta Hadrian, 27.1

50. Cassius Dio Book 69 23.2
51. Historia Augustus, Antoninus Pius 5.3
52. Birley, 2005: 139
53. Breeze, 208: 36
54. Breeze, 208: 22
55. Breeze, 208: 21
56. Southern, 2016: 377–81
57. Arrianus, Ektaxis kata Alanon
58. Breeze, 208: 35
59. Breeze, 208: 18
60. Breeze, 208: 40
61. Breeze, 208: 48
62. Tomlin, 2018: 129
63. Tomlin, 2018: 169
64. Tomlin, 2018: 209
65. Tomlin, 2018: 143
66. Birley, 2005: 147
67. Birley, 205: 148
68. Birley, 2005: 155

Chapter 5
1. Cassius Dio, book 72.36
2. RIB 1149
3. Birley, 2005: 154
4. RIB 1737
5. Birley, 2005: 355
6. Cassius Dio, book 74.3
7. Elliott, 2020: 100
8. Pollard and Berry, 2015: 93
9. Pollard and Berry, 2015: 94
10. Pollard and Berry, 2015: 83
11. Breeze and Dobson, 2000: 267
12. Historia Augusta, Life of Pertinax, 2
13. McHugh, 2015: 57
14. Moffatt, 2017: 206–7
15. Birley, 2005: 166–7
16. Cassius Dio book 73.4
17. McHugh, 2015: 97–8
18. Historia Augusta, Commodus, 6.1
19. Cassius Dio, book 73.9
20. Birley, 2005: 261
21. CIL vi. 41127
22. Birley, 2005: 171
23. Historia Augusta, The Life of Pertinax, 5–9
24. Webb, 2011: 56
25. Webb, 2011: 57
26. Webb, 2011: 109
27. Crabtree, 2018: 31
28. Naismith, 2019: 43
29. Webb, 2011: 132
30. Bailey in Bassett, 1989: 110

31. Cassius Dio book 73.12
32. Herodian 1.12.4–5
33. Cassius Dio book 73.13.6
34. Herodian 1.13.3
35. Herodian 1.13.8
36. McHugh, 2015: 126
37. McHugh, 2015: 167
38. Herodian 1.15.1
39. Herodian 1.17.1
40. Sullivan, 2022: 154
41. Cassius Dio, book 76
42. Herodian 2.15.3
43. Grant, 1997: 117
44. Herodian 3.5.8
45. Historia Augustus, The life of Clodius Albinus, 13
46. Herodian, 3.5.2
47. Herodian 3.5.4–5
48. Herodian 3.6
49. Cassius Dio, book 76.6
50. Herodian 3.7.2
51. Herodian, 3.7.3
52. Cassius Dio, book 76.6.7
53. Birley, 2005: 184

Chapter 6

1. Grant, 97: 108
2. Grant, 97: 113
3. Cassius Dio book 76.8
4. Herodian 3.8.7
5. Birley, 1999: 170
6. Herodian 3.14.1
7. Cassius Dio, book 77.11
8. Cassius Dio book 77.12
9. Birley, 1999: 178
10. Herodian 3.14
11. Elliott, 2020: 146–7
12. Elliott, 2020: 147
13. Birley, 1999: 179
14. Elliott, 2020: 151
15. Elliott, 2020: 152–6
16. Herodian, 3.14.8
17. Cassius Dio, book 77.15
18. Birley, 1999: 180
19. Birley, 1999: 180
20. Historia Augusta, Geta, chapter 4
21. Herodian book 4.3
22. Ottaway, 2004: 26
23. Ottaway, 2004: 31
24. Ottaway, 2004: 24
25. Herodian 3.15–4.6
26. Cassius Dio, book 78

27. Cassius Dio book 78.2
28. Historia Augusta, Caracalla 9.3
29. Birley, 2005: 181
30. Birley, 205: 333
31. RIB 1265
32. Scarre, 1995: 207
33. Historia Augusta, Life of Severus Alexander, 59
34. Aurelius Victor, Life of the Caesars 24.4

Chapter 7
1. Historia Augusta, The Lives of the Thirty Pretenders, Postumus
2. RIB 605, Birley, 2005: 364–5
3. Southern, 2013: 270
4. Birley, 2005: 364–6
5. Grant, 1997: 175
6. Grant, 1997: 173
7. Zosimus 1.68.3
8. Elliott, 2022
9. Elliott, 2022: 87
10. Elliott, 2022: 89
11. Birley, 205: 371
12. Elliott, 2022: 92–3
13. Aurelius Victor, *De Caesaribus*, 39.20
14. Eutropius, Breviarum, 9.21
15. Birley, 205: 373–4
16. Elliott, 2022: 97–8
17. Elliott, 2022: 99
18. Panegyrici Latini, 8.12 in Casey, 1994: 193–4
19. Elliott, 2022: 107
20. Elliott, 2022: 109
21. Elliott, 2022: 114–5
22. Elliott, 2022: 116–7
23. Elliott, 2022: 121
24. Elliott, 2022: 131
25. Aurelius Victor, De Caesaribus, 39.21 in Elliott, 2022: 123
26. Panegyrici Latini, 8.12 in Casey, 1994: 192–3
27. Casey, 1995: 127
28. Birely, 205: 386
29. Casey, 1995: 129–35
30. Birley, 205: 383
31. Casey, 1995: 137
32. Birely, 205: 390
33. Hughes, 2020: 15
34. Birley, 205: 397–8
35. Gerrard, 2016: 215
36. Rippon, 2018: 327
37. Bedoyere, 2006: 89
38. Salway, 2001: 230
39. Birley, 2005: 413
40. RIB 1912 in Birley, 2005: 405

41. Goldsworthy, 2000: 168
42. Hughes, 2020: 27

Chapter 8
1. Eutropius, book 10
2. Grant, 1998: 16
3. Grant, 1997: 216
4. Orosius, book 7 chapter 15
5. Hughes, 2020: 153
6. Grant, 1998: 15
7. Lanctantius, *De mortibus persecutorum*, chapter 28
8. Lactantius, *De mortibus persecutorum*, chapter 24
9. https://orbis.stanford.edu
10. Grant, 1998: 23
11. Birley, 2005: 410
12. Eusebius, *Vita Constantini*, 1.19–20
13. Birley, 2005: 411
14. Birley, 2005: 412
15. Eusebius, *Vita Constantini* 1. 8. 2
16. Eusebius, *Vita Constantini*, 1. 25. 2
17. Grant, 1998: 156–7
18. Grant, 1998: 82
19. Grant, 1998: 105
20. Grant, 1998: 107
21. Eutropius, Short History of the Roman Empire, 10.6
22. Grant, 1998: 84
23. Southern, 213: 313
24. Birley, 2005: 414
25. Birley, 2005: 414

Chapter 9
1. Eutropius, Short History of the Roman Empire, 10.9
2. Birley, 2005: 420–3
3. Dark, 1994: 10
4. Goldsworthy, 2010: 344
5. Dark, 2000: 17
6. Gerrard, 2016: 55
7. Dark, 1994: 16
8. Dark, 1994: 15
9. Halsall, 2014: 457
10. Salway, 2001: 277
11. Ammianus Marcellinus, book 20.1
12. Ammianus Marcellinus, book 26.4.5
13. Ammianus Marcellinus, book 27.8
14. Salway, 2001: 280–281
15. Gerrard, 2016: 23–25
16. Higham, 2014 :21
17. Salway, 2001: 293
18. Hebblewhite, 2021: 15–6
19. Hebblewhite, 2021: 16

20. Grant, 1997: 272
21. Grant, 1997: 273–4
22. Hebblewhite, 2021: 1
23. Grant, 1997: 274
24. Salway, 2001: 297
25. Zosimus, *Historia Nova*, book 4
26. Grant, 1997: 275
27. Claudian, Panegyric on Stilicho's Consulship, book 2
28. Salway, 2001: 316
29. Gerrard, 2016: 168
30. Higham and Ryan, 2015: 42
31. Orosius, Book 7, 40.3
32. Sozomen, Historia Ecclesiastica, Book IX.11
33. http://www.vortigernstudies.org.uk/artsou/orosius.htm
34. http://www.vortigernstudies.org.uk/artsou/chron452.htm
35. http://www.vortigernstudies.org.uk/artsou/zosim.htm
36. Oosthuizen, 2019: 27
37. http://www.vortigernstudies.org.uk/artsou/procop.htm
38. Birley, 2005: 460
39. Grant: 1997: 287
40. Birley, 2005: 457–60

Chapter 10

1. Goldsworthy, 2010: 337
2. Evans, 2000: 26
3. Hughes, 2020: 34–35
4. Storr, 2016: 56
5. Swanton, 2001: 10
6. Lapidge and Dumville, 1984: 52
7. Lapidge and Dumville, 1984: 47
8. Lapidge and Dumville, 1984: 50
9. Pace, 2021: 25–35
10. Wood in Dumville and Lapwood, 1984: 8
11. http://www.vortigernstudies.org.uk/artsou/prosp.htm
12. Charles-Edwards, 2014: 227
13. O Croinin, 2017: 46
14. Dumville, 1999
15. Mathisen, 1993: 68–69
16. Brown, 2012: 448
17. Brown, 2012: 446
18. Halsall, 2014: 480
19. Charles-Edwards, 2014: 370
20. Todd, 2004: 208
21. Eagles, 2018: xxxiv
22. Hills 2011: 10
23. Bede volume 5 chapter 9
24. Hughes, 2020: 130
25. Snyder, 1998: 230
26. Snyder, 1998: 107
27. Orosius, History against the Pagans, 7.42.5

References

Beard, Mary, *SPQR A History of Ancient Rome*, (Profile Books, London, 2016).
Berresford-Ellis, Peter, *Caesar's Invasion of Britain*, (Constable, London, 1994)
Birley, Anthony, *Garrison Life at Vindolanda, A Band of Brothers*, (Tempus, Stroud, 2002).
Birley, Anthony, *Septimius Severus the African Emperor*, (Routledge, London, 1999).
Birley, Anthony, *The Roman Government of Britain*, (Oxford University Press, Oxford, 2005).
Bishop, M.C., *The Secret History of the Roman Roads of Britain*, (Pen and Sword, Barnsley, 2020).
Bishop, M.C., *Lucius Verus and the Roman Defence of the East*, (Pen and Sword, Barnsley, 2018).
Breeze, David, J. and Dobson, Brian, *Hadrian's Wall*, (Penguin Books, London, 2000).
Breeze, David, *Edge of Empire, Rome's Scottish Frontier, The Antonine Wall*, (Birlinn, Edinburgh, 2008).
Bruun, Christer and Edmondson, Jonathan, The Oxford Handbook of Roman Epigraphy, (Oxford University Press, Oxford, 2015).
Carver, Martin, *Formative Britain, An Archaeology of Britain, Fifth to Eleventh Century* AD, Routledge, London, 2019)
Casey, P.J., *Carausius and Allectus*, (Yale University Press, New Haven, 1994).
Charles-Edwards, T.M, *Wales and the Britons 350–1064*, (Oxford University Press, Oxford, 2014).
Chrystal, Paul, *A Historical Guide to Roman York*, (Pen and Sword, Barnsley, 2021).
Clearly, S., *The Ending(s) of Roman Britain* in Hamerow, H, Hinton, D, and Crawford, S, *The Oxford Handbook of Anglo-Saxon Archaeology,* (Oxford University Press, Oxford, 2011).
Collins, Rob, *Hadrian's Wall and the End of Empire*, Routledge, New York, 2012).
Collins, Rob, *Living on the Edge of Empire*, (Pen and Sword, Barnsley, 2020).
Crook, J.A., *Law and Life of Rome, 90 B.C. – A.D. 212*, (Cornell University Press, New York, 1967).
Crow, James, Housesteads Roman Fort, (English Heritage, 2012).
Crummy, Philip, City of Victory: The Story of Colchester – Britain's First Roman Town, (Colchester Archaeological Trust, Colchester, 1997).
Cruse, Audrey, *Roman Medicine*, (Tempus, Stroud, 2004).
Cunliffe, Barry, *Britain Begins*, (Oxford University Press, Oxford, 2011)
Cunliffe, Barry, *The Ancient Celts*, (Oxford University Press, Oxford, 1997)
Czajkowski, Kimberley, Eckhardt, Benedikt, *Law in the Roman Provinces*, (Oxford University Press, Oxford, 2020).

Dando-Collins, Stephen, *Legions of Rome, The Definitive History of Every Imperial Roman Legion*, (Thomas Dunne Books, St Martin's Press, New York, 2010).
D'Amato, R. and Negin, A., *Decorated Roman Armour, from the Age of the Kings to the Death of Justinian the great*, (Frontline Books, Barnsley, 2017).
D'Amato, Raffaele and Sumner, Graham, *Arms and Armour of the Imperial Roman Soldier, from Marius to Commodus, 112 bc- ad 192*, (Frontline Books, London, 2009).
Dark, K.R., *Civitas to Kingdom; British Political Continuity 300–800*, (Leicester University Press, London, 1994).
Dark, Ken, *Britain and the End of the Roman Empire*, (Tempus Publishing Ltd, Stroud, 2000).
Davenport, Caillan, *A History of the Roman Equestrian Order*, (Cambridge University Press, Cambridge, 2019).
Davies, Hugh, *Roman Roads in Britain*, (Shire Archaeology, Oxford, 2008).
De La Bédoyère, Guy, *Domina*, (Yale University Press, New Haven, 2018).
De La Bédoyère, Guy, *Eagles over Britannia*, (Tempus Publishing, Stroud, 2001).
De La Bédoyère, Guy, *Gladius, Living Fighting and Dying in the Roman Army*, (Little Brown, London, 2020).
De La Bédoyère, Guy, *Roman Britain, A New History*, (Thames and Hudson, London, 2006).
De La Bédoyère, Guy, *The Real Lives of Roman Britain*, (Yale University Press, New Haven, 2015).
Dumville, David, *Saint Patrick*, (Boydell Press, Woodbridge, 1999).
Elliott, Paul, *Everyday Life of a Soldier on Hadrian's Wall*, (Fonthill, 2015).
Elliott, Paul, *The Life of a Roman Soldier in Britain AD 400*, (Spellmount, Stroud, 2007).
Elliott, Simon, *Pertinax*, (Greenhill Books, Barnsley, 2020).
Elliott, Simon, *Roman Britain's Missing Legion*, (Pen and Sword, Barnsley, 2021).
Elliott, Simon, *Roman Britain's Pirate King*, (Pen and Sword, Barnsley, 2022).
Elliott, Simon, *Roman Conquests: Britain*, (Pen and Sword, Barnsley, 2021)
Elliott, Simon, *Roman Legionaries, Soldiers of Empire*, (Casemate, Oxford, 2018).
Elliott, Simon, *Romans at War*, (Casemate, Oxford, 2020).
Elliott, Simon, *Sea Eagles of Empire, The Classis Britannica and the Battles for Britain*, (History Press, Stroud, 2016).
Elliott, Simon, *Septimus Severus in Scotland*, (Greenhill Books, Barnsley, 2018).
Esposito, Gabriele, *Armies of the Late Roman Empire AD 284–476, History Organisation and Equipment*, (Pen and Sword Books, Barnsley, 2018).
Gerrard, James, *The Ruin of Roman Britain an Archaeological Perspective*, (Cambridge University Press, Cambridge, 2016).
Goldsworthy, Adrian, *Caesar*, (Phoenix, London, 2007)
Goldsworthy, Adrian, *Pax Romana*, (Weidenfeld and Nicolson, London, 2016).
Goldsworthy, Adrian, *The Fall of the West*, (Phoenix, London, 2010).
Goldsworthy, Adrian, *The Complete Roman Army*, (Thames and Hudson, London, 2003).
Goldsworthy, Adrian, *Roman Warfare* (Phoenix, London, 2000).

Grant, Michael, *Constantine the Great, the Man and his Times*, (Barnes and Noble, New York, 1998).
Grant, Michael, *The Antonines*, (Routledge, London, 1994).
Grant, Michael, *The Roman Emperors*, (Phoenix, London, 1997).
Halsall, Guy, *Barbarian Migrations and the Roman West 376–568*, (Cambridge University Press, Cambridge, 2014).
Hamilton, Walter, *Ammianus Marcellinus, The Later Roman Empire ad 354–378* (Penguin Books, London, 1986).
Haywood, John, *Dark Age Naval Power, A Reassessment of Frankish and Anglo-Saxon Seafaring Ability*, (Routledge, London, 1991)
Hebblewhite, Mark, *Theodosius and the Limits of Empire*, (Routledge, London, 2021).
Hobbs, R. & Jackson, R., *Roman Britain*, (The British Museum Press, London, 2015).
Hoffmann, Birgitta, *The Roman Invasion of Britain, Archaeology versus History*, (Pen and Sword, Barnsley, 2013)
Hopkins, Keith and Beard, Mary, *The Colosseum*, (Profile Books, London, 2005).
Hughes, Ian, *A Military Life of Constantine the Great*, (Pen and Sword, Barnsley, 2020).
Hughes, Ian, *Patricians and Emperors*, (Pen and Sword, Barnsley, 2015).
Istvanovits, Eszter, and Kulcsar, Valeria, *Sarmatians, History and Archaeology of a Forgotten People*, (Romisch-Germanisches Zentralmuseum, Germany, 2017).
Kershaw, Stephen, *Barbarians, Rebellion and Resistance to Ancient Rome*, (Robinson, London, 2019).
Laing, Lloyd and Jennifer, *The Origins of Britain*, (Book Club Associates, Thetford, 1980).
Lapidge, Michael and Dumville, David: *Gildas, New Approaches*, (Boydell Press, Woodbridge, 1984).
Laycock, Stuart, *Britannia The Failed State*, (The History Press, Stroud, 2011).
Levick, Barbara, *Claudius*, (Routledge, Abingdon, 2013)
Levick, Barbara, *The Government of the Roman Empire*, (Routledge, London, 2000).
McHugh, John, *The Emperor Commodus, God and Gladiator*, (Pen and Sword, Barnsley, 2015).
McLynn, Frank, *Marcus Aurelius, Warrior, Philosopher, Emperor*, (Vintage, London, 2010).
Milner, N, P, *Vegetius: Epitome of Military Science 2nd Ed* (Liverpool Universety Press, Liverpool, 2011).
Moffatt, Alistair, *The Wall, Rome's Greatest Frontier*, (Birlinn, Edinburgh, 2017).
Moorhead, Sam, and Stuttard, David, *The Romans who Shaped Britain*, (Thames and Hudson, London, 2016).
O Croinin, Daibhi, *Early Medieval Ireland 400–1200 2nd Edition*, (Routledge, London, 2017).
Ottaway, Peter, *Roman York*, (Tempus Books, Stroud, 2004).
Pace, Edwin, *The Long War for Britannia, 367–664, Arthur and the History of Post-Roman Britain*, (Pen and Sword, Barnsley, 2021).
Pearson, Andrew, *The Roman Shore Forts*, (The History Press, Stroud, 2010).
Penrose, Jane, *Rome and Her Enemies*, (Osprey Publishing, Oxford, 2005)

Pitassi, Michael, *The Roman Navy, Ships, Men and Warfare 350 bc – ad 475*, (Seaforth Publishing, Barnsley, 2012).
Pollard, Nigel and Berry, Joanne, *The Complete Roman Legions*, (Thames and Hudson, London, 2015).
Richards, Mark, *Walking Hadrian's Wall Path*, (Cicerone, Cumbria, 2015).
Richardson, John, *The Romans and the Antonine Wall of Scotland*, (Lulu.com, 2019)
Rivet, A.L.F., and Smith, Colin, *The Place-Names of Roman Britain*, (Batsford, London, 1982).
Rogan, John, *Roman Provincial Administration*, (Amberley Publishing, Stroud, 2011).
Sage, Michael, *Septimius Severus and the Roman Army*, (Pen and Sword, Barnsley, 2020).
Salway, Peter, *A History of Roman Britain*, (Oxford University Press, Oxford, 2001).
Scarre, Chris, *Chronicle of the Roman Emperors*, (Thames and Hudson, London, 2007).
Shotter, David, *The Roman Frontier in Britain*, (Carnegie Publishing, Preston, 1996).
Southern, Patricia, *Roman Britain, A New History 55 bc- ad 450*, (Amberley Publishing, Stroud, 2013).
Southern, Patricia, *The Roman Army, A History 753 bc- ad 476*, (Amberley Publishing, Stroud, 2016).
Sullivan, Tony, *The Real Gladiator*, (Pen and Sword, Barnsley, 2022).
Summerton, Nick, *Greco-Roman Medicine*, (Pen and Sword, Barnsley, 2021).
Swanton, Michael, *The Anglo-Saxon Chronicles*, (Phoenix Press, London, 2000).
Symonds, Matthew, *Hadrian's Wall, Creating Division*, (Bloomsbury, London, 2021).
Syvanne, Ilkka, *Caracalla, A Military Biography*, (Pen and Sword, Barnsley, 2017).
Syvanne, Ilkka, *Military History of Late Rome 425–457*, (Pen and Sword, Yorkshire, 2020).
Tacitus, *Agricola and Germanis*, (Penguin Classics, London, 2009).
Taylor, Don, *Roman Empire at War*, (Pen and Sword, Barnsley, 2016).
Todd, Malcolm, *A Companion to Roman Britain*, (Blackwell Publishing, Malden, USA, 2007).
Tomlin, R.S.O., *Britannia Romana, Roman Inscriptions and Roman Britain*, (Oxbow Books, Oxford, 2018).
Travis, Hiliary and Travis, John, *Roman Body Armour*, (Amberley, Stroud, 2012).
Travis, Hiliary and Travis, John, *Roman Helmets*, (Amberley, Stroud, 2016).
Travis, Hiliary and Travis, John, *Roman Shields*, (Amberley, Stroud, 2016).
Wacher, John, The Towns of Roman Britain, (BCA, London, 1995).
Webb, Simon, *Life in Roman London*, (The History Press, Stroud, 2011).
Webster, Graham, *The Roman Invasion of Britain*, (Routledge, London 1993)
Webster, Graham, *The Roman Imperial Army*, (A & C Black, London, 1981).
Webster, L & Brown, M, *The Transformation of the Roman World ad 400–900*, (British Museum Press, London, 1997).

Index

Agricola, first century Roman general 13, 40, 52, 57, 62, 64, 74
Alexander Severus 107-8, 124, 126, 178
Allectus xii, 116, 132-6, 141, 174, 178
Ambrosius Aurelianus 176-7, 179
Antonine Constitution 124
Antonine wall 28, 52, 59, 63, 76, 78-80, 84-5, 87-8, 109-10, 121, 175
Antoninus Pius 67, 76, 82, 84
Augustus, Emperor 3, 11, 15-7, 38, 42, 84, 109
Aulus Plautius 19-23, 26, 29-32, 36, 39-40, 43-4

Barbarian conspiracy 151
Boudicca xi-xii, 31, 33, 55-6, 117, 179

Caerleon 52, 62, 75, 85, 92, 111-2, 124
Caligula 13-8, 33, 36
Camulodunum, see Colchester
Caracalla 38, 52, 101, 107-10, 112, 114-7, 119-24, 128, 137, 154, 178
Caratacus 17, 19, 21, 25, 36-7, 128
Carausius xii, 128-34, 148-9, 161, 178
Carausius II 150
Cartimandua, Queen of the Brigantes 31, 118
Cassivellaunus 7-8, 12, 23, 26
Chester 62, 75, 85, 92, 112, 124, 154
Chichester 31-2
Classis Britannica 18, 96, 112
Colchester 17, 21-4, 28, 30-3, 37, 41, 44, 55, 93
Claudius xi, 9, 12-3, 15-23, 25-37, 39-42, 44, 54, 134, 178
Clodius Albinus xii, 52, 82, 85, 98, 100-3, 105, 108-9, 149, 178
Commodus 2, 43, 68, 78, 82, 88, 90-2, 97-101, 107, 115

Constans I 139, 147-9, 151, 154, 178
Constans II 161-5, 179
Constantine I xi-xii, 52, 86, 116, 119, 136-7, 139-47, 174, 178
Constantine II 147-9
Constantine III 86, 157, 159, 161-6, 169, 173, 175, 177, 179
Constantius Chlorus xii, 116, 119, 130, 132-7, 139-44, 146, 148, 154, 178
Constantius II 147, 149-50
Constantius III 162-3, 165, 169-72, 177, 179
Corbridge 62-5, 68, 80, 82, 85, 89-90, 106
Cunobelin 17-8

Diocletian 52, 86, 116, 128-9, 131-3, 136-42, 144-7
Dorchester 48, 50, 52

Edict of Caracalla see Antonine Constitution
Edict of Milan 146
Elagabalus 52, 107-8, 123-4, 178
Exeter 32-3,

Fishbourne Palace 32

Gallic Empire 126-7, 129
Geta 107-9, 111-2, 115-7, 119-22, 154, 178
Gratian, usurper in Britain c. 409, 161, 164, 177, 179

Hadrian xii, 59, 60-81
Hadrian's wall 52, 59, 61-81

Julius Caesar xi, 1, 3-4, 9, 12-4, 16-7, 19, 22, 26, 29-30, 51-2, 84, 112, 134, 169, 178-9

Legions
  Legio VII Claudia (the Seventh) 5, 7, 21, 23
  Legio X Equestris (the Tenth) 5, 178
  Legio II Augusta (the Second) xii, 19, 32-3, 36, 39, 51-3, 63, 74, 77-8, 85, 112, 124, 130
  Legio VI Victrix (the Sixth) xii, 41, 62-3, 66, 69-70, 74, 76-9, 81, 83-5, 87-91, 106, 112, 124, 130, 144, 154, 178
  Legio IX Hispania (the Ninth) 19, 74-5, 118-9
  Legio XIV Gemina (the Fourteenth) 19, 74
  Legio XX Valera Victrix (the Twentieth) 19, 25, 55, 74, 77, 85, 112, 124, 130
London 37, 55, 64, 66, 75, 93-6, 90, 92-7, 124, 130-3, 135-8, 152-4, 171
Lugdunum, battle of, 52, 102-9

Magnentius 149-150, 178
Magnus Maximus xi, 156-61, 165, 170, 175-9
Marcus Aurelius 2, 67, 76, 81-3, 99, 101, 115, 122
Mark, usurper in Britain c. 409, 161, 164, 177, 179
Maximus, Emperor in Hispania c. 409, 163, 165
Mons Graupius, battle of, 13, 40, 52, 62-4, 74, 78, 111

Notitia Dignitatum 52, 71-4, 79, 86, 97, 134, 144, 166-7
Noviomagus see Chichester

Perennis, 2nd century praetorian prefect 90-3, 97
Priscus, 2nd century governor of Britain 82-3

Priscus, 2nd century legate proclaimed emperor by troops 88-92
Postumus 126-7, 149, 178

Richborough 20, 29, 36, 53, 66, 152, 167
Rutupiae, see Richborough

Septimius Severus xii, 52, 85, 98, 100-1, 107-9, 111-7, 119, 142, 150, 154, 178
Silchester 52, 135-6
Saint Alban 171, 176
St Albans 25, 55, 93, 116, 171

Tetricus, emperor of Gallic Empire 127
Theodosius I 146, 151-60, 178
Titus xii, 33, 35-7, 39, 41, 43, 45-7, 49, 51, 53-5, 57-9, 67, 78, 85, 171
Togidubnus, Tiberius Claudius 31
Togodumnus 17, 19, 21, 36-7

Ulpius Marcellus, 2nd century governor of Britain 88, 90-2

Verulamium, see St Albans
Vespasian xii, 19-21, 32-3, 35-9, 41, 43-55, 57, 59, 63, 77, 85, 178
Vindolanda 63-5, 68, 72, 77, 79, 86-7, 118
Viroconium see Wroxeter
Vortigern 176-7, 179

Watling Street, battle of 55
Winchester 44
Wroxeter 33

York xi-xii, 41, 52, 61-2, 64-5, 67, 70, 74-5, 80, 84-6, 88-90, 92, 112, 114, 116-20, 124, 133, 137-8, 142-4, 146-7, 153-4, 167, 169, 178